THE VODKA-COLA COWBOY

THE VODKA-COLA COWBOY

Trucking Russia 1990–1995

Mick Twemlow

First published 2016

Published by
Old Pond Publishing,
An imprint of 5M Publishing Ltd,
Benchmark House,
8 Smithy Wood Drive,
Sheffield, S35 1QN, UK
Tel: +44 (0) 0114 246 4799
www.oldpond.com

A catalogue record for this book is available from the British Library

ISBN 978-1-910456-53-8

Book layout by
Servis Filmsetting Ltd, Stockport, Cheshire
Printed by Replika Press Pvt, Ltd, India
Photos by Mick Twemlow

Cover image: Mick's truck in a queue at the Belarus–Polish border, waiting to enter Poland.

Contents

About the Author

HAVING left school in 1966, at the age of 15, Mick joined the British Army. He served with the 2nd Royal Tank Regiment, until leaving in 1972. He then spent the next three years alternating between working as a truck driver in the U.K. and as a professional musician.

In 1975, he drove the John Surtees formula 1 team car transporter to European Grand Prix. He also made his first road haulage trip to Yugoslavia. From 1975 to 1978 he worked virtually exclusively in European haulage.

Joining Pro-Motor Europe in late 1978, he drove trucks for the company to every country in Europe, as well as making ten trips to Iraq and one to Moscow, in 1981. Specialising in the Eastern European side of the company, he went on to make 86 trips to Yugoslavia.

Having been made redundant by Pro-Motor in late 1983, he joined David Croome Ltd and worked as a driver on mainly West European operations. However, due to his experience he did undertake some East European exhibition work for Croome, on behalf of Kepstowe Freight Services.

Becoming an owner-driver in 1987, he worked initially on U.K. haulage, but by 1989 he was running to Germany, on a permanent basis for Lep.

In 1990 he was approached by Croome to operate to Moscow on behalf of Kepstowe Freight. The years 1990 to 1995 were spent working and living in Russia.

Having moved his family to England from Moscow, in 1995 he then undertook a variety of jobs so that he did not have to leave them alone in the U.K. These positions included running a staff agency, working for the benefits agency, being a probation service officer, and finally a prison officer.

He took early retirement from the Prison Service in 2010 and returned to truck driving, for agencies and then for Morrisons supermarkets.

Mick has now retired from full-time employment and spends his time writing and constructing model railways.

In his youth Mick Twemlow was a highly successful amateur boxer and footballer. As an ex-serviceman, like many others, he had the self-sufficiency necessary to complete long distance transport operations across Eastern Europe, Russia and the Middle East. As a competent linguist who speaks six languages, his main interest has always been communication with others, regardless of nationality.

Orsha Hill, Belorussia
12th February, 1991 – Temperature: -42 Celsius

I had lost all the feeling in my left hand. It had become totally frozen. The blood had entirely ceased to circulate within the hand. My body was protecting itself by withdrawing the blood flow from the affected area. This is the natural reaction of the human body when any of its extremities freeze.

Lack of blood circulation would lead to frostbite, which in those extreme circumstances could trigger gangrene. That can result in needing to have the infected part of the body amputated if it cannot be saved.

Where I was, stranded in a desolate snow-covered wasteland many miles from any habitation or medical assistance, I was actually in real danger of dying. I desperately needed to revitalise the circulation in my hand and get warmth extremely quickly. Hypothermia was the next inevitable stage that would affect me. In those conditions, that would have been lethal.

The heavy-duty cotton Rigger glove encasing my left hand had become saturated in Soviet diesel, which contained a high water content. Having frozen, in the bitter sub-Arctic temperature the glove had become a casement of ice. I had not noticed this development due to the complete lack of sensation in the hand.

This occurred while I was changing my truck's diesel filter. The filter had waxed up due to the freezing cold temperature and had blocked the supply of diesel to the engine. It had brought the truck to a complete and utter standstill in this frozen deserted wilderness.

There was absolutely no other traffic on the road from which to gain assistance. The adjoining fields were a complete sea of white where the deep snow covered the earth. A constant blizzard of snow blew across the road. It was driven by the freezing Arctic winds howling westward from Siberia.

I came to the desperate conclusion that I might not survive this severe situation. I realised that perhaps my time had finally come in the harsh frozen wastelands of Russia.

What had led up to this dangerous situation and what happened after it?

Dedication

THIS book is dedicated to Margarita, Lloyd and Eddie.

I would like to express my deepest love and gratitude to my wife, Sue, for her continuous support and belief throughout the writing process, particularly cutting down the profusion of commas that I had inserted.

With my extremely special thanks to Rachel Turner, Commissioning Editor at 5M/Old Pond Publishing, for her highly appreciated level of guidance, assistance and encouragement, which has successfully brought this book to publication.

Also my heartfelt thanks to everyone at Channel Commercials PLC, Daf U.K. and Daf Europe, for supplying me with a terrific truck. This was matched by a superb level of aftercare and support that enabled me to successfully complete more than five years of arduous operations within Russia and the ex-Soviet Union.

I have written this manuscript in lasting memory of my very good friends and companions in the Russian adventure, Peter Newlyn, Gordon Jones and Mike Mudie. May they rest in eternal peace.

Foreword

BRITISH road transport undertakings to Russia in the early 1990s appear to be a part of the history of U.K. international haulage operations that are little remembered, known about or documented.

Therefore, I decided to write this book as an acknowledgement of the part played by British truckers, including myself, in opening up Russia to road movement of freight by U.K. companies.

Unlike the British involvement in Middle East haulage, which spawned numerous television documentaries and books, this major chapter in our past has gone mostly unnoticed and unrecognised.

The reason for this is probably that during the 1970s and 1980s, when Middle East haulage was so prevalent, vast numbers of U.K. trucks and drivers were engaged in those operations. By comparison, the number of British trucks running to Russia and the other states of the ex-Soviet Union in the 1990s was very small. Probably far fewer than 100.

Before U.K. hauliers could become fully established in carrying the rapidly expanding amount of British goods being imported by the Russians the work had been largely hijacked by East European hauliers.

The East Europeans, with much lower overheads and costs, vastly undercut British transport companies. This appealed greatly to freight agents and exporting companies. As Britain was undergoing a recession at the time most of the work was passed to the East Europeans as a means of cost cutting. Generally, they would carry out the operations for less than half the price of a British haulier.

Not all U.K. exporting companies used the East Europeans, however. Those that did not used British hauliers on principle, preferring to have a British driver accompanying their goods for reliability. These were in the main but not exclusively Blue Chip companies, such as Kodak and Rank Xerox. This left room for U.K. trucks and drivers to take part in and open up operations to and within Russia. However, the rapid increase in Russian imports saw borders allowing access into the old Soviet Union and between the ex-member states become swamped with freight traffic. This led, in turn, to journey times increasing dramatically as days were actually wasted by trucks sitting in border queues. Obviously, that impacted heavily upon the profitability of operations.

The collapse in the value of the Russian rouble in 1997 was, in fact, the last straw and virtually signalled the end of Russian operations for most British companies. This was especially as it coincided with the beginning of mass freight movement from the U.K. to North Africa.

The height of the British involvement in Russian haulage was, therefore, extremely short-lived in comparison to the halcyon days of Middle East operations.

Introduction

AS an owner-driver I spent the period April 1990 to June 1995 driving my truck exclusively on trips to, from and within the ex-Soviet Union. In addition, I actually lived in Moscow for most of those five years with my future wife, Elena.

We lived together in a flat in an area of the city known as Voikovskaya. This was situated in the Leningradski District of north-west Moscow. Our daughter, Margarita, was born in Moscow in June 1992.

My Daf 95, 350 ati, twin-steer tractor unit had been supplied to me by Channel Commercials, of Ashford, Kent, on Valentine's Day, 14th February 1990. I had taken it on a five-year lease-purchase agreement. Within just over two months I was running to Russia with it.

The truck was superb and Channel Commercials went on to provide me with excellent support, service and aftercare during my time trucking to Russia, as did the Daf European support network.

During that period of time, 1990–95, the Soviet Union changed dramatically and was ultimately broken up. I witnessed most of those changes, first hand. Sometimes being at the very centre of them.

Taking the opportunity to learn to speak, read and write Russian allowed me to communicate with Russian people from all walks of life and social status.

When people discover that I actually lived in Russia they are intrigued. Generally, this is because of the lack of understanding of Russia and its people caused by the Soviet Government's imposed secretive isolation.

Living in Moscow myself, as opposed to merely passing through the country, as most foreign truckers did, I was deeply immersed in the culture. Rather than merely seeing the situation in abstract; through the windscreen of my truck, I was completely involved in it.

The title of this book is a tongue in cheek reference to my friends, "The Cola Cowboys" who drove for Astran in the 1970s. A T.V. documentary series was made about them and this was followed by a book. It followed a group of Astran drivers as they travelled to the Middle East and back together.

The book was named "The Cola Cowboys", because the drivers, as did all of us who carried out Middle East work, carried cases of Coca-Cola to drink while operating in the oppressive heat.

In comparison, while in Russia I dressed like a cowboy in checked shirts, jeans and boots and regularly drank vodka-cola, so my Russian acquaintances regarded me as a "Vodka-Cola Cowboy".

Prior to working in Russia I had 15 years of international truck driving experience, my first trip being to Yugoslavia in 1975.

From 1978 until 1983 I was driving for Pro-Motor, the leading British company specialising in East European transport, among its other work. This included show tours – exhibition freight and vehicle launches in West Europe. I was involved in many of these jobs. However, the bulk of my work was carried out in Eastern Europe.

For Pro-Motor I made 86 trips to Yugoslavia, ten trips to Baghdad and drove in every country in Europe, including my first trip to Moscow in 1981.

Leaving Pro-Motor in late 1983, I then drove for David Croome until 1987, when I became an owner-driver.

In 1990 I was offered a one-year contract to run to Russia. The one year became five. This book attempts to explain the conditions under which we worked in Russia and the difficulties and problems that occurred in carrying out our work. For example, obviously, the extremely low temperatures and arduous conditions in which we operated, during the six-month long, winter periods.

Also, at that time all international movement of goods, even just within the E.U., were controlled by customs procedures. Each load was accompanied by customs documents that had to be presented at every border that you crossed. When large numbers of vehicles were doing this at the same time large queues of stationary trucks formed, some as long as 20 miles. This added greatly to our problems.

This is a compilation of a mixture of events that took place over a five-year period. I have also included incidents from my previous experiences within Eastern Europe, so as to provide background to the events in the early Nineties.

Where I have used Russian words, I have set them in italics. They are phonetic and reproduce the sound of the word. Obviously, they are not the Russian spelling, which would be in the Cyrillic alphabet.

The reader will discover that this book contains a description of many different situations, ranging from funny to harrowing and ultimately to tragic.

I hope that you enjoy reading my story and that it proves to be informative.

1

1990 "The Beginning of an Era"

MY first trip to Moscow was in 1981 when I was a company driver for Pro-Motor (Europe). At that time trucks crossed over the Polish–Soviet border between Terespol in Poland, and Brest in the U.S.S.R. This was an urban crossing. Therefore, your first view of the Soviet Union was the city of Brest. However, returning to Russia in 1990, I discovered that trucks were no longer allowed to cross over at the Terespol–Brest border as they had done on my previous trip.

So now, as an owner-driver, my first view of the Soviet Union on this trip came as I drove my brand new truck along a narrow, single carriageway road. This passed over the crest of a ridge in Eastern Poland. I had been driving along the main road from Warsaw to Terespol when, just before Terespol, I saw a road sign diverting trucks off the main road. Following this diversion I turned left and climbed to the top of the ridge, passing through a heavily forested area during the ascent.

Once on top of the ridge the woodland thinned out and I had a panoramic view of miles of flat open countryside that lay before me. I knew, from previous experience of the area, that the border crossing was not that far ahead. Therefore, by deduction, the land in the middle and far distance was Soviet territory.

I descended a gently sloping 3-mile stretch of road that had the occasional curve and bend. At the bottom of the incline, as the surrounding land flattened out, the roadway was carried the remaining 200 yards to the border gate upon an embankment. I had arrived at the freight vehicle-only border at Kukariki.

I stopped at the border gate, which was closed and studied the Polish border post that stood in front of me. There was no activity within the border area. No sign of vehicles or people, other than the gatekeeper. He was a Polish soldier, who was sitting in a gatehouse to the right of the gateway.

The soldier left his gatehouse and opened the gate for me. As I pulled forwards he reached up and passed me a small coarse sheet of paper, which was my border pass. Pointing to a bridge at the far right-hand side of the border complex, he indicated that I was to drive over it.

The Polish custom service was obviously not using the buildings on the Polish side of the border. I pulled away from him and drove across the tarmac surface of the border complex. Arriving at the bridge I drove up the incline and passed over what I found out to be a river known as "The Western Bug".

On the top of the bridge there was a sentry box, which was manned by a Soviet K.G.B. border guard. He merely waved for me to drive down the opposite side of the bridge into the Soviet border compound. From the top of the bridge I looked down on to the Soviet border complex below and mentally noted the layout of the enormous site.

In the centre of the vast expanse of tarmac stood a double-storeyed central building that housed all the Soviet bureaucracy and at that time the Polish authorities as well.

To either side of the building I could see open-sided canopies housing inspection pits and gantries. In front of the canopies, lanes were marked upon the tarmac. Here you waited before being called into the inspection area.

I then looked to my right. In the distance I could make out the buildings of the Soviet city of Brest. Turning my head to look out of the nearside window I noticed how, on the Soviet side of the river, there were open fields that led to thick woodland on the horizon.

Running away from the border complex were two parallel, five-metre-tall barbed wire fences. These had a ten-metre gap between them. The gap was a killing zone and would have contained anti-personnel land mines. The fences were alarmed so that anyone attempting to cross them set off an alarm on the Soviet side of the border. This, as I would later see, would send a group of highly armed Soviet K.G.B. Border Guards hurrying off along the fences to inspect the attempted crossing. I slowly drove down to the parking area, pulled into one of the marked lanes and stopped.

I had arrived at the border from Venray in Holland. There I had loaded from Rank Xerox's European Distribution Centre, for the Xerox Distribution Centre at Klyazma, just outside of Moscow. My trailer was loaded with a range of Xerox office equipment.

This was the initial load, in what was meant to be a one-year contract. I was meant to load from Venray every alternate Thursday and deliver to Klyazma as and when I got there.

The Xerox contract had been awarded to Kepstowe Freight Services, who were based in Wandsworth, south London. They were highly experienced freight forwarders who specialised in, and were the original pioneers of, haulage from Britain to the Soviet Union. They also carried out operations throughout the whole of East Europe, particularly exhibition transportation.

Kepstowes had in turn subcontracted a major share of the work to David Croome, who was an international road haulier based on the Isle of Sheppey. Croome operated a large fleet of vehicles but these were mainly wagon and drags.

The Xerox contract called for two 13.5-metre trailers to be used, so Croome had engaged John Dicks and myself, who were owner-drivers with our own tractor units. We were to pull the trailers and service the contract for him. And here I was entering the U.S.S.R. again. Nine years after my first trip to Moscow. Then I had been involved with an exhibition load to the Krasnaya Presnaya exhibition centre in central Moscow.

As with the Polish side of the border, the Soviet side was devoid of other trucks. I carried out the border procedure in just over an hour. Firstly, a K.G.B. guard led a sniffer dog around the vehicle. The dog was searching for the smell of drugs, human stowaways or secreted weapons.

Then, you were called forwards and drove into

the canopied area, where you parked over one of the empty pits. Here, the Polish officials carried out the passport control and a cursory cabin control. Then a Soviet officer climbed into the cab, took my passport and carried out a more thorough cab search.

The Sov' then climbed out and carried out a control of the exterior. Climbing down into the pit, he checked the underside of the truck. He then mounted the gantry so that he could inspect the top of the truck and trailer. Satisfied that I was not carrying anything illegal, I was guided out of the inspection area and told to park between the canopy and the exit gate. I then entered the main custom building, carrying my document folder.

Inside the large cavernous custom hall I presented my custom documentation to the Polish customs officers. It was duly stamped to confirm that I had completed the transit of Poland with the goods that were in the trailer.

I then reported to the Sovinteravtoservice office. Sovinteravtoservice was the Soviet Government Department responsible for the provision of services to all foreign motorists, be they travelling by car, bus or truck. They operated a chain of Motels throughout the U.S.S.R. that were manned by Sovinter' staff. The motels also included garage facilities where cars could be repaired. However, trucks could not be repaired at the motels. They had to be repaired at the local Sovtransavto depot. Sovtrans' was the state transport company.

It was at the Sovinteravtoservice office where my Russian trip permit had the route that I was to take to my destination marked upon it. The permit authorised you to drive, within the U.S.S.R., on a single return trip, to your point of unloading. You could then drive to a further point for reloading and return to the border. The stipulated route was written upon it because, at that time, foreign vehicles were only allowed to use a few specifically designated major roads.

Here, I also bought diesel coupons. These were necessary so as to legally obtain fuel within the Soviet Union. You purchased the coupons from Sovinter' at the border and redeemed them at the official refuelling points. This way the government received the money for the fuel. Alternatively, I could use the black market.

In 1990, the price of buying diesel coupons on the border was 1 Deutschmark per litre. This equated to 2.5 litres for £1. However, the black market price was 100 litres for £1. You could see where the attraction was to bend the rules slightly (slightly being an understatement).

With this procedure completed I made my way to the Soviet customs office, where I underwent the custom procedure. Here, my freight documents were registered and stamped. This showed that I had entered the U.S.S.R. at Kukariki and was under custom control until I presented the documents, at the final custom destination. In this case this was the Xerox terminal near Moscow.

Having changed some Deutschmarks into Roubles at the bank, I left the building and returned to my truck. Driving out of the border gate I emerged into the Belarus Soviet Socialist Republic, which was one of the fifteen republics that made up the U.S.S.R.

The single carriageway road that led 15 kilometres from the Border to the Brest–Moscow main road was mainly carried on an embankment. As the surrounding countryside was so flat this was to avoid the road becoming submerged below deep snow when winter was in full force.

Just before arriving at the main highway I filled my diesel tank at a roadside fuel station. Fortunately, the women running the station were amenable to selling their diesel for hard currency. Having bought 200 litres for five Deutschmarks I drove on.

So, having only been in the country for less than thirty minutes, I had already carried out a totally illegal act. It was not to be the last. Some people said that I had a "Criminal Intent". I would reply that I had never ever owned a tent.

Arriving at the main road, I was pleasantly surprised. I discovered that since my previous trip to Moscow the single carriageway arterial road that ran from Brest to Borisov, north-east of Minsk, had been replaced by a concrete motorway. This covered the first 430 kilometres of the 1,045 kilometres between Brest and Moscow. It had greatly improved the travelling time. In addition, it had improved driver comfort. But not my temper.

Cruising the 345 kilometres along the motorway from Brest to Minsk, the journey was continually interrupted by the police. They were hell-bent on relieving me of money.

I had decided to stop for the night at the Minsk motel. This was situated on the western outskirts of the city. My plan was to leave Minsk the following morning and complete the journey to Moscow that day.

I had bought a folding paper map of the western Soviet Union at the Sovinter' office and a book that contained the details of every Sovinteravtoservice motel and Sovtransavto depot throughout the whole U.S.S.R. However, having stopped at the Minsk motel in 1981, I knew exactly where it was.

The Minsk motel was built to the same pattern as all Sovinteravtoservice motels. These were situated in every major town and city throughout the U.S.S.R.

These motels supplied accommodation, secure parking areas and good food in their restaurant.

On arrival at Minsk, I left the motorway and drove to the motel. Having eaten in the restaurant and slept in my cab, I left the next morning and drove the 700 kilometres to Moscow. I needed to unload at Klyazma the following day, Monday 30th April. If not, I would be stranded in Moscow over the three-day May Day holiday.

Upon entering the U.S.S.R. I knew that I was driving into the largest nation in the world. But I had not realised that it comprised of 15 republics and covered an area of 8,650,000 square miles. It stretched 6,800 miles from east to west, which was 10,900 km. From north to south it stretched some 2,800 miles, 4,480 kilometres.

The population of the Soviet Union was just under 287 million people. When the Soviet Union was dissolved in December 1991, Russia alone became the largest country in the world with an area of 6,592,800 square miles. The population of the Russian Federation itself stood at 143 million people.

I learned these facts from a Soviet T.V. documentary that I watched in Moscow some years later.

Having left Minsk, it was a bright, sunny day as I drove through the low-lying Belarus plain. Firstly, on the concrete dual carriageway to Borisov and then from where it became an extremely wide single carriageway. It was wide enough in most places for eight trucks to have driven along it side-by-side.

This wide, arterial road, which stretched all the way to Moscow, was mainly a well surfaced, length of tarmac. There were the occasional potholes but within a very short time of beginning the contract I had learned where all of these were and avoided them.

What I also learned rather rapidly was where all of the G.A.I. (*Gosudarstveny. Avto. Inspectoret*) police posts were situated between Brest and Moscow. Also, where the hidden speed traps between the G.A.I. posts were. The G.A.I. were the traffic police; as opposed to the militia, who were the ordinary police.

The G.A.I. police posts were situated at every major crossroad, along the length of every highroad in the U.S.S.R. They were also to be found at the junctions where roads ran off from the main road to enter towns and cities.

The G.A.I. manning the M1 – the highway from Brest to Moscow – appeared to have made it their mission to stop every western truck using that road. The reason behind this practice was so that the police officers could amass a fortune in foreign currency.

This was through a combination of tactics such as catching trucks genuinely speeding, using a radar gun. Or by pretending to catch them speeding, carried out by falsifying the radar gun's reading. Once they had gained possession of your passport and visa they would simply demand money for their return. Or they would pretend that they were collecting foreign coins for their coin collection (once they had collected the right amount of coins, they got a western driver to change them for a note of the same value). Banks would not take coins.

Where this practice involved fining you, the fine was 10 Deutschmarks, which was £4. Therefore, it was in my greatest interest to avoid paying these uniformed bandits anything. In fact, on that first trip, I was stopped on no fewer than 30 occasions on the return trip from Kukariki to Moscow and back. Although I blagged my way out of some of the situations, it still ended with me having parted with around £100. Not only did this severely annoy me, but it ate into my profit margin.

Eventually, I arrived at Moscow in the late evening, having driven the 700 kilometres from Minsk to the Soviet capital. Other than at the interminable G.A.I. controls I had only stopped once. That had been at Smolensk, where I had topped up my diesel tank.

I was averaging somewhere near to 3.6 kilometres per litre, which equated to more than 10 miles per gallon. However, this was not an entirely accurate figure as the amounts that I had put in at Kukariki and Smolensk had both been 200 litres and neither had filled the tank completely.

The reason for this had been that you could not use coins at the fuel stations. Therefore, the minimum amount that I could purchase was 200 litres, for either a 5 Dm note, or 3 U.S. Dollars. The next amount that

I could buy would be 400 litres, for a 10 Dm note, or 6 U.S. Dollars. But as the tank only held 400 litres I would have to have been running on fumes to buy the larger amount.

Reaching Moscow – or Vodka City, as I was soon to begin to call it – I turned on to the M.K.A.D., (*Moscovnaya Klitzovaya Avto Daroga*). This was their answer to London's M25 and I drove clockwise to the north-east sector of the city. There, I left the outer ring road and took the Yaroslavl road heading north away from the city. Xerox's depot at Klyazma was approximately 20 kilometres along this road.

Close to my destination, I stopped at a G.A.I. post to ask for directions. While the officer on duty at the post was explaining to me the route that I needed to take a police car pulled up next to the post. Two uniformed officers dragged a male prisoner from the car, opened the door of the building and literally threw the man into the unlit police post. I heard him crashing about in the darkness. I pulled away from the scene as soon as the officer had finished explaining the route to me and I did not look back. I can only wonder what happened to the prisoner once I had left the scene.

Arriving eventually at my destination I parked the truck in the street and went to bed.

The next morning I received some particularly bad news. The Russian custom officers who were employed at the depot had decided to extend their May Day holiday, from three to four days, by taking the Monday off as well. This meant that I would be unable to tip the load until the Friday. I was left with four days to kill. They told me this in the office block boardroom where I had been taken after being allowed to enter the complex and park the truck. I had found six men seated around the large walnut boardroom table.

Three were to become very important to me. The first, Mikael Molkov, was the owner of the company Molkom. He provided the warehousing and distribution services to Rank Xerox. Weirdly, Molkom shared the depot with a Russian Army unit. Molkov allowed me full use of all of the site's non-military facilities.

Then there was Molkov's warehouse manager and English language interpreter, Piotr. Piotr was important as initially he translated for me and occasionally taught me some Russian. Then there was Boris, the depot's duty dog handler. He taught me more Russian and we had an enormous amount of fun together during the time that I delivered to Molkom.

My four days of enforced attendance at Molkom all basically followed the same routine. They started with coffee in the boardroom accompanied by the same six men. I then went to the dog handlers' accommodation where Boris would teach me basic Russian.

I would then leave the complex in my tractor unit and recce Moscow. This took the form of carrying out circuits in either direction of the complete length of the M.K.A.D., or heading into central Moscow and carrying out circuits of the inner ring road, which was called the *Sadovaya Klitzovaya* (The Garden Ring).

On the last two days, I drove into Moscow and proceeded to drive along all of the main roads that linked the M.K.A.D. to the Garden Ring. This gave me a perfect knowledge of the local layout and was to prove extremely beneficial later in my time in Moscow.

Many parts of the city were familiar to me from my previous trip to Moscow, when I had spent a week there, particularly, the Mezhnuarodni Hotel situated upon the eastern bank of the Moskva River close to the *Krasnaya Presnaya* exhibition ground. I drove there on the Monday and Tuesday to use the communications facilities. On the Monday, I sent a telex to Croome informing him that I could not unload until Friday and why. In the communication suite on Tuesday I was handed a reply from Croome instructing me that once I had unloaded at Molkom I was to drive to Siedlce, a small town between Brest and Warsaw and contact them from there.

For the other two days I did not return to the Mezh', as we called it for short.

My new friend Boris was actually a soldier, attached to the unit who shared the depot with Molkom. He taught me Russian through use of the German language. Like many members of the Army, G.A.I. and Militia, he had been stationed in East Germany and had learned the language there. As we both spoke German, he would tell me the word in German and then Russian. Crude but simple.

He also took me shooting in the woodland inside of the enormous complex. One day we shot with air rifles and on another we used Kalashnikov AK-47s on a target range at the extreme end of the depot. We had a terrific time together.

On May Day night he came and got me and took me on to the roof of the highest building on the site. Up there we looked south towards Moscow and saw a magnificent fireworks display. From launching sites all over the city thousands of rockets were sent into the night sky. The effect was spectacular; it was the finest firework display that I had ever seen.

On the Friday morning the Russian custom officers arrived at Molkom. The custom procedures were carried out and my cargo was discharged into the warehouse. Just as I was preparing to leave Molkom, the depot's electric gate slid open to admit five Croome trucks. They drove on to the site and parked around the central, tarmac square.

The drivers were all long-time friends of mine: Ronnie Seymour, Cyril Gardner, Tony Merry, Mike Mudie and Martin Dobie. I spent a short time with them and then left to drive to the Mezh'.

Between 1990 and 1992 the Mezh' was the recognised parking place for western drivers in Moscow. The hotel had been actually built by the Americans in preparation for the 1980 Olympics in Moscow. Ironic then that the U.S.A. boycotted those Olympics in protest over the Soviet invasion of Afghanistan.

Beside the extremely important communication centre, which was one of the only few places in Moscow where you could get immediate contact with the west, the hotel had other attractions. These included an English Pub, the John Bull. There was also a German bar, a sports bar and the Fortune bar. The Fortune bar was full of one-armed bandit machines and the working place of the $500-a-night prostitutes. They gathered at the bar so as to meet wealthy American businessmen who were using the hotel. The hotel also boasted a Chinese restaurant, coffee lounge and a fully stocked duty free shop. Everything was paid for in hard currency. I used to buy chocolate and sweets from the duty free shop to use as bribes so as to keep the wheels turning. A very worthwhile investment. However, of most importance was the health centre. Here, you could use the indoor swimming pool, showers, sauna and washing facilities. This amenity was exclusively for the use of hotel guests only. However, for 20 Marlboro cigarettes the manageress would allow western truck drivers access to the centre.

The Mezh' was situated on a corner where *Ulitsa 1905* met the *Krasnaya Presnaya* embankment on the eastern edge of the *Moskva Riyeka* (Moscow River). A kilometre north of the Mezh', along the river embankment road, stood the enormous Krasnaya Presnaya exhibition ground.

A kilometre south along the river you could see the *Bee-Yelli-Dom* (The White House). At the time, this was the Commi-Con building where the Trade Council of the Warsaw Pact met. It later became the Russian Parliament Building. And on the opposite side of the river from the White House stood the Ukraina Hotel, a skyscraper building and one of nine in the city built under Stalin.

At that time we used to park on the riverside embankment in front of the Mezh' hotel. I had just pulled the truck up and parked by the river when a battered little green Lada Zhiguli came and parked in front of my cab. The driver, Vlad', was a black market entrepreneur who I had actually done business with on my first trip to Moscow nine years previously. The boot of Vlad's car was crammed full with cartons of American cigarettes and bottles of

Sovietskoy shampansku (Soviet champagne). I bought six cartons of Marlboro Red cigarettes and twelve bottles of Shampansku from him. I also changed up some Deutschmarks for Roubles at black market rate.

He then drove away; his little car belching out clouds of dirty black smoke while it kangaroo hopped along the embankment road. I stowed my contraband in the wardrobe behind my driver's seat but took one of the bottles and went to sit in the sunshine. I perched on the riverside wall to wait for the Croome drivers to arrive.

My purchases had cost me £1 per carton of cigarettes and £1 per bottle of champagne. The entry to the health centre equated to one packet of Marlboro, which had cost me 10p. Not a bad price, for a sauna and shower.

I spent the evening drinking with the Croome drivers in the Mezh'. The following morning I set out for Poland on my own. They were going to spend the Saturday night in Moscow and asked me to stay with them, but having lost so much time at Molkom's I needed to put in some mileage. Although I would receive £50 per day demurrage for sitting in Klyazma, that was not comparable to what I earned when the truck was mobile. I could easily make a return trip to Moscow from London, say, in under ten days. For that I received £3,000. So, as long as I was moving I could make at least £300 per day. As I told the Croome lads, "Sorry boys. Time is money. My bloody money!"

Leaving Moscow I crossed the river and passed the Ukraina Hotel and the Pizza Hut building. After the Pizza Hut I passed Moscow's Triumphal Arch. This was a massive monument modelled on the Arc de Triomphe in Paris. The Moscow replica also had the horses and chariot on top of the arch. It was a memorial to Tsarist Russia's defeat of Bonaparte's French Army in 1812.

After the arch I passed the Soviet War museum park. I then passed through boring suburbs until I eventually drove across the bridge over the MKAD and headed out of the Soviet capital. Once free of Moscow I put the hammer down and headed for my first stopping point, Smolensk.

Having filled my water container with pure spring water at a layby just before Smolensk, I drove on to Minsk where I spent the night. That evening I ate in the Minsk motel restaurant and had the usual three-course meal. I unwillingly drank the cheap raw vodka, which I mixed with cola, the waitress having informed me that there was no champagne.

That night, as upon others, there was a drought of champagne in Minsk. Strangely though, during the course of the evening I watched as locals passed through the restaurant and went into the kitchen. They would emerge later with a full shopping bag, from the top of which would protrude the tops of champagne bottles. Obviously, the motel staff were reserving the champagne for friends and family at the expense of patrons of the restaurant.

However, it was quite a good night because all Sovinteravto' motels provide musical entertainment in the evenings, with a resident band. This brought out the locals and the restaurants were usually well patronised. I spent the evening dancing occasionally with a couple of the local women. They signified that they wanted me to dance with them in a strange manner. They would look directly at me and then thrust their head forward, forcefully, so as to fully grab my attention. They would then nod towards the dancefloor. A crude but effective gesture. Like using a sledgehammer to crack a pair of nuts.

As I had noticed in Moscow, the women in Minsk were always extremely well dressed. They either wore smart dresses, or a jumper and skirt or jeans combination. On the other hand, the men were extremely poorly dressed, in shabby suits, or cheap denim jeans and even cheaper cotton shirts normally buttoned right up to the top button. The men, generally, looked extremely skanky.

I realised that I had stood out from all of the other male patrons of the restaurant due to my western clothing. I always wore smart jeans, Wrangler, Lee Cooper or Falmer, usually with either an expensive checked shirt not buttoned to the top, or a T-shirt.

I carried a suitcase of clothes in the truck and a grip containing underwear and socks. I never had fewer than ten pairs of jeans with me at any time.

In Soviet society I had sartorial class. And certainly, more and better casual clothes than any of them.

Arriving at the turn-off from the M1 on to the link road to Kukariki, I drove into the fuel point and filled the tank to the brim. To do this I used Sovinter' diesel coupons, which were in 100 litre denominations. I then drove to the border. Once again, the truck crossing point was empty. Obviously, due to the May Day holidays.

I lied to the Sovinter' staff saying that I only had 50 litres in my diesel tank when in fact, it was brimful with 400 litres. Presumably due to institutionalised idleness, they did not go out to the pits and dip my tank. They merely accepted me at my word. I imagine that they could not be bothered to go outside where the temperature was only +2C.

Soon, I had cleared both sets of customs and had driven over the bridge into the new Polish compound. When I had reached the top of the bridge, I stuck my right arm out of my driver's window and gave the Soviet Union a formal, two-fingered, salute. This was a demonstration of my anger at the continuous police controls that had broken up my driving shifts unreasonably. It also signified the resentment that I felt at the amount of money that had been taken from me, mostly under spurious circumstances. To be honest, I was bloody angry.

Looking forwards, from the top of the bridge I noticed that the new Polish layout was similar to the Soviet's, with a central building, which had canopied pits and gantries on either side of it. Traffic heading into Belarus would use the nearest side to the roadway, from the Polish gate to the bridge. Trucks heading into Poland would drive to the rear of the building for their formalities. The Polish customs were working on the Soviet side until their own new facility was completed. Then it would be all change. This time I just drove directly to the gate and exited the border.

Reaching Siedlce, (Pronounced *Shiltza*), I turned off the bypass and drove towards the centre of the town. The Hetmann motel stood beside the road, 500 metres from the bypass. There was only one other truck in the enormous tarmac motel car park. I recognised that it was John Dicks'. For some reason he had separated his tractor unit from the trailer.

Entering the motel building, I discovered him in the restaurant. We had dinner together and drank quite a few half litres of Polish beer during the evening. I was just glad to be able to drink decent quality beer after the raw Russian vodka.

John told me that although we had applied for our Soviet visas at the same time, his had still not come through. Therefore, the plan was for me to turn around and head back to Moscow with his trailer. He was going to take mine back to the U.K..

Early the next morning, we swapped trailers and he headed off towards Warsaw. I drove back in the opposite direction towards Kukariki.

Swapping trailers in Poland and returning to Russia was to become a major feature of my work because each driver's Soviet multi-entry visa cost £385 for a year. Kepstowe saved a fortune by turning me around and making the most of mine. This was to work to my advantage, as you will see.

2

"Back in the U.S.S.R."

DRIVING from Siedlce back to the border at Kukariki, I was not feeling overly happy. My first trip as an owner-driver had been successful up to a point. I had made some Russian friends who could teach me Russian and socially it had not been a bad experience. However, the persistent activities of the greedy G.A.I. officers relieving me of hard-earned cash had marred my enjoyment. So much so that I would not have turned round at Siedlce if John was in possession of his Soviet visa. I would have quite happily have gone back to England and forgotten all about Russia. However, things would improve virtually immediately and I could then begin to enjoy working and living in the country.

I completed the border formalities and drove to the M1 junction. Turning on to the M1, I headed for Minsk. Predictably, I was pulled over at the first G.A.I. post that I came to. I now put into practice an idea that Boris at Molkom, had suggested and that I had refined.

At the Minsk motel, on the way back from Moscow, I had bought four small Soviet Union flag stickers, with the gold hammer and sickle logo, on a red background. I had attached two of them to the front of the truck, at each corner, just above the radiator grille. Outside of them, towards the edge of the grille I had fixed two Union flag stickers, which were the same size.

Now my truck had a plain white cab with a dark grey chassis, steps and front underskirt. It was unmarked and showed no sign writing to indicate who the truck belonged to. In that way, it was similar to the joint venture vehicles that operated out of Moscow.

Joint venture companies were business entities, half-owned by a Soviet company, or individual and half-owned by a Western company or individual. Their vehicles were generally unmarked, presumably to stop them from being robbed by Russian criminals, thinking that the driver would be carrying wads of hard currency.

Also, their registration numbers were different from Soviet numbers. The Soviet plates featured white letters and numbers, upon a black background. Their newer plates had black writing upon a white background with a segregated area number. Moscow was 77.

However, the J.V. numbers were made up of a single letter, followed by two or three numbers, followed by a further two or three letters. Black characters, upon a white plate. Therefore, my registration number, G642TKJ, resembled a J.V. number plate with its black letters on the front white plate.

Virtually all G.A.I officers spoke German, having served in the D.D.R, while in the Army. So, when stopped at that first G.A.I. post, I told the police officer, in German, that far from living in England, I actually lived in Moscow, with my wife, who was Russian. I was driving for an Anglo–Soviet J.V. company and was paid in Roubles. Taking me at my word, he fined me a Rouble and allowed me to proceed. I was getting 50 Roubles to the pound on the black market, so my fine had been 2p. Much better, from my point of view, than £4.

I drove past Minsk, keeping to the motorway, and made my way to Smolensk. I then turned off the main road and parked at the Smolensk motel for the night. Here, I made the acquaintance of the local black marketer, Igor, and his friends, Arkadie, Gennie and Piotr. I was to conclude some very interesting deals with them over the coming years.

Driving from the border to Moscow I was taking notice of the countryside. I realised that unlike the flat, marshy lowlands of the majority of Belarus, once that you had passed Borisov you began to climb up into hilly land. The open countryside that you had passed through then turned to a mixture of dark, brooding pine or birch forests. These hemmed in the long, straight, broad roadway. This was interspersed with stretches of open countryside and made the drive less boring than crossing Belarus.

Occasionally I drove through small villages comprised of crude wooden bungalows, all of which were painted in insipid pastel colours; faded pale yellows, or light blues or light greens.

I had crossed from Belarus into the Russian Federation between the villages of Goryani, in Belarus, and Kurgan, in Russia. Either side of the border line there were police posts. However, there were no custom formalities there at that time. Once you had entered the Soviet Union, you were able to drive directly to your destination point.

An old tatty metal sign indicated to you that you were leaving Belarus and another told you that you were entering Russia. Basically, it was like crossing from one county to another in Britain. I was stopped at both police posts for the customary attempt of fleecing me of hard currency. Both times the "living in Moscow" routine worked and I was extremely pleased. It was only the incessant stopping to deal with the G.A.I. that now irritated me. But I gained immense pleasure from conning them and that compensated somewhat for the delays.

An interesting fact was that although the G.A.I. persecution continued for a couple of months, it suddenly stopped. The police lost all interest in Western trucks and their drivers. This may have been because, as I knew, the Dutch, German and French drivers trucking to Moscow complained bitterly about it to their embassies. Presumably, the embassies took the matter up with the Soviet authorities. I am not sure whether this was the actual reason but it would seem feasible. The Soviets, particularly their government, were importing ever-increasing amounts of goods and may have stamped down on G.A.I. activities to demonstrate that the U.S.S.R. was a normal law-abiding country (as if).

Once safely in Moscow, I parked at the Mezh', where I socialised with some Dutch drivers from the company Nesotra. This was Netherlands–Soviet–Transport, a Dutch subsidiary of the Soviet company Sovtransavto. Sovtrans' also owned a German subsidiary Desotra, Deutsch–Soviet Transport.

In 1990, there were only a limited number of

Western drivers who were running exclusively between the West and Russia; ten Dutch, ten French, four German and ten British. Of the ten British drivers, three of us, Paul Cantwell, Dave Lloyd and myself, had all been stationed at Hohne in West Germany at the same time in the late 1960s. Dave was with 32 Armoured Engineers and Paul and I with the 2nd Tanks. Some coincidence. But by the middle of 1991, I was to be the only one of those ten British drivers still running exclusively to Russia.

Having delivered my cargo of photocopiers at Molkom and having a short Russian lesson with Boris, I left Moscow and headed back to Poland. I had received a telex from Croome instructing me to make my way to Siedlce. There I was to wait for another trailer coming up from Venray, loaded for Molkom.

At Kukariki there had been two trucks heading back into Poland at the same time as me. One was Czechoslovakian and the other Hungarian. Strangely, the Sovinteravtoservice officer, on duty, who was named Luda', short for Ludmilla, went out to the pits and dipped both of their tanks.

Obviously, they were both at it, because they were called into the open fronted office and I saw wads of notes changing hands.

My truck was not dipped. This may have been because when reporting to the Sovinter' desk I had handed over some sweets and bars of chocolate that I had bought in Moscow. One of my little mottos is; "get to know the rules of the game and then use them to your own advantage".

In a rabidly corrupt society such as the Soviet Union virtually everybody was corruptible. The

Sovinter' staff could be bought for a few sweets or bars of chocolate to ensure that they turned a blind eye to the contents of my diesel tank.

For Vlad' in Moscow the police patrolling the area of the Mezh' were obviously being bought to turn a blind eye to his black market operation. The same was no doubt true for Igor at the Smolensk motel and his counterpart at the Minsk motel, Sergei, who was their local spiv.

The G.A.I. officers manning the M1 were also obviously as bent as corkscrews. Their activities of relieving foreign drivers of hard currency were not legal. Fiddling radar gun readings was hardly legal. And what little bullies they were in that they threatened to take you to court if you refused their spurious demands. Boris "the dog" told me that if that happened to me I should refuse to pay the fine up to the moment that they told me to get into their car to be driven to the local courthouse. If it got to that stage I should then have a change of heart and pay up. He assured me that if I was actually taken to court then I would be relieved of a lot more money than the police had demanded, because the court would want their cut.

The other likely outcome, which Boris pointed out, would be that the police would not take me to the court, at all, but drop me off miles from my truck and I would have to find my way back on foot. In the process of this abduction I might also receive a roughing up, which if I retaliated, would result in a good beating being meted out to me. This could then lend itself to me, rather than being dropped off and left to fend for myself, being dragged before the court and charged with "assault of a police officer". The fact that I was the one who had received the said "assault of a police officer" would be neither here nor there. I would be remanded in custody, which would prove to be extremely bleak and my truck would be left at the roadside, open to the goods being stolen from the trailer and the cab ransacked for anything of value.

Therefore, in all of my dealings with the G.A.I. officers I was pleasant and apparently respectful at all times, although I actually had no respect for them whatsoever.

I arrived at Siedlce, where I had to wait for my next trailer to arrive. Then, once again, I was under way back to Moscow. I repeated this trip a further three times before eventually having a complete change from the tedious monotony of shuttling between Siedlce and Moscow. I had to drive to Moscow but from there did not return directly to Siedlce. I passed through it after I had been to Ukraine and was on my back to the U.K. And beyond, actually.

3

It's a Long Way to Cyril Gardner

M Y next trailer change saw me return to Moscow again but the trailer was loaded with exhibition goods bound for the Krasnaya Presnaya Exhibition ground. I took over the trailer in Siedlce and headed back to Moscow. At Siedlce I had found not only a driver there with my next trailer, but my friend Cyril Gardner, a Croome driver, was waiting for me. We were to run to Moscow together. He was unloading at Klyazma and then we were to drive down to Kiev, capital of Ukraine. There we were to load bales of cotton bound for either Tipperary in Ireland, or for Devon.

We travelled to Moscow and parked up at the Mezh'. The following morning, he headed off for Rank Xerox, while I drove down to the exhibition ground. At Krasnaya Presnaya the agent's staff unloaded the trailer that afternoon. Once empty I drove out of the exhibition ground and parked up beside the Mezh', where I waited for Cyril to return from Klyazma.

This load to Krasnaya Presnaya was the beginning of a complete change of direction in the work that I carried out for Kepstowe Freight and Croome. The

Rank Xerox contract had been altered because its business with the Soviet Union had picked up dramatically. Instead of sending a trailer per week into Venray it now required much more haulage from Kepstowe on a weekly basis. In order to accommodate Rank, Kepstowe used Croome's vehicles more due to the extra carrying capacity of his road trains. I was put across to carry out Kepstowe's other work, which was great, because it offered me more variety. As well as loads to Klyazma I was also going to deliver to other destinations in Moscow and beyond.

Cyril returned from Klyazma and the following morning we left Moscow en route for Borispol, near Kiev. A day later we arrived in Borispol and located the factory of Femtech, the company we were loading for.

Femtech was a J.V. company, set up between Tampax in the U.K. and a cotton producing company in Ukraine. Tampax had exported all the production line equipment to Borispol so the company could produce tampons to be marketed locally. This was in return for bales of cotton. We were to load some of those bales of cotton and take them to Tipperary.

From the Femtech factory we drove to the town of Cherkassy, a distance of 200 kilometres. We were accompanied by a Ukrainian named Victor. He was high up in the management structure of the company on the Ukrainian side of the business. Cyril led the way, with Victor in the cab beside him to give directions.

When we arrived at our destination, Viktor guided us to a hotel, where we were to spend the night. Victor spent his night with a girlfriend from the Cotton company.

The following day we set out for the cotton baling plant, where we loaded the cotton for Ireland. The loading took all day and Viktor suggested that we stop the night at the hotel again. As the hotel had no restaurant or bar, I refused. Had I liked Viktor, who wanted to spend another night with his girl-friend in Cherkassy, I would probably have agreed. Unfortunately, I did not like him because he had basically inferred that I was not clever enough to learn Russian. I was to prove him completely wrong.

That evening we drove through the gathering gloom back to Kiev. Most of the gloom was Viktor's.

Having spent the night in the Femtech compound we then drove to Borispol airport, where Victor, who by now would hardly talk to me, carried out the customs procedure.

Afterwards, Cyril took him back to Femtech and dropped him off at the gate. Then, we both drove away, heading for Kiev.

Kiev was an ancient city and at one time had been the capital of the Russian Orthodox Church. When the Christian religion had spread, from the Middle East to Europe, the Catholic Church, based in Rome, had spread the religion throughout Western Europe. In the East, the Orthodox Church had spread it through Eastern Europe and Russia. The centre of the Orthodox Church had been Constantinople, which had been in Greece, until the Turks invaded and it then became part of Turkey. The Muslim Turks had split the Orthodox Church into two factions by driving a wedge between Greece and Russia.

The head of the Greek Orthodox Church was then based in Athens, while the Russian Orthodox

Church based itself in Kiev before moving eventually to Moscow.

Old Kiev is set on a hilltop, on the western bank of the Dnieper River. The modern suburbs have now spread on the western side and over to the eastern bank, creating modern Kiev.

On the hilltop of Old Kiev there are numerous white-walled churches with towers topped with golden globes. These are religious Byzantine-styled buildings, typical in the ex-Soviet Union.

As Cyril and I approached Kiev from the east we could see an enormous statue that dominated the hillside on the western bank of the Dnieper River. It was a 100-metre high statue of a Soviet soldier who was holding a broad sword aloft. This was a tribute to the Red Army, who had liberated Kiev from Hitler's fascist forces during the Second World War.

We crossed the river and bypassed the centre of Kiev by following the southern ring road.

Having passed Kiev, we headed for Rovno.

Two days later we came to the Polish–East German border at Swieco–Frankfurt Oder. We completed the Polish custom formalities and then drove across the river, where we undertook the German procedures.

The Germans had now introduced the T form – E.E.C. custom documents – to East Germany. This harmonised the custom services in East and West Germany. They had sent West German customs officers into the east to teach their eastern brothers the system.

As we had travelled from Ukraine on C.M.R.s we now had to use a German customs agent and have

T1s made. We then presented the documents to the German customs for registration.

On that day Cyril and I made history. We were the first Englishmen to have T1s created at that border. Also, our T1s were the first made at Frankfurt Oder with goods from Ukraine. As well as that, they were the first created at Frankfurt Oder for goods travelling to Ireland.

Yes. We were going to Tipperary. And that was a long, long, bloody way.

Having cleared customs we pushed on to Michendorf services and the following day we drove to Zeebrugge to get the ferry to England. En route we stopped at Locheren in Belgium, situated between Antwerp and Ghent, where we put the trucks through the truck wash. Having driven through the thickly dusted roads of Ukraine both of our trucks were filthy.

Having washed the trucks we drove to Zeebrugge. At the P&O freight office we booked land bridge tickets. Land bridge meant that we were transiting England to get to Ireland. We would take a ferry to Dover, drive to Liverpool and then take a B & I ferry from Liverpool to Dublin.

We booked in with P&O, received our tickets and headed back to our trucks. Immediately, we were called forward for loading and drove on to the ship, which was destined for Dover.

We had booked in with one truck each, which contained one driver each. Return. Zeebrugge to Dublin and back again. This was to become an important distinction, for Cyril.

At Dover, we lodged our custom paperwork with the clearing agent and went to bed. By now, it was 6 in the morning. When I awoke at 4pm Cyril had gone. I retrieved my papers from the agent and then I drove to Croome's yard in Queenborough on the Isle of Sheppey.

The next morning, Cyril turned up at 10 accompanied by his wife, Doreen. Cyril told me that neither of them had been to Ireland before so he was taking her with him. We started our trucks and drove to Liverpool.

Having arrived in Liverpool, we drove to the docks and entered the B&I complex. Parking in the waiting bays we entered the B&I office. I booked in first at the loading desk and the clerk checked my paperwork.

Having satisfied himself that all was in order he prepared to print out my loading document for the ship. "How many drivers?" he asked, looking across at Cyril and Doreen.

"One," I replied. He printed off the loading slip.

"Food on the boat is free," he said, passing me the tickets and added, "Loading will start at around 10pm. There is a driver's rest cabin next door with food and drinks machines." I thanked him and walked away from the counter. Cyril took my place.

This was when the distinction as to how many drivers per vehicle had booked in at Zeebrugge came into effect. As Cyril had booked one driver on his ticket in Belgium, he was asked to pay extra for two drivers crossing the Irish Sea and back. £54 extra, in fact.

Cyril changed colour. Actually he changed many colours and ended up with a pallid white complexion tinged with green. He passed over the money with a serious lack of grace.

We made our way to the drivers' lounge; a shabby Portakabin that contained a few vending machines and a television. We sat in the lounge, which was full of Irish drivers, and watched the World Cup semi-final between England and Germany. England lost on penalties, following a 1-1 draw at the end of extra time. This was met with wild cheering by the Irish, who had all become supporters of Germany for some reason.

When I pointed out, rather loudly, that the Irish football team had an English manager, Jacky Charlton, the wild celebrations subsided.

Just then, we were called out to drive down to the loading quay. All the vehicles parked in the waiting lanes drove one behind the other down to the berth. The scene was a typical night loading operation. The boat was anchored at the end of the jetty. Arc lamps highlighted the scene as trucks, their headlights on, moved through the dark to load upon the ship. Dock machinery moved around the quay hooking up unaccompanied trailers and running them up the ramp to load them on the vehicle decks.

Men in high vis jackets spoke into hand-held radio receivers organising the loading. Eventually, both Cyril and I had driven on to the ship and parked among all of the other vehicles. Climbing out of our cabs Cyril, Doreen and I made our way up to the accommodation deck.

We found our way to the drivers' lounge, where heaps of food were waiting to be eaten. The cooks had filled the stainless steel receptacles with piles of bacon, egg, sausages, toast, tomatoes, beans and mushrooms.

Cyril supervised Doreen as they passed along the row of food containers, ensuring that she filled her plate so that it was brimming over with breakfast items. He did the same with his own.

When we sat down to eat, they sat side by side and I sat opposite to them. I could not see their faces, because they were each hidden behind a mound of food.

I ate my modest meal, drank a couple of beers and left them chewing their way through enough food to feed Africa for two weeks. This was Cyril's method of recouping some of the money that he had paid out for Doreen's ticket. As the food was free, I did not see the point.

We landed in Dublin at around 6am and after the Irish customs had cleared our customs paperwork we drove through the city and emerged on the road to Tipperary. En route we stopped for breakfast at a country pub. From there we drove to the Tampax factory at Tipperary.

When you enter the town there is a white sign with black writing that says, "Welcome to Tipperary. You have come a long, long way". I thought to myself, "I bloody well know."

We found the Tampax factory and parked inside the compound. A young Irish lady in a white laboratory coat took samples from the cotton bales on both my truck and Cyril's. She went off to analyse them in her laboratory and the site manager informed us that they had received bales from Ukraine that had contained mould. If our loads were found to contain mould, then we were going to have to take them back across the Irish Sea and deliver them to a Tampax factory in Devon.

While we were waiting for a decision, Cyril said to me, "Viktor would have loved that."

"Loved what?" I said, disinterestedly.

"That sign. 'Welcome to Tipperary. You have come a long, long way'."

"Why?" I asked, without enthusiasm.

"Because, before we left Borispol I asked him, are we going to Tipperary, or Devon," Cyril said, adding, "and he replied Cyril, you are going to Tipperary and that is a long, long way."

Eventually the young lady scientist was content that the bales did not contain mould and they were unloaded there in Tipperary. While the bales were unloaded, Cyril rang David Croome's office to let them know that we were unloading. He was told that we were to make our way back to Dublin and to call Croome's office before we loaded on to the B&I ship. Under no circumstances were we to go on to the ship without ringing.

Realising that we would not make it back to Dublin in time to catch the evening ferry, we stopped the night at the country pub where we had eaten breakfast. The next morning, we drove to the ferry port.

We booked in at the B&I office and when we were called we drove down to the quay to load on to the ship. While we were waiting to load Cyril was called back to the B&I office. As he drove away I was instructed to drive on to the ferry.

With my truck safely loaded on the truck deck I went up to the drivers' lounge and began to have breakfast. Shortly afterwards I was joined by Cyril and Doreen. Cyril informed me that David Croome was less than happy with me as I had not phoned him before loading on to the boat. It turned out that he had a load arranged from Limerick to London that I should have loaded on the following Monday. Now, he would have to let the load go as it would not be worthwhile making me return across the Irish Sea.

No doubt, I was not flavour of the month in Croome's office that Saturday morning. Although, looking on the bright side, I did not have to spend the weekend in Limerick.

When the ship landed there was a message waiting for me at the B&I office, in Liverpool. This told me to report to Kepstowe's office in Wandsworth on the Monday morning.

Kepstowe Freight Services Ltd was a pioneer in haulage to Eastern Europe and particularly Russia, during the 1970s, '80s and '90s. It specialised in exhibition forwarding throughout the Commie bloc. In fact, it actually had a worldwide operation shipping exhibition goods around the globe. The business had grown because having successfully shipped exhibition goods for customers, it had then become the transporters of choice for those clients. This had necessitated it expanding its haulage operations to accommodate the increase in business.

In 1990 it was running four trucks of its own and using Croome and Johnny Dicks and myself to carry the excess for East European destinations and now Russia.

Kepstowe's premises were off Garrett Lane in Wandsworth. The company was owned and run by Neil Richardson, a forthright, larger than life character who was an ex-public schoolboy. He was assisted by his wife Marta, a wonderful Hungarian lady.

There were three other main characters at Kepstowe: Rob, Charlie and Henry. They too were ex-public schoolboys. Charlie and Henry were brothers. Not only did these three help to run the business from the office in Wandsworth, but they also acted as exhibition site reps alongside Neil.

I had worked with all of them on numerous exhibition sites throughout Eastern Europe. Sometimes I had been carrying their goods and at other times had been there for other exhibition forwarders. This was mostly in my days with Pro-Motor.

The whole exhibition site and Eastern Europe scene was a bit incestuous. Everyone knew one another and people moved between companies engaged in the same work.

Besides those five who ran the company, there was Marion, a nice middle-aged woman, who was the bookkeeper and Steve, a guy in his mid-twenties, who ran the warehouse operation.

The main driver was my good friend, Pete Newlyn. A large guy, with white hair and beard, he actually resembled the country singer Kenny Rogers, although I told him that he looked more like Dolly Parton.

I reported to Rob, who informed me that they would load the trailer during the afternoon, with groupage for Kiev and So-Fin, in Moscow. Therefore, the morning was basically my own to do as I pleased.

I spent the morning walking up to the shopping centre by the South Circular and doing some retail therapy. I bought some new clothes and. most importantly, I found a bookshop that was selling foreign dictionaries and language learning books. Here I purchased a Russian–English dictionary and a book titled Learn Russian in three months. It actually took me six months to master the whole contents of the book but by that time my Russian was virtually fluent.

Content with my purchases, I made my way back to the truck and sat in the cab studying my Learn Russian book. I could already understand and speak some Russian, which I had learned from Boris the Dog and Piotr, at Klyazma. I was also learning from Julia, an office worker at So-fin.

The Cyrillic alphabet I had learned during my many trips to Yugoslavia and Bulgaria, where they used the same script as in Russia.

In Russia, most people did not speak a foreign language. Therefore, it was important to learn the language in order to communicate. That ensured that you could get what you wanted, whether it was directions, fuel, food or anything else that you needed.

The Hugo manual started you off with a small scenario. It used phonetic spelling so that you could pronounce the Russian words, as well as having the script written in English and Russian.

As you progressed throughout the book, it built, lesson by lesson, on what you had already learned and then added to it.

Due to the amount of time spent sitting around, at warehouses, factories, borders and customs depots, I had more than enough time to learn. I made it a priority to spend at least an hour every day, reading and learning. Usually it was two or three hours of bloody hard work.

4

Full Spid Ahead

BY 6pm that evening, the trailer had been loaded. I had been given my customs documents and I was driving away from Wandsworth, heading for Dover.

I crossed the channel during the night and parked the truck in Zeebrugge. When I woke in the morning, I set out for Kiev, not realising that I would not be bringing the truck back into England for at least nine months.

I arrived in Kiev and made my way to Mykhaila Hrushevskovo Street. Parking in the street, near the central library, I crossed the road to a small hotel, where I had dinner and a few drinks. I then went back to the cab and went to bed.

In the morning I drove to the railway goods yard near Ivana Fedorova Street, where it had been arranged that I would meet people from the Kiev SPID clinic. The goods that I had on board for them turned out to be syringes, needles and medical equipment.

The guy, from the clinic, who was organising my customs clearance, spoke very good English and informed me that SPID meant Aids in English. He explained to me that in the Soviet Union there was a sense of denial regarding Aids. The official line was that there were only about 300 cases in the whole of the Soviet Union, whereas, the actual number of cases in Ukraine alone was more than 3,000. Therefore, taking the U.S.S.R. as a whole, the true figure would be astronomical.

I asked him why there were so many cases and he explained that the Soviet Union sent thousands of people to Africa and Asia to assist communist regimes in those parts of the world. Obviously, these technicians, observers and military personnel formed sexual relationships with natives of these countries, where Aids was rife. The Sovs became infected and brought the disease back home and spread it further by sexual contact within their own country.

There was also the effect from the rampant drug taking within the Soviet Union, which the government denied vehemently. Some Soviet soldiers serving in Afghanistan during the Soviet occupation in the 1980s had turned to drug taking to alleviate the situation they encountered. During my time in Russia I met a large number of ex-Soviet soldiers who had served in Afghanistan and they informed me of the brutality that they had witnessed first-hand. These incidents involved cold-blooded murder, decapitation, torture, massacres, rape and the killing of innocent bystanders, by both sides.

Afghanistan, the world's major grower and supplier of poppies, whose seeds are the base of opium, was awash with opiate-based drugs such as heroin. Afghans, keen to make money, willingly supplied Soviet troops with drugs. The Soviet soldiers, having become hooked upon these narcotics, returned to the U.S.S.R. requiring supplies to feed their habit.

As Afghanistan's northern border was shared with the southern border of the Soviet Union and this frontier was not totally secure, drugs were transported by smugglers to feed this lucrative market. In Russia it was controlled by the Russian Mafia.

We unloaded the four pallets for the SPID centre and I drove back to the library, where I parked the truck. On the way I had passed Kreshatik Square, Kiev's main central feature. This was just down the hill from the library.

I walked to Kreshatik Square where Ukrainian nationalists were demonstrating in support of the nationalist demand for separation from the Soviet Union and Ukrainian independence.

Gorbachev's philosophy of Perestroika and Glasnost had made it possible for dissenting voices to be heard within Soviet society, when previously all political dissent had been suppressed. This was a new age of political freedom, up to a point, within the U.S.S.R.

There were also communist counter-demonstrators in the area. I did not stay long in case the situation became violent. They would not be amused to find a foreigner involved.

The following day I drove to Moscow.

Upon arriving at the Mezh' I found a number of Western trucks parked up. There were two other British trucks that belonged to Barry Martin Trucking, who were based near Gatwick. There were also a couple of Dutch trucks and a French truck.

Although their trucks were parked near the hotel, there was no sign of the drivers. I presumed that they were sightseeing in central Moscow. Not long after I had parked up, Vlad arrived with his little car stocked up with goodies. I purchased some champagne and cigarettes, which I stowed in my duty free locker.

However, as it was a beautiful sunny afternoon I kept one bottle of champagne out, opened it and sat upon the parapet wall beside the Moskva River, drinking it. As I sipped the Soviet sparkling wine I watched the sparkling dots of the sunlight reflecting from the waves in the river. Just before I finished the bottle, I noticed a David Croome truck making its way across the river bridge, up near the Ukraine hotel. Shortly afterwards, I saw it driving along the embankment road heading for my location. It arrived at the Mezh', drove past where my truck was parked and turned around, out of sight, further along the embankment. It returned to park behind my truck. The driver climbed from the cab and I saw that it was my great mate, Ronnie Seymour.

5

Who Dares Grins

RONNIE was a very good, long term, friend of mine. We usually managed to have a few laughs together. Straight after his arrival Vlad returned and Ronnie bought some champagne and cigarettes. He opened one of his bottles and we drank it, sitting in the sunshine on the parapet.

As afternoon turned to evening we decided to go to The Arbat restaurant for dinner. Entering the large foyer of the Arbat building, we looked towards the main wooden-doored entrance to the restaurant hall. Standing in front of the double doors were a group of waiters. They were dressed in white shirts and black trousers.

Before entering the restaurant you made a deal with one of them, usually the one who quoted the lowest price. You told them what you wanted, for example, a three-course meal with champagne. They then told you whether they could supply it and at what price. Normally the food was not a problem, but it depended upon whether they had champagne. This evening there was no champagne, so we settled for a half litre of vodka each.

The price was $15 (£10) each, which we

agreed with and we were led in by our waiter and seated.

The restaurant hall was enormous. At one end there stood a stage for the cabaret acts to perform upon. In front of the stage was a wooden-floored dancing area, for when the cabaret entertainment ended and the resident band played music to dance to. The restaurant tables, with their white tablecloths, were laid out in long lines as in a banqueting hall. High-backed oak dining chairs were lined along the rows of tables, for the patrons to sit upon.

The waiter seated us so that Ronnie sat opposite to me. He was facing the stage, while I had my back to it. We were seated close to the middle of the long run of tables, but there were no other diners to either side of us. It was a quiet night by the Arbat's standards.

Sitting at the row of tables two rows behind Ronnie were two men and a girl. One of the men had his back to me, while the girl and the other man were facing me. The girl was slim, with long black hair and a glorious, beautiful, high cheekboned face.

Our waiter brought us our carafes of vodka, which we began to drink before the food started to arrive. The cabaret began and I turned in my chair, to watch it. It began with a female dance troupe and this was followed by a female Russian singer, who sang only American and English songs without a trace of a Russian accent.

The star turn was a male gymnast, who performed an exemplary routine, using two ropes that hung from the ceiling above the stage. I would imagine that he had been a specialist on the rings when he had been competing. I was to see his act a number of times and never tired of watching it. He concluded by rolling himself up the ropes until he was virtually at ceiling height above the stage.

When he had finished his act the band began to play dance music. I noticed the girl behind Ronnie get up and join the guy who had his back to me at the end of the line of tables where they were sitting. They made their way on to the dance floor and began to dance. Ronnie and I sat eating our meal and drinking the vodka. We finished our carafes and the waiter brought us a litre carafe of brandy, for which we negotiated an extra price.

While the band played their music the girl and her male friend retook their seats and I became aware that when the man was not watching she was staring at me. Soon, she began nodding her head towards the dance floor and obviously wanted me to ask her to dance.

Just then, the man facing her got up and she went with him towards the end of the row of tables. He was slightly ahead of her and she looked in my direction and tossed her head. It was as if she was saying that she had to dance with him because I had not asked her to dance.

I was puzzled by this reaction. Neither Ronnie nor myself were exactly small in stature and we were no strangers to an occasional act of violence. However, we were out for a night out and a good drink and not for a Sunday night brawl. I did not know how the girl's companion would react if I had the brass neck to ask her for a dance. So I did not bother.

However, I told Ronnie what was happening and when the man and the girl had returned to their seats he casually turned round to have a look. She was once again nodding her head to signify that she wanted to dance with me.

"She definitely wants you to dance with her," said Ronnie.

"I could do without a punch in the mouth, though," I replied.

By this time the band announced that they were going to play their last song of the night and our waiter arrived, wanting us to settle our bill.

Once again, the girl gave me a look of disappointment as she went to join her friend on the dance floor. Ronnie had turned around to face the waiter, who was standing at his shoulder, and saw the look. He said, "She really does fancy you mate."

I just shrugged my shoulders.

Ronnie and I finished our brandy as the band brought their performance to an end. As soon as they had finished the main lights in the hall came on, bathing the place in unnatural, bright light.

The girl and her friend returned to their seats as Ron and I stood up, preparing to leave. Ronnie looked me square in the face and said, "I dare you to go and ask her for her phone number."

Knowing that as he had dared me I would have to pay a forfeit, if I did not ask her, I replied, "Don't dare me Ronnie, because you know I will have to do it and if that bloke gets nasty, then I might end up with a fight on my hands." Continuing I added "And there are two of them."

Ronnie smiled, then chuckled and said "I dare you!"

I shook my head and said, "O.K., but if a fight starts don't leg it and leave me to it."

"I dare you," he said again, the look on his face telling me that I would not be on my own.

Resigned I walked along my side of the row of tables, to the end. He walked down his side and we met at the far end. Together we made our way past the next row and then walked along the aisle, between the tables, until I was standing beside the man who had been sitting with his back to me. I was facing the girl that he had been dancing with.

The other man, who was sat beside the girl, looked at us with a slight smile upon his face.

"*Priviet*," I said, which is the Russian for hello. "*Rutshky yest?*" I continued. This meant "Have you a pen?"

The man sat beside me, who had been dancing with the girl, reached into his jacket pocket and produced a biro. He passed me the pen. "*Spasiba* [thanks]," I said.

The girl smiled sweetly at me and I leaned forwards looking directly at her, not daring to look at the guy seated beside me. I asked "*Tvoya nummer telefon, nee mozhna?*" Basically this was, "Your telephone number, not possible?" The Russians generally make a request, using the negative "not possible".

The girl smiled a beaming smile and replied "*Da. Mozhna. Koneshna* [Yes. Possible. Of course.]"

She reached into her handbag and produced a piece of paper and then took the pen that I was holding out to her. She passed me the piece of paper, upon which she had written her name and telephone number. As I read it, she placed the man's pen upon the dining table in front of him. I did not look at him, at all, but noticed that the man seated beside her was beaming a wide smile, as was the girl.

Having read her name, I said, "*Spasiba Tanya, Dobra Notch.* [Thanks Tanya. Good night.]"

Smiling broadly she replied, "*Perjalista. Dobra notch* [Don't mention it. Good night.]"

Still not looking at the man beside me, I turned and Ronnie and I walked towards the exit. We left the restaurant hall, crossed the foyer and made our way out into the Moscow night air. As we reached the street, the adrenaline that had been coursing through my body subsided and I felt a great sense of relief.

Ronnie and I looked at one another and burst out laughing. My laughter was probably due to nervous release as I had been expecting to receive a punch in the side of the head from the cuckolded dancing partner.

Ron and I walked along Kalinin heading for the White House.

"Did you see that bloke, when you asked for his girlfriend's phone number?" Ron asked.

"No mate," I replied. "I made sure not to look at him."

"As soon as you asked for her number he burst out crying and cried his eyes out," Ron told me.

"Oh good. That makes me feel bloody great then," I said. "You are going to pay for this," I told him.

"Let's go to the Fortune bar and have a couple of beers," he said.

"Fair enough," I replied, laughing and we made our way back to the Mezh'.

Seated upon bar stools at the Fortune bar, we were drinking our second beer when I had an idea. There was a metal tray on the bar counter. It was a couple of feet in diameter and painted gloss black. In the centre of the tray a bunch of yellow and red flowers had been hand painted. Green-painted leaves and stems completed the artwork.

I looked at Ronnie seated beside me and said, "I dare you to nick that tray for me Ronnie."

"Don't dare me," he said, "because you know that I will have to do it."

"Exactly," I said, adding, "Exactly what I said to you at the Arbat."

Ronnie did no more than stand up, pick up the tray, pull out the front of his jeans waistband and stuff the tray down the front of his trousers. Turning away he said, "I'm going to the toilet," and he disappeared in the direction of the gents.

While Ronnie had been carrying out this impressive magic trick, observed by everybody in the bar, Lev, the barman, had been standing behind the counter at the opposite end of the bar. He had been drying glasses with a tea towel and watching every move that Ronnie had made.

When Ron disappeared into the gents, Lev strode forward until he was standing on the opposite side of the bar counter to me, looking directly at me.

"Here we go," I thought, expecting the Militia to arrive in force and arrest me and my erstwhile magician friend at any moment. To my surprise, Lev bent down and reached below the counter of the bar. I expected him to stand up holding a weapon of some kind in his hand. Instead, he was holding an exact replica of the tray that Ron had removed from the bar top. Placing the replacement tray on the bar in the exact position that the purloined one had been, he gave me a serious stare then walked back across the bar floor area and resumed drying glasses. I noticed that he was smiling.

Ronnie returned from the gents, where he had removed the tray from the front of his jeans and moved it to the back. Looking down at the bar, he saw the new tray. Automatically his hand went to the back of his trousers, to check that the one that he had taken was still there.

Having finished our beers, we made our way out of the hotel and when we were back by our trucks he passed over the tray that was secreted in the back of his waistband.

I still have the tray as a souvenir of that night.

6

Some Local Colour

WHEN Ronnie and I awoke, the next morning, we found that Pete Newlyn was parked near us. Pete was loaded for the same exhibition in Krasnaya Presnaya as Ronnie. They set off along the river bank to the exhibition ground and I drove out of the city, heading for Butova and the Sofin site.

Butova was famous for being the site of the modern headquarters of the K.G.B. You could see the K.G.B. complex as you passed by it on the M.K.A.D. A tall, ten-storeyed tower jutted up from a lower level base building. It was surrounded by other buildings, making a large complex. On the roof of the tower block, aerials, antennae and satellite dishes sprouted.

I carried on past this and then turned on to the M4. The So-Fin's depot was just beside the M4 and I could see its premises beside the road below me. I entered the site, lodged my custom papers and waited to offload the full load of groupage. The trailer was tipped during the afternoon and I was ready to go.

However, I had a passenger for the trip back into central Moscow: Julia, who worked in the So-Fin office. I gave her a lift to Kutovsky Prospekt where she lived, close to the Pizza Hut building. On the way she taught me some Russian.

When I dropped her off at Kutovsky, she turned to me and said, "You need to be careful Micky. There are big changes going to happen in this country and I do not want anything to happen to you. Take very good care of yourself and avoid any kind of trouble." With that, she opened the door and was gone.

As I drove away from the kerb, pitting my wits against the rush hour traffic, I thought, "Don't worry about me, Julia, self-preservation and survival are my middle names."

Well, in fact, they aren't. Patrick is my middle name. But self-preservation and survival will do to be going on with. Until we get to the time when I became known as Mikael Petrovich Tvemlov that is.

Back at the Mezh' I found Pete and Ronnie. They had not tipped at the exhibition and were going to have to go back there the following day. We went to the Mezh' Communication Centre, where I discovered that I had a telex telling me to make my way to Siedlce immediately and to contact Croome from the Hettman. "All in good time," I thought because I had been working consistently without a day off for weeks.

I had decided that I was going to take the following day off and wait for Pete and Ronnie so that we could leave Moscow together.

Yes, of course, I was making good money from the constant work. This money was paying off my debts, running my truck and allowing me to eat well. But, as the Russians say, "All work and no play makes Jack a *Geroy Soviyet Soiyooz* [Hero of the Soviet Union]."

Due to the Soviet Union spending so much of its natural wealth upon defence – more than 80% – it needed to improve the output of its heavy industries. Therefore, workers in those industries were exhorted to work harder than their contemporaries and vastly increase their personal output. Anyone who did so, by cutting that extra tonne of coal, or welding that extra 100 rivets in a day, was awarded the Honour of Hero of the Soviet Union.

I did not want to be a hero of the Soviet Union. I did not want to be a hero of the U.K. I did not even want to be a hero within my own truck cab. No, I just wanted a day off. And I was going to take it.

The following morning, I went to the Mezh' information desk and asked the girl on duty where there was anywhere of interest that I could visit other than Red Square.

She ran through an itinerary of interesting places in Moscow and finally told me about the Pushkin Art Gallery, near to Red Square. I decided that the Pushkin Gallery was the ideal place to spend a few hours.

Some people may think it strange that a truck driver would be interested in art. However, the old stereotype of a trucker having little education and living a basic existence, making his way through life and relying upon his brawn to earn his wages was completely outdated.

Although the music that I played in my truck was usually rock music, I actually liked some, but not all, classical music. Tchaikovsky was a particular favourite of mine, especially the 1812 Overture. I also liked Wagner's work and Bach.

With regard to art, I like Flemish painting and the

girl at the information desk informed me that there was a Flemish exhibition being held at the Pushkin at that time. The Pushkin Gallery it was then.

As it was a fine day, having left the hotel I walked to Red Square.

At some stage in your life you will have seen pictures of the Kremlin or Red Square on a news bulletin on T.V. You may even have been there in person. The media in the West use the images to signify Russia.

The Kremlin, with its red brick walls, green tile roofed clock towers and white cathedrals, topped with gold onion shaped domes, is the seat of ultimate power in Russia. It is where the modern presidents of Russia operate and, prior to the modern style of government in Russia, was where the Supreme Congress of the Soviet Union sat.

The white-walled cathedrals within the grounds house the tombs of the ancient rulers of Russia, the tsars. The Kremlin also houses historical artefacts of Russia, such as suits of armour, weapons, carriages and clothing that belonged to the tsars and their supporters.

Red Square, which is not a square but a rectangle, paved with grey cobble stones lies beside the Kremlin. It is generally known as the site of Soviet and now Russian military parades, particularly on May Day and May 9th. The latter is the day that Russia celebrates the end of the Second World War.

Standing to the side of Red Square beside the Kremlin Wall is Lenin's tomb. This salmon pink, marble building houses the embalmed body of Vladimir Iliyich Lenin, the first leader of the Soviet Union. Lenin's body lies in its coffin, which is open, so that his embalmed face is visible. Behind Lenin's mausoleum, other heads of state are buried.

Opposite the Kremlin wall and Lenin's mausoleum, on the other side of the square, stands the grey building of the G.U.M. The G.U.M, (*Gosudarstveny Universalniy Magazine*) is generally regarded as a department store. However, it is actually a warren of small, individual shops. Built on two levels, small ornate bridges link the upper levels to each other over the passages below. In the centre of adjoining passages on the lower level, fountains decorate the environment. The small individual shops sell a multitude of goods, mainly clothes and tourist souvenirs.

Red Square runs from the north-west to the south-east. At the north-west end of the square stands the Russian History Museum. The bright red-bricked building dominates that end. At the opposite end stands St Basil's cathedral, with its multicoloured domes topping the red brick façade. This is another of the iconic images of Russia, renowned throughout the world.

To me, Red Square and the Kremlin epitomise the power and governance of Russia. It is the hub of the country. From here the massive landmass of the Soviet state was run. All roads led from Moscow and this area of Moscow was the heart of the country's government.

Kreml, the Russian name for Kremlin, means fort and in the 900s A.D. the original fort was built there, with timber walls, on the banks of the *Moskva* River. It was built as a protection against the Mongol hordes that had spread westwards from their own country, far to the east of the small state of Russia, and threatened Russia's security and well-being.

Initially Russia had been formed as a small state, in

the west of what is now mainland Russia. It was populated by Scandinavian settlers called the Rus who mainly had red hair; the word "Rus" meaning red. This is where the name Russia came from.

The interesting thing about the Rus is that they were a Scandinavian tribe who decided that their fate lay in heading eastward and trading in the area that they created as Russia.

When the Rus headed eastward to populate Russia, the other half of the tribe decided to head south. This part of the tribe were the Norsemen, who moved from Scandinavia and settled in Normandy – the part of France that we now call Brittany and Normandy. They were the tribe that invaded Britain in 1066 and are known to us in the U.K. as the Normans.

My surname Twemlow is of direct Norman decent, therefore, not only am I directly descended from warriors who fought for William the Conqueror, but I am also descended from the Rus who moved into Russia at that time.

I feel that my ability to learn the Russian language so quickly and my affinity with the country and the people was a direct consequence of my heritage.

The initial capital of Russia was Novgorod. This was a city north of Moscow en route to the city of Leningrad/St. Petersburg. Possibly the only claim to fame of Novgorod in the annals of Russian history was that it was the first city in the world to have proper roads and not dirt tracks.

Novgorod was paved with wood; not gold but wood.

Between 1990 and 1995 I drove through Novgorod many times and obviously by that time they had replaced the wooden roadways with tarmac equivalents. However, the tarmac roads were atrocious and full of potholes and trench-like cracks.

They would probably have been better to have stuck to the original wooden roads.

Having walked through Red Square I turned right and followed the Kremlin wall to make my way to the Pushkin art gallery. Beside the art gallery, named in honour of Aleksandr Pushkin – a Russian nobleman, regarded as the finest Russian poet of all time – there was also Pushkin Square. The square was situated on Ulitsa Gorki, where a statue of Pushkin took pride of place. It was in Pushkin Square where the first McDonald's restaurant in Russia was opened, providing the citizens of Moscow with even more culture. Or not.

Entrance to the gallery was free and I made my way inside. Before long I found myself in a room that contained paintings by the Flemish masters, such as Rubens, Brueghel and the Van Eyks. This was my particularly favourite form of painting, especially the winter scenes they created; people skating and fishing on frozen rivers and lakes.

I was studying one of the paintings intently, totally lost in thought as I analysed it, when I became aware that a woman beside me was speaking in Russian. I thought that she must have been talking to a companion. My concentration having been broken I turned and found that there was only her and I in that section of the hall. It became obvious that she was speaking to me. I thought that she must have been a curator or guide who worked for the gallery.

I turned to her and, speaking English said, "I am sorry I only speak a little Russian. I am English."

7

The Beginning of an Anglo-Soviet Relationship

THE woman, standing in front of me was tall and slender, five foot nine. She had shoulder length brown hair, framing a long, high cheekboned face. Her lips were full and her eyes were deep. She wore a fawn coloured jumper, blue jeans and brown ankle boots.

Speaking in English, she said, "I was asking whether you like this painting."

"Very much so," I replied.

"I find it very interesting," she said, continuing, "Have you seen the upper floor?"

"Not yet," I said.

"Come on then," she said, turning and putting her arm through mine. She led me to the exit door of the salon, out into the corridor and up the sweeping, wide staircase that led to the first floor of the building. She introduced herself. Her name was Elena.

Anybody watching us would have thought that we had known each other for a long time.

Having studied the contents of the upper floor we made our way out into the street and went to a nearby cafe. Here we drank wine and ate red caviar, spooned on to bread and butter.

Elena looked at me and asked, "How much Russian do you actually speak?" I realised that we had been speaking together entirely in English.

"*Nim noshka* [a little bit]," I said and then she began speaking Russian, rattling away for about two minutes, non-stop. Occasionally I nodded, smiled, or shook my head, taking my cue from her facial expression.

Eventually she stopped and sat looking at me, waiting for a reaction, or a reply. When none came she asked, "How much of that did you understand?"

I looked into her eyes and said, "*Vapshee Niyet* [absolutely nothing]," then smiled, disarmingly. She looked at me, her lips pursed and her eyes narrowed as a frown came over her face. Suddenly, she began to laugh. A bright smile lit her face.

"*Mee – yi – kee,*" she said, which was how she pronounced Micky, "You is crazy."

From that moment on, our friendship was cemented, although I should not have been so pleased that she had identified so quickly and so accurately that I was crazy.

Elena gave me her telephone number as we sat at the cafe table. Then she accompanied me to the underground station and rode with me to the station at 1905 Ulitsa. We left the station and in the bright Moscow sunshine, she pointed across the massive intersection to the road that I needed to take to walk down to the Mezh'. Then she went back into the station to travel home.

The day had been a pivotal point in my life. I had visited a wonderful art gallery, met an interesting woman and taken my first ride on the Moscow underground.

Unlike the phone number of Tanya, the girl in the Arbat restaurant, which I had thrown away I placed Elena's phone number in my wallet so that I could call her when I returned to Moscow.

Walking down the hill to the Mezh' I felt extremely happy.

The next morning Pete, Ronnie and I drove out of Moscow heading for Poland.

When we arrived at the Hettman the following day after overnighting at the Minsk motel, I found a telex informing me that I was to swap trailers with another driver in Poznan. Ronnie was to make his way to Germany and load from Nurnberg. Pete was to head for Brno in Czechoslovakia and load from the exhibition ground.

We drove together to Lodz, where Pete turned off and headed for Bytom and the Czech border. Ronnie and I drove on to Poznan.

After Ronnie left, heading for Germany, I stayed at the motel waiting for my next trailer to arrive. When it turned up it was a refrigerated trailer, loaded with food for Aeromar, at Sheremetyevo airport.

Aeromar was a joint venture company that comprised of elements of Aeroflot, the Soviet state airline, and Marriott, the American hotel and catering company. Aeroflot had enlisted Marriot's expertise to provide the in-flight meals on its flights to the U.S.A.

To ensure that the ingredients were of high quality they were carried at chilled temperatures on refrigerated trailers. They were sourced from the U.K. and Germany. Not Russia, for some reason.

I could not think why.

Upon delivery to Aeromar the produce was

cooked, packaged and transported to the planes. The vast majority of the staff working at Aeromar were Russians but the operation was overseen by the unit manager, who was an American called Bob. A small squat balding man, Bob was probably the most miserable person that I ever met in Russia. He was continually complaining about everything.

On the other side of the coin, Aeromar was a great place to tip. Firstly, we drivers had free use of the staff canteen. The customs clearance was instantaneous because of the Aeroflot involvement. When they were ready to unload you, you merely switched off the fridge, opened the two back doors and reversed on to the loading bay. The palletised goods were unloaded by their staff using electric pallet trucks, generally, in less than an hour. Then you were on your way.

Arriving in Moscow with the Aeromar load, I drove to the Mezh'. Wim, a Dutch friend of mine, was there with his truck and I reversed my trailer on to the back of his, so that the fridge doors could not be opened and the load pilfered.

I telephoned Elena and we arranged to meet in front of the hotel at 7.30pm. We walked to the Arbat restaurant, where we had dinner, watched the show and then danced to the music provided by the resident band.

During the evening I discovered that Elena worked for an engineering company where she translated technical details into English. As part of her job she worked on exhibitions at Krasnaya Presnaya and the other major exhibition grounds in Moscow, such as V.D.N.K.

The following night, having tipped at Aeromar, I telephoned Elena again and we met in front of the hotel. This time we went to the Ukraine hotel, on the opposite bank of the river. where we dined and then danced to the resident band's music.

While we were dancing to one of the numbers Elena spoke to a Russian man who was dancing with a girl beside us. It turned out that the man was the husband of one of Elena's friends. However, the girl he was dancing with was not Elena's friend. It was a somewhat embarrassing incident as he had been caught red-handed, although not literally with his trousers down. That probably happened later.

The band at the Ukraine had been excellent. They played all American and English music and the musical ability and the vocals had been amazing. As we strolled back over the bridge between the Ukraine and the White House, Elena asked me what sort of music I listened to.

I told her that I liked a wide variety. When I had been younger I had played bass guitar in a number of bands. One of them had been professional and I played with them for some 18 months. My taste was eclectic and varied from pop music to heavy rock, with everything in between. However, my favourite was commercial rock and R&B, such as The Stones, The Who and E.L.O. I also liked The Sweet and Roy Wood.

When we arrived back at the Mezh' Elena got up into the cab of my truck and I played her some of the music that I had on cassette.

The next morning, I was drinking coffee in the Mezh' coffee bar when I was joined by a young lady.

She was short, probably not even five feet tall, with blonde hair and a finely chiselled, pretty face. However, her face was marred by a prominent scar that she had received in a car accident, as I found out later.

"My name is Mona," she said. "I work for Barry Martin's office here in the Mezh'. And you must be Mick?"

She went on to explain to me that one of the Barry Martin trucks had broken down on its way to Femtech in Kiev. Barry Martin had arranged with Kepstowe that I would go to Kiev and load upon its behalf. She showed me a fax sheet from Kepstowe confirming this.

"How did you know that I am the Mick that you needed?"

"Paul Cantwell told me about you. He said that you dress like a cowboy," she responded.

I laughed. I was dressed in my usual boots, jeans and a checked shirt. I suppose that is like a cowboy.

"I think that you look more like a Russian hero, from our history," she said, "with your fair hair and square jaw."

"Perhaps I am a Russian cowboy then," I said, laughing aloud but thinking to myself, "because I am out here in the Wild, Wild Bloody East."

I left the Mezh' and headed out of Moscow. I reached Borispol late that night and was allowed into the Femtech compound.

The following morning, they loaded the fridge with pallets of tampons, which were destined for Havant. Once fully loaded and the customs procedure was complete, I headed towards Kiev. On the way I stopped at a service area and filled the tank with diesel again.

The girl on duty in the service area was called Julia. When I paid for the diesel, I gave her a couple of bars of chocolate that I had bought in Moscow. Having filled up, I went back inside the service station office and gave her a bottle of Sov' champagne. She was extremely happy to be given these presents and later on it transpired that this was a decidedly good investment.

Back on the road again I headed for Poland, but, instead of driving to Brest, I drove to Lvov and crossed the border into Poland.

Here, I found myself in familiar territory as I drove past Jaraslav Zheshov and the Wooden Hut at Tarnow. I stopped for the night in Krakow.

Passing the Wooden Hut at Tarnow I recalled nights that I had spent there. The Wooden Huts were restaurants and had at one time also been hotels. Their design was based upon old Polish hunting lodges and the one at Tarnow actually had wild boar and bear on the menu.

These restaurants, which were dotted throughout Poland, were actually built on stone foundations and had stone walls. Usually three storeys high, the upper floors were clad in timber and they had timber eaves and balconies. The eves and balconies were attractively carved and varnished.

My favourite Wooden Hut was at Buk, just to the west of Poznan. Back in the late '70s and '80s, while working for Pro-Motor, I had been a regular customer there. In fact, at one time, I was the only person who could get a lock-in once the restaurant had closed for the night. This was because I was supplying the waitresses with lipstick and tights, which they could not buy in the Polish shops at that time.

I was always guaranteed a late drink there. I was quite a little spiv, really.

My experience of Poland had begun in 1978. This merely entailed me making occasional trips to Poznan or Warsaw.

However, my involvement in Poland increased dramatically in 1980. Martial law was imposed in the country because of the activities of *Solidarnosc* (Solidarity), the Polish trade union, led by Lech Walesa. The Government under General Jaruzelski tried to starve out the protestors. In response, the Catholic Church in Poland arranged for consignments of basic foodstuffs to be sent there so the people could survive. These foodstuffs were paid for by various sources, such as the Catholic Churches in Britain, the U.S.A. and Canada and by the European Community, now known as the E.U.

Originally, the Canadian and U.S. churches had sent the foodstuff direct from their own countries in 40-feet containers. Ironically the container ships carrying them had docked in Gdansk, the home of *Solidarnosc*, and then the containers had been transferred on to Polish trucks for onward delivery. However, the trucks and their drivers had then disappeared, never to be seen again. So the Canadians and Americans decided they would send the money to the British Catholic Church, who would purchase the foodstuffs and ship it directly to Poland on British trucks. For this contract, the Church appointed Pro-Motor.

Between early 1980 and late 1983, every Sunday

evening of the year, ten to fifteen articulated trucks would leave our depot in Dunton Green, near Sevenoaks in Kent. and head to Wroclaw, in south-west Poland.

Basically, we carried staple foodstuffs, such as sugar, rice, baby milk powder and porridge oats. This was to help the starving Polish people survive.

For some reason, rather than deliver a full load to Wroclaw as the other trucks did, I would have a part load. I would then have to drive further into Poland to tip at other destinations such as Katowice, Krakow, Rzeszow, or Torun. This gave me a more in-depth knowledge of Poland, which proved to be advantageous when I began to haul to Russia.

The worst incident of the *Solidarnosc* crisis, which I recall from that time, came once after tipping at Wroclaw and Rzeszow, when my last delivery was to Lublin. I had unloaded there and my trailer was empty. I left the town and picked up the main road for Warsaw, just as darkness began to fall.

As I left Lublin, 20 to 30 Polish police vans passed me on the other carriageway, heading in the opposite direction. The officers in the vehicles were dressed in riot gear. Obviously, they were on their way into Lublin, where a demonstration was being staged. They sped along, blue lights flashing, driving at breakneck speed.

I later discovered that the occupants of these vehicles carried out an unbelievable atrocity. Using live rounds of ammunition, they murdered innocent people who were merely holding a peaceful demonstration. They were protesting against the poor conditions, poverty and starvation that they were being forced to endure under what was, to all intents, a socialist government.

It was said at the time that these police officers were in fact Soviet soldiers disguised as the Polish Police. That may well have been true, because it might not have been possible to get the police to have fired against their fellow citizens.

One thing that I did notice in 1981 was that the Polish shops were almost completely empty and had virtually no goods to sell. For instance, a shoe shop in Wroclaw that I passed regularly normally had only three pairs of shoes on display for sale. However, unbelievably there were four members of staff working there.

This was in great contrast to the shops in Moscow, which at the same time were bulging at the seams with products to sell. How the tables had turned though when I returned to Moscow in 1990.

Fortunes had reversed completely and the Polish shops were crammed full of stock, while the Moscow shops were virtually desolate and empty.

Driving along from Rzeszow to Tarnow and on towards Krakow was a trip back into the past. The same old single carriageway road with the extra strips either side. There was slick tarmac that had been laid by an expert in ripple plastering.

Reaching Krakow I decided to stop there for the night. I parked the truck beside the river and walked into the middle of town.

In the central square of Krakow there was the market place. An ornate single-storeyed, multi-arch-sided building housed the market. In one corner of the square there stood a tall clock tower. Beneath the clock tower there had been a cavernous under-ground building, which had been a bar. After eating in a nearby restaurant, I made my way down the wide stone stairway to the underground cavern. Here, I was confronted by numerous staff who informed me that I could not have a beer.

Mortified because I was not pissed, I remonstrated with them and started to get the hump that I was not going to be able to have a beer. It was then that they informed me that since my previous visit some seven years previously, the place had ceased to be a bar and was now merely a coffee bar. That was why I could not get an alcoholic drink.

They offered me a coffee or tea, but I politely declined the offer.

Climbing back up the stone stairway, I headed for my truck, where I sat in the cab and drank a couple of cans of German beer. Sod coffee and tea!

The next morning, I departed for the German border at Cottbus. I was heading for West Berlin, which was the future. Conversely, Russia, Ukraine and Poland were definitely 30 to 50 years in the past.

Shortly after leaving Krakow I came across signs diverting me away from the main highway, which I realised was closed for road works. The diversion meandered around through narrow country lanes and suddenly I entered the urban enclave of Oswiecim.

At first this meant nothing to me, until I thought about it further and realised that I had arrived at the place that the Germans called Auschwitz, the most prolific killing ground of all of Nazi Germany's deadly concentration camps. Of all of the six million Jewish people killed by the Nazis in the Second World War, more than 1.1 million were exterminated at Auschwitz.

Slipping away from the diversion route, I made a few turns through residential areas and found myself parked in front of the infamous gateway to hell. I stopped the truck on the tourist parking area and sat in the cab, looking at the arched entranceway to the camp.

In front of me stood a single-storeyed red brick, tile-roofed building. In the centre rose a tower with an archway, through which ran a railway track. This was how thousands of people entered Auschwitz, in railway cattle trucks, on their way to the gas chambers during the Second World War.

To the sides of the central entrance building, barbed wire fences stretched away. Beyond these fortifications stood rows of red-brick bungalow style buildings. These were the accommodation blocks, occupied by inhabitants of the camp who had been lucky (or unlucky) enough, not to be selected for immediate extermination upon arrival at the camp.

I sat staring at the entrance to the camp for probably some 30 minutes, deep in thought. Then, returning to my normal state of mind, I started the truck engine and drove away from this terrible place. Determined never, ever to return.

Pushing on through southern Poland, which was known as Silesia when it had been German territory, I crossed the border into Germany at Cottbus. Heading north-west, I took the atrocious, broken concrete motorway to Berlin.

I entered the city in the south-west at Drei Linden and parked on the service area. Dropping the trailer, I drove into the city with my tractor unit, heading for a launderette that I knew. Here, I had my clothes laundered while I had a meal. I then drove back to Drei Linden to wait for my next trailer.

The following morning the trailer appeared hot foot from Venray and shortly I was on my way back to Klyazma while the fridge trailer full of Femtech tampons was rocking and rolling its way towards the white cliffs of Dover. All in all, I reckoned that I was heading in the right direction.

Once again I travelled through Poland and headed for Moscow. The borders were still quiet and I passed through them with relative ease. It was August 1990, a hot sultry summer.

I stopped for the night at the Hetmann in Siedlce. Parked in the truck park were two of my Dutch mates, Arri and Yap.

Having showered, I went into the restaurant and joined them at the table near to the window. I sat with my back to the window, facing them. They were already eating, so I ordered my dinner and beers all round. In addition, I asked for three brandies and the waitress, Anouska, a beautiful, slim-figured girl, with long blonde hair went off to get the order.

As I sat looking towards the unused stage at the far end of the room, I noticed a well-dressed woman enter the restaurant. She looked around and then strode purposefully toward a table where a man and woman were sat eating. Reaching their table, the well-dressed woman shouted something in Polish and then slapped the man alongside his face. Moving over to the next table she picked up a half-empty glass of beer that the guy at that table had been drinking. Returning to the other table she poured it over the man's head. With that she turned on her heel and left the restaurant.

I looked at Yap and Arri and realised that they had been so busy eating that they had not seen any of this carry on.

When Anouska returned with our drinks I asked her, "What was that all about?"

She replied, "I don't know. They do that every week."

With that she shrugged her shoulders and made her way back to the bar.

Yap and Arri were on their way home, so the following morning I set off for Moscow alone.

I had made an early start so stopped the next night in Smolensk. The following morning, I rolled on towards Vodka city and arrived there mid Sunday afternoon.

Vlad turned up and supplied me with champers and fags. After he had gone I sat on the riverbank wall and drank champagne.

I was at a loss because Elena had gone away on holiday to the Black Sea. Her firm owned a hotel at Sochi and she had jetted off for a free holiday, where all she had to pay for was her alcohol.

Realising that I was on my own in Moscow, I was wondering what to do with myself when

Ronnie Seymour turned up, driving towards me along the river bank.

"Bloody hell," I thought. "Not more bleeding dares."

As it happened we had a very subdued evening. We went to the Ukraine hotel, had dinner and enjoyed the music of the resident band. The next day we drove to Klyazma and unloaded.

Back in Moscow, that night we went to the Arbat, much against my will in case we ran into that bird

Tanya whom I had asked for her telephone number. However, Ronnie told me not to be a baby.

Fortunately we did not see her because no doubt further dares would have been issued.

Again that night we returned to the Fortune and had a few levellers. Lev, the barman, welcomed us like long-lost brothers, although he was probably thinking more about his long-lost black metal tray with the hand-painted flower design.

I had instructions to report to the cultural attaché at the British Embassy the following afternoon.

Ron had decided to take the day off, before heading back towards Poland.

Strangely, we discovered that we were both virtually out of sugar and decided to visit a local shop in the morning and purchase some so that we could use it for brewing up in our cabs.

We walked along the river bank and saw a shop signed "*Produkti* (Food)". We went into the shop and milled around like a couple of peasants, until we worked out the system under which the shop operated. There were no supermarkets in Russia in 1990.

Actually, virtually all Russian shops were the same at that time. To buy something, you firstly told the shop assistant behind the counter what you wanted. She wrote this down on a slip of paper and added the price. You then made your way to the cash till clutching your slip of paper. At the cash till you paid for the goods. The lady there (it was all women working in shops at the time) took your money and then stamped the piece of paper to indicate that you had paid for your purchase. You then made your way back to the original counter and handed your slip of paper to the first shop assistant as proof that you had paid. She then gave you the article that you had purchased and you walked away smiling happily, even though you had aged somewhat.

However, being the prat that I am, I had forgotten that Elena had told me that at that point in time Moscow was undergoing severe shortages in most basic foodstuffs, including sugar. Therefore, a ration card system had been introduced and only legitimate citizens of Moscow could have one. Although Ronnie's and my visas gave us a legitimate right to be in Moscow, they did not give us the right to coupons for foodstuff, so we could not buy sugar.

One of the old ladies working in the shop could speak English and explained the situation to us.

"However," she trilled, obviously overawed to be in the company of two handsome, athletic Englishmen (I don't know where they had got to, but me and Ronnie were there), "there is no reason why you cannot buy a cake, because cakes are not on ration."

I said, "That will be wonderful. What cake can we have?"

"Any one of those," she replied, waving in the direction of a whole section of cakes.

We selected a bloody enormous chocolate cake, went through the protracted caper of purchasing it and left the shop, with it neatly packaged in a box with a large pink ribbon on it (sweet).

Back at the trucks I brewed a couple of cups of black coffee on my filter coffee machine, while Ronnie sliced the cake. The practice, so our new Russian girlfriend had explained to us, was that in the absence of sugar you could drink your coffee and eat the cake, which would provide the sweetness in place of sugar.

However, when we ate the cake it had the consistency of cardboard and tasted like crap. Whatever crap tastes like. Well, obviously, like that cake (not sweet).

Within a very short period of time the cake found itself floating on top of the river Moskva and then it quickly disappeared below the surface, never to be seen again. Interestingly though, some weeks later a barge running up the river sank without trace at that very spot.

What a bleeding coincidence!

8

Hard Labour

THAT afternoon I drove the truck to the British Embassy. It stood on the Sofiyskaya embankment directly across the River Moskva from the Kremlin. The main building was set back behind wrought iron railings and had wide stone steps that led up to a pillared entrance way. The Union flag flew proudly from a flagpole on the roof. The sight of the flag fluttering in the breeze had been seen regularly by Stalin from the windows of the Kremlin. It had greatly annoyed him.

To the right of the main entrance compound stood the consular section, where people applied for visas. Queues of Russians were waiting to enter it, but I made my way past them to the main building. I met the cultural attaché, Penny Steer, who told me that I needed to come back to the embassy the next morning for 9am. We were then going to drive to Prospekt Mira where we were to load 40 wooden cases containing a clothing exhibition that was going to the British Embassy in Bucharest. The clothes were iconic '60s fashion, as modelled by Twiggy, etc.

I left the embassy and drove back to the Mezh',

where I found Ronnie sitting on the embankment wall.

The following morning, Ronnie headed for England and I drove back to the embassy. I met the ten-man labour crew, who were going to drive to Prospekt Mira in a minibus. Penny was driving there in her own car. I was going to tag along behind, but expected to get separated from them by traffic. I could find my way to Prospekt Mira, no problem. All I wanted them to do was to wait on the corner of the road that I needed to turn off at so that I did not miss it. With this in mind we set out through the morning's city traffic.

When I had first gone to Moscow in 1981 you were not allowed to sleep in your truck. You had to stay in a hotel so the authorities knew exactly where you were. I had stayed at the Hotel Cosmos on Prospekt Mira for my seven-day stretch. The Cosmos was a large hotel that catered for foreign tourists. The semicircular frontage of the building made it stand out from those around it. The Cosmos was just up the road from *V.D.N.K.*, the science and technology exhibition ground. This was also known as the Space and Technology museum.

V.D.N.K. was pronounced *VeDenKa* and I was to work there numerous times over the coming five years, taking trailers into the grounds for exhibitions. *V.D.N.K.* and *Krasnaya Presnaya* were the two main exhibition sites within the city.

Heading out from central Moscow you took the Yaroslavl road, which became Prospekt Mira. Driving along Prospekt Mira from the city centre you passed *V.D.N.K.*, which stood on your left. In front of

V.D.N.K. there was an extremely tall, gold-coloured monument of a space rocket taking off.

Then you drove past the Cosmos, which was on your right. After the Cosmos there was a large statue of a man and a woman on your left. They were dressed as agricultural workers. The man was holding a hammer aloft and the woman a sickle, the symbols of the Soviet Union. It was a propagandist masterpiece, demonstrating the power of the heroic agricultural workers who fed mother Russia and the U.S.S.R.

A picture of this statue was used as a test screen on the All Soviet Television channel.

The turning that I wanted was just past this statue on the left-hand side of the road. I turned into the road and entered a large high rise housing estate. The entrance to the storage place, which was actually an underground nuclear bomb shelter, was at the end of a small tarmac spur road on the left. I reversed up as close as I could get to the entrance and stopped.

I accompanied the crew down two levels to where the goods were stored. All in all, there were apparently six levels to the bunker. Each level had chambers off it that could be sealed by massive steel doors. When we reached the chamber where the clothing exhibition cases were stored a caretaker opened the huge, heavy steel door and turned on the lights. We peered into the cavernous chamber where the forty wooden cases stood.

The embassy work crew were not overly impressed by the situation. They walked out tutting and muttering. Apparently, as they had no handling equipment they were not prepared to carry the cases up the slope to the surface by hand. A brief conversation took place between Penny and the leader of the workmen and then we all returned to our vehicles, started them and drove back to the embassy.

Back at Sofiyskaya Nabob I was informed that the following day we were going to return to Prospekt Mira with handling equipment. I went back to my truck and returned to the Mezh'.

The next day I parked near the embassy. Penny appeared and two of the *dvorniks* (Russian for yard workers); basically unintelligent people who can just about master sweeping a yard as long as they are constantly supervised and instructed, wheeled the two pump up pallet trucks across the road and we stowed them in the back of the trailer.

We then set off for Prospekt Mira again. The *dvorniks* in their minibus, Penny in her car and me bringing up the rear, in the truck. The other two vehicles had soon left me behind, with me getting stuck at traffic lights.

When I arrived at the nuclear shelter I reversed up to the entrance and opened the rear of the trailer. The *dvorniks* got their pallet barrows out of the tilt and wandered down the two levels to the storage chamber, while I inspected a notice board on the inside wall of the entrance. The notice board displayed numerous posters that described the action to take in the case of a nuclear strike. It also explained the warning system that would trigger people taking refuge in the bunker. There would be a constant wailing of a siren. There was a picture of the siren with a man winding the handle to make it work. I presumed that this was for the benefit of deaf people. They would not hear the siren but would see the guy winding it. They would then know that it was time to leg it to the sanctuary of the bunker.

Having inspected the faded, tatty, simplistic posters, I made my way below ground, to where the cases of clothes were situated, as were the tatty, simplistic, lazy embassy *dvorniks*.

As I arrived at the storage chamber, the head *dvornik* had engaged Penny in conversation, while the others muttered ominously in the background. It appeared that they considered that they could not complete the task before knocking off time. Therefore, the operation was to be abandoned.

Back on the surface Penny told me that she was abandoning the exercise and that I should contact Kepstowe to arrange an alternative load. She, meanwhile, would think of another way of getting the goods to Bucharest, possibly through Sovtransavto.

Now, having been to Rumania on numerous occasions, either to tip or reload from exhibitions in Bucharest, or in transit through the country, I knew it well. To say that I was no great lover of the place was an understatement. It was internationally recognised as the most impoverished country in Europe. The road surfaces were awful and when it rained they became lethal; it was like driving on a skating rink. This was due to whatever it was that they mixed with the tarmac.

Mind you, to be fair, in the past I had more than my fair share of laughs in Rumania. As much as I did not like the place, the chance to take the load of '60s fashion to Bucharest offered me an escape from the routine of driving back and forwards from Moscow, to Poland. Not that I minded shuffling back and forwards from Vodka City but, as they say in snooker terms, a change is as good as a rest.

Plus, there was obviously money to be made here.

With this in mind I made a proposition to Penny. No! Not that kind of proposition, she was a British diplomat, for god's sake! No, what I proposed was that we drove to Molkom to see whether they would be prepared to supply the labour to load the goods. As I told her, she would need to engage people to actually do the heavy work of lifting the cases and bringing them to the surface ready to load them on whatever trailer was going to carry them to Bucharest.

While she had my trailer available, we might as well ask Molkom if they would supply that labour. She decided that it was worth a try because, as I pointed out, the embassy in Bucharest was expecting the goods.

We left my truck at the Cosmos Hotel for a 5 Deutschmark parking fee. I knew that it was safe at the Cosmos because the place was crawling with K.G.B. officers who were spying on and watching the foreign guests. Getting into the suicide seat of Penny's car, I guided her to Molkom.

Within a very short space of time we were seated in the boardroom discussing the situation with Mikhail Molkov. Once he had been informed that the operation was for the British Embassy, Molkov offered his staff's assistance without hesitation and at a very reasonable price.

I think that he probably thought he might get a knighthood out of it. Whatever the reason for his alacrity to help, it was arranged that a crew of his men, complete with handling equipment, would meet us on Prospekt Mira at 9am the following morning. We exited the boardroom with Molkov actually bowing and scraping to Penny in utter deference.

We left the office block and climbed back into Penny's car for the trip back to the Cosmos Hotel. Penny was ecstatic that the loading could be successfully undertaken.

"Why do you think that the embassy crew would not load the goods?" she asked, as we approached the M.K.A.D. underpass.

"Because they are a bunch of no good, lazy, bolshie, bloody communists," I replied. We laughed all of the way to the Cosmos.

The next morning, Friday, I arrived at the bomb shelter at 8.30. I had just backed into position and begun opening the side of the trailer for loading when the Molkom team arrived. They climbed out of their minibus and unloaded a few pump up pallet trucks. Just then Penny turned up and the shelter's security guy appeared as well. Soon, the Molkom crew had brought all the cases to the surface and we had stowed them safely in the trailer. The cases were feather light, which went to show how idle the embassy crew really were.

By 1pm the operation was complete and I had closed the trailer. The Molkom team were preparing to get into their minibus when Penny called them over to the boot of her car. They lined up to be presented with a carrier bag each containing two cartons of 200 cigarettes and a bottle of Scotch. They were absolutely delighted to be rewarded so magnificently. They were so grateful to Penny and you could actually see that I had gone up immeasurably in their estimation for giving them the chance to be so rewarded.

They took it in turn to shake my hand and hug me in a very Russian display of gratitude. They climbed into the minibus and a few of the bottles were opened before they even left the site. "*Nastrovia,*" I called to them, as the bus pulled away, the crew waving happily. *Nastrovia,* means good health and is the equivalent in Russian to us saying "cheers" when you are having a drink.

It was too late to drive to the diplomatic customs depot at Butova and carry out the customs clearance for the goods. Therefore, I was stuck in Moscow for the weekend and would have to go to Butova on Monday morning. Penny would arrange for embassy staff to take the requisite documents to Butova and meet me there at 9am. She asked me what my plans were for the weekend.

I said that I did not have any but would probably spend the weekend sightseeing and eat at the Arbat or the Ukraina. She asked me whether I would like to have Sunday dinner at her flat. She promised me roast beef, roast potatoes and Yorkshire puddings, as well as a couple of glasses of beer. Naturally, I could not refuse and she gave me her address and telephone number. We arranged that I would turn up at her flat at 1pm on Sunday to have dinner. Her flat was actually on Kutovsky Prospekt, just up and across the road from the Ukraine Hotel and a gentle two kilometre walk from the Mezh'.

We parted company, her to drive back to the embassy and me to return to the Mezh'.

That evening, I made my way to the Hotel Belgrade, where I had decided to have dinner. The Belgrade was an extremely exclusive establishment and did not normally admit Westerners. It was for the cream of Russian society: politicians, sport stars and entertainers.

However, having given the doorman my calling card, a 10 Dollar note, I was admitted immediately. The waiter who had seated me walked away but kept looking back at me. It was as if he recognised me, but could not remember where from. When he returned to the table to take my order he enquired, "So how was the caviar?"

"Caviar?" I queried.

"Yes, I sold you two jars of Beluga caviar in ..." he thought for a moment, "1981," he concluded.

"Yes," I replied, "It was very, very good," thinking to myself, "Just like your memory."

"*Harashaw* [good]," he responded, laughing, then took the order and left again.

I spent the Saturday sightseeing. I did the normal haunts around Red Square: the Bolshoi, the Kremlin Dzerjinski Square and the old K.G.B. building, the Lubyanka.

What I also found, alongside the Kremlin Wall, was the eternal flame memorial to the Russian soldiers killed in the Second World War.

At this impressive monument, newly-wed couples came to pay their respects to the fallen after their wedding ceremony. The brides laid their beautiful bouquets on the commemorative site. They did this as a tribute to all the soldiers who had died in the conflict before they had the opportunity to be married themselves. It was a touching gesture.

At Sunday lunchtime I made my way to Kutovsky Prospekt. I was carrying a bottle of Soviet champagne and a bunch of flowers as a gift for Penny. I was really looking forward to a proper English roast lunch after so long out of England. I wasn't disappointed.

The meal was excellent and topped off with real Oxo gravy. For afters we had profiteroles. Following lunch, we sat chatting, while listening to classical music. Penny, in her official capacity, was spending the evening at a concert. So, at around 5pm, I took my leave and went back to the Mezh'.

I spent the evening, in my cab, getting my business books up to date. As a self-employed road haulier, i.e. owner-driver, I had to keep track of my accounts for the purposes of paying any income tax due to H.M.R.C.

I was also V.A.T. registered and had to keep records for that and supply quarterly statements. I ran the business from the cab of the truck during the whole five years that I was operating in Russia.

The income and outgoings I recorded in an account ledger. I attached any receipts that I had to this and when I was in England following the end of a tax year I handed them to my accountants, who were based in Sittingbourne. They completed the accounts and submitted them to H.M.R.C. upon my behalf.

The V.A.T. returns I sent in quarterly, handing the envelope to whichever driver I was swapping trailers with at the time. Upon their return to England they would post them for me, as I had given them cash to cover the stamp. As all my operations involved working outside of the E.E.C. borders, I did not have to charge V.A.T. to my customers. However, I was paying V.A.T. on my truck lease, spare parts and servicing, all of which I could reclaim. Therefore, I received a V.A.T. rebate every quarter.

Having ensured that my accounts were up to date I

then turned to my Russian language book and spent a couple of hours studying from that. My Russian was coming on due to my friends teaching me and studying from this book.

I am a very self-confident person and thought nothing of practising Russian upon every Russian that I now came into contact with. To me, communication was the key to everything. I did not care overly whether I was speaking the language badly at that time. Speaking it was the priority. And generally they understood me. If not, I battered them into submission. However, what I now needed to master was understanding what they said in reply.

The next morning, I drove to the customs depot at Butova. Eventually, two Russian female members of staff from the embassy turned up. They took my part of the paperwork and disappeared into the custom hall. Three hours later they returned with a Soviet customs officer in tow, who sealed the tilt cord, while one of the ladies from the embassy gave me all my documents back.

The documents included an official British Government certificate that stated in Russian that I was carrying diplomatic goods on behalf of the British Government. This signified that I was not to be stopped or hindered in the performance of my duties for whatever reason.

Having checked that all of the paperwork was correct, I left the compound and headed for the M.K.A.D. As I drove along the street that linked Butova customs compound with the M.K.A.D. I thought to myself, "Here we bloody go then. Bucharest. And with diplomatic bleedin' immunity."

9

By Royal Appointment

HAVING left Butova, I spent that night at Smolensk and the following day drove down into Ukraine. As I neared Kiev I passed Chernobyl, the site of the 1986 nuclear disaster. In fact, over the five years of driving in the Soviet Union I passed Chernobyl many times. So many times that I am surprised that I don't glow in the dark.

I ripped past Kiev, carrying on along the Odessa road. Odessa is a major coastal city in south-west Ukraine. It is also a Black Sea port with industrial docks and a docking point for cruise liners. The Odessa road was typical of Soviet civil engineering; an asphalt road with trenches and potholes built in. You could maintain a steady 65–70 miles per hour on it but only as long as you were switched on enough to be on the lookout for dangerous holes in the road.

Reaching the small town of Lyubashivka, I decided to throw my hand in and stop for the night. I pulled off the road and turned into a wide square, which was an area of just plain dirt. Probably because I had covered 580 miles that day, I fell asleep as soon as my head hit the pillow.

It was August after all and the temperatures had been in the 40s Centigrade all day. This had been draining in itself. I had been heading directly southward, towards the Black Sea and the temperature was rising as I headed south. When I had left Moscow it had been 35 degrees.

I woke the following morning to find that my truck was surrounded by small vans. The vans were being loaded with trays containing loaves of bread. Unknowingly, I had parked the night before next to the local bakery. Surprisingly the noise of the vans coming and going, coupled to the sounds of the drivers loading their vehicles, had not woken me. I entered the bakery and bought a hot white loaf which had only just come out of the oven. Tearing strips off the loaf and eating them, I started the truck and pulled out of the dirt square, picking up the road south.

I had 70 miles to do to get to the border between Ukraine and Moldova. At 30 miles past the border I would come to Kishinev, the capital of Moldova. From Kishinev I would have to travel about 50 miles and then I would come to the border at Vama Leuseni, where I would cross from the Soviet Union into Rumania. Bucharest was 220 miles from the border, so hopefully I would be able to get there that night and park outside of the embassy. That was the plan. But we know a song all about plans, don't we?

The scenery had changed as I headed south. The dark pine forests and rolling green fields of Russia and northern Ukraine had given way to a harder, harsher type of landscape of dust and sandy dirt, which was strewn with rocks and stones. The dust drifted on to the road in the breeze. As you drove along, swirls of dust would rise into the air. At night the dust hung in the air and distorted your vision. Dust and the oppressive heat were your constant companion in the summer months in Ukraine. Russia was as dusty but marginally cooler.

I headed further south, on the M05, until I reached the junction with the M13. Turning west here, I drove towards Moldova. The Ukraine–Moldova border was at Hulyavko. There were no border formalities because you were still driving within the Soviet Union. There were police posts on each side of the border but they were totally disinterested in me. On the way from the border to Kishinev, I passed over a road bridge spanning a river. The next time that I entered Moldova I would not be able to pass over it as it would be the scene of fighting between ethnic Rumanian nationalist Moldovan and ethnic Russian separatists.

Entering Kishinev, I was taken aback by the sight of communist slogans written on hoardings and banners that were attached to buildings. All of these slogans were written in white upon post office red backgrounds. They extolled communism and socialism and the virtues of the mighty Soviet state. You did not see this kind of propaganda in Russia or Ukraine. It was common in the East European communist states such as Czechoslovakia, during the '70s and '80s, but by 1990 had disappeared from those states as well. Kishinev was a mundane town and from what I saw of it had very little to offer except a few ornate water fountains, statues and outdated propaganda.

Totally underwhelmed by Kishinev, and indeed the whole of Moldova that I had seen, I passed through and headed for the Moldovan–Rumanian border. It was early afternoon and it looked likely that I would make Bucharest that night.

I reached the border at Vama Leuseni late in the afternoon. This was a different type of border crossing compared to Kukariki. The border was directly on the edge of an urban area, unlike at Brest. The Soviet side was more chaotic than at Kukariki because cars and coaches were using the same crossing point. Trucks were funnelled into their own area and the procedure was similar to Kukariki. There were the usual cab control and vehicle control over the pits between the gantries. K.G.B. border guards patrolled with dogs and one was led alongside my trailer carrying out a search.

A Sovinteravtoservice woman dipped my diesel tank, which was full right to the top but I had declared this to them. They did not question the amount of diesel coupons that I had bought at Kukariki or the fact that I had managed to carry out all the extra mileage on so few coupons.

Jesus turned water into wine. I turned Deutschmarks into diesel.

With the custom paperwork stamped and fully authorised I crossed over into the Rumanian section.

Here the atmosphere was completely different. Unlike the Soviets, who were functional and business like, the Rumanians were lax and slack. Their attitude was different as well. The Sovs treated you with a certain amount of respect but the Rumanians were totally offhand.

Unlike the interior of the Soviet customs buildings, which were clean, full of light and freshly painted, the Rumanians' buildings were dark, dank and dingy. The border formalities completed, I had the choice of pulling out of the border and parking for the night or ploughing on to Bucharest. I decided to head for Bucharest. I drove out of the border and headed for Husi, the nearest big town.

As soon as I left the border the sky darkened, the heavens opened and it poured with rain. This was not a good omen.

I drove from the border to Husi. Although it was only early evening the rain-laden clouds overhead had made the sky ominously dark. In Husi there were no streetlights and it was torturous going navigating the streets with the holes in the road. You also had the added danger of pedestrians walking in the road dressed in dark clothes. They were extremely hard to spot in the driving rain until you were right upon them.

As I navigated my way through Husi I noticed a drunk on the pavement, just ahead of me, further along the road. As I approached him, he staggered to the edge of the kerb and then fell, head long, into an enormous pothole in the road. The pothole was full of water and he created a huge splash as he entered it. Water shot up into the air and then came down again, right on top of him. Keeping well away from him, I drove past and looked down at him, getting to his knees in the pit of water, after having been face down in it. He could have drowned but I wasn't stopping to check his state of health. No doubt he was sobering up by now. I ploughed on.

Leaving Husi I came across another hazard that you encounter on Rumanian roads: the horse and cart. Generally, it is a beaten up old horse pulling a dilapidated wooden cart, which would be carrying corn on the cob. The corn stems would be piled high in the cart and there would be a few people riding on top of the corn.

The danger is that in Rumania at night these carts are never carrying lights and, like the pedestrians, you cannot see them until you are right on top of them. When you are on a good piece of road and travelling quite quickly you come upon them so fast that you need to take emergency measures to avoid hitting them. It was a hazard that I had experienced many times previously. I had probably made twenty to thirty trips to or through Rumania when I worked for Pro-Motor.

I drove on through the night. The weather conditions and the roads were conspiring to ensure that I travelled very slowly. It was approaching midnight and I realised that I was getting nowhere fast. I was actually more likely to have an accident than to get to Bucharest that night.

I had just passed the town of Focsani and was driving through a wooded area. Suddenly, I saw a restaurant ahead. It was on the opposite side of the road, but there was parking either side of the road. Relieved to be able to stop, I pulled on to the parking area to my right.

In the '70s and '80s it had always been the wisest course of action to park at proper restaurant facilities in Rumania so as to have secure parking. There were a lot of criminals in Rumania, particularly among the Romas.

I had just switched off the engine when, out of the darkness of the woods, a curious figure appeared. He was probably about 5ft 4in tall. He was dressed in a cape and had a hat like a deerstalker on his head, Jodhpur-style trousers and knee-high boots.

However, the most striking thing about him was that he was carrying a pickaxe helve. It did not have the pickaxe head on it, rather it had a long, sharp spike protruding from it.

"F@ck me, what is this all about?" I thought, locking the driver's door.

Standing beside the truck in the teeming rain, he spoke in German and introduced himself to me as Vlad. He then asked whether I was parking for the night. If I was, he continued, it would cost 50 Deutschmarks (50 DMs was £20).

"You are joking." I thought, having already nick-named him Vlad the impaler due to his homemade weapon. I restarted the engine, ready to pull out of the parking area, and he waved his arms and shouted "Woh". I turned off the engine and he said, equably, "10 DMs, then."

I said, "O.K. 10 Deutschmarks". Ten was much better than 50.

"Five now and five in the morning if you and the truck are O.K.," he said.

I pondered that point. What did he mean, "If me and the truck were OK?" But, I needed to sleep and this sounded like a better deal. I passed him a 5 DM note out of the driver's window.

"Do you want *Maidschen* (German for woman)?" he asked cheerfully, describing the form of a nubile young woman, with his hands. While he did this he nearly stabbed himself with the spike in his pickaxe helve.

"No", I replied, "I just want to sleep".

"Ballon?" he enquired.

"Ballon," I replied, the tone and inflection of my voice indicating that I did not understand what he meant. What I thought was, "Christ, he wants to have a kid's birthday party."

"Ballon," he stated, as if to someone who was slightly special needs. Special needs of a ballon.

He made the mime of pulling on a condom. I understood then what he meant.

"No," I said, mock seriously. "I am Catholic. The Pope doesn't let us use them."

"*Ich verstere* [I understand]," he said.

"What time does the restaurant open?" I enquired.

"8," he replied.

"Can you wake me at 8 then?" I asked.

"Yes," he replied. "Good night," he added and then turned and disappeared into the blackness of the night. Gone like a spook.

I opened a can of German beer from the duty free locker, lit a cigarette and thought to myself,

"I am in a parallel bleeding universe."

That night I slept like a log. When I woke up, I looked at my watch and the time was 9am.

"So much for my call at 8," I thought, opened the curtains and looked around. Nothing.

The night before there had been two trucks and a beaten up old Ukrainian-registered Mercedes car on the parking area. They had gone. Everything was quiet.

"Well I am still here," I thought.

I opened the door and got out of the cab. I toured the trailer and truck, looking for damage or the signs of pilfering. Nothing. The truck and trailer were fine.

Back in the cab, I looked across the road. The restaurant was not open. It was closed down and looked derelict. I started the truck and drove away from the site, heading on towards Bucharest. I wondered what had happened to Vlad.

It took me two and a half hours to cover the 100 miles to Bucharest. The road surfaces were fairly good and the traffic light. En route from Focsani to Bucharest I passed through the town of Buzau, where I had once loaded a consignment of metal.

From there I knew my way into Bucharest and the route to take in the city to reach the British Embassy. I had delivered furniture to the embassy twice, in 1982.

Driving in the daylight I could see that I was passing continuous cultivations of corn on the cob. The fields of corn cobs stretched as far as the eye could see. Small trucks, horses and carts plied along the road, each loaded to the gunnels with corn stems. This was the impoverished Rumanians' staple diet. The corn, when milled, produced their coarse black bread.

At that time in 1990, Rumania was rated as the poorest country in Europe. Since then, they have had to fight off the challenge for that title from Moldova and Albania.

Rumania had been ruled by Ceausescu, the puppet leader of the country, installed by their communist masters in Moscow. Presiding over a bankrupt country, Ceausescu had done nothing to relieve the poverty of his people but had spent millions of pounds upon grandiose building projects, creating a series of presidential palaces and government buildings.

When the break-up of the East European network of communist satellite states had occurred in 1989 and Gorbachev had allowed the satellites their freedom, Ceausescu and his corrupt regimes had been swept from power, after initially allowing his army to shoot the protesting people.

Ceausescu himself had been caught and executed for this murderous act against his own people. No great loss to anyone.

During the uprising, Bucharest University students had initiated a peaceful protest in University Square, in the heart of the city. Ceausescu's response had been to allow his forces to open fire upon them. A large number of unarmed, peacefully protesting students had been killed by the security forces' gunfire. My route to the British Embassy took me directly through University Square.

As I entered Bucharest it began to rain again. Driving through the city, the rain got heavier.

When I entered University Square the rain was teeming down.

The traffic was heavy and I kept having to stop at traffic lights. As I did so, even the pouring rain could not stop me from witnessing the tributes paid to the dead students.

The square was awash with small wooden crosses and candles set in glasses, placed in memory of the martyrs who had lost their lives in a peaceful protest against a corrupt and authoritarian regime.

It was an extremely sobering sight.

Eventually I arrived at the British Embassy. It was situated in what is to all appearance, a side street: Strada Jules Michelet. However, the embassy was substantial, set back behind a low wall mounted with iron railings. Looking at it from the front, the entrance way into the compound was to the right and this was guarded 24 hours a day by Rumanian police officers. They had an ornate police guard box in which to shelter from the elements.

Within the embassy grounds the main building was centrally positioned, while to the right and rear ancillary buildings stood. Opposite the embassy were normal dwelling houses where everyday residents of Bucharest lived.

I parked in the street directly in front of the embassy. The police protection officers ensured that there was nothing parked in front of the site. This was to ensure that terrorists couldn't park a car bomb there. However, a British truck was allowed to park as long as it was on official business and as I was carrying virtually diplomatic cargo, I was OK.

I climbed from the cab taking with me my custom documentation and passport. Locking the cab door, I made my way to where the police officer was sheltering in his guard hut against the rain, which was driving down.

Having inspected my paperwork and seen my passport the officer allowed me to enter the embassy grounds.

Entering the embassy grounds in 1990, the first person that I met was Maria. She was the only member of staff who remained from my previous times there in 1982. As I sat in her office while she prepared the custom papers she said, "You must have left the border very early this morning Mick, because you were not parked here when I turned up for work this morning."

"No," I replied, "I left the border yesterday afternoon."

"What?" she said. "So, where were you last night?" Her tone incredulous.

"I stopped at a restaurant near Focsani," I said, oblivious to why this seemed to present a problem.

"Then you are very lucky that you and the truck are O.K.," she stated.

"Why?" I enquired, not seeing why my safety would be in doubt.

"Because," she said, "when Ceausescu fell, they opened up the prisons and released all of the convicts that had been locked up under his regime."

She looked at me intently. Continuing she said, "Not only did they release all of the political prisoners, who had protested against the way that he ran the country but they also released all of the murderers, robbers and rapists under a general amnesty. There are gangs of cut-throats roaming the countryside who would think nothing of murdering you and ransacking your truck."

I laughed in disbelief.

"Mick," she said sternly, "I am not joking. It is not like eight years ago when you were last here. Everything has changed and the country is very, very dangerous. You need to be extremely careful. Do not park out in unprotected places."

I looked at Maria and realised that she was serious. I thought about Vlad from the Focsani restaurant. I wondered what he was really up to. When he was talking to me I had not got out of the cab. It is taken for granted that truck drivers carry weapons so as to protect themselves. Maybe he was a brigand and had I got out of the cab I might have ended up feeling the spike of his pickaxe helve. Maybe that was why there was no 8 o'clock wake up. He had made 5 DMs without being confronted by any weapon that I carried and thought that he would not chance his arm in case I was tooled up. Whatever the story, I would never know.

★

The trailer was unloaded that afternoon and I was free to leave Bucharest. A telephone call to Croomes from the embassy office resulted in me being given an address in Brasov. I was to load metal there the following day. Brasov was 114 miles from Bucharest.

I decided to stay outside the embassy overnight and to drive to Brasov in the morning. Maria's warning had worked.

The Tour De Romania

I arrived in Brasov at 7.30am and quickly found the factory where I was to load the pallets of metal. By 1pm the goods were loaded and customs procedures carried out. I was free to drive to the border and escape from Rumania. However, when I had phoned Croomes the day before they had said that, as the metal consignment was only 10 tonnes, there was a possibility that I might also have to travel to Belgrade, the capital of Yugoslavia. There I would load exhibition goods, which were to return to the U.K. The metal factory did not have a telex and international phone calls had to be booked in advance. The waiting time for a call was at least 24 hours. I was in no mood to wait overnight in Brasov so I drove to the main street in the city where there was a P.T.T. office. From there I could telex to England immediately.

I parked the truck in the main street, locked the cab doors and made my way to the P.T.T. I paid the clerk at the counter £2 in Rumanian Lieu and she went off to send the telex. When she returned I told her that I would go off and return in an hour to see if there was a reply. I went back to the truck and sat in the cab. I noticed that the street that I was in was a wide boulevard with buildings to the left, but open parkland to the right. On either side of this street grandstands had been erected. From the street lamps, Rumanian flags and bunting had been hung, running along the length of the street on either side. I thought that, as it was Friday, there was probably some kind of festival taking place over the weekend and did not give it any more thought.

Back at the P.T.T. there had not been a reply so I sent another telex to Croome. I wrote, "Loaded at Brasov. Do you want me to go to Belgrade? If no reply within one hour will make my way to Budapest and contact you tomorrow."

The girl sent the telex and I returned to my cab. As I sat in the truck, playing music and smoking I watched as the grandstands filled up to capacity and the people standing alongside the roadway increased in number. There were crowds of people beginning to mill about in the vicinity. Obviously, what was about to happen was going to take place that afternoon and not over the weekend, as I had originally thought.

I also noticed that there was no traffic driving along the street any more. The roadway was completely empty.

At the end of the hour I made my way back to the P.T.T. to discover that I had still not received a reply. Feeling slightly pissed off that I had lost two hours sitting in Brasov for no good reason, I sent a terse message, "Gone to Budapest". I paid the girl and returned to the truck.

By now, thousands of people were flocked along the street on either side of the road. Police officers were lining the pavement edges to keep the crowds back.

I climbed into the truck, started the engine and pulled away from the kerb. Ahead of me stood the grandstands. As I drove forward, all the police officers waved at me. "What a friendly bunch of people," I thought.

Picking up speed, I passed the grandstands and looking ahead realised that some 500 metres in front of me there was a right-hand bend. More and more people waved to me as I passed by. Feeling like royalty I waved back, surprised that there was no other traffic on the road considering that it was late afternoon.

I reached the right-hand bend and followed the road round to the right. In front of me there was a crossroads controlled by traffic lights. The lights were on red. On my side of the road, the right, there were two lanes. The right-hand lane had an arrow indicating that it was for people who wanted to turn right. The left-hand lane, of the two, was signed for traffic that wanted to carry straight on. I moved to my left and occupied this lane.

Stopping at the halt line, I realised that there were a number of police officers standing around. They were shouting and waving for me to move over to the right and actually turn right. I did not want to turn right as my road was straight ahead, so I sat there in the middle of the road.

One of the police officers came over to the cab and began to speak to me but I could not understand what he was saying because I do not speak Rumanian. Suddenly, one of the other police officers shouted out something urgently and the cop beside my cab, sprinted for the kerb. I looked at him, watching him run for his life, and then turned my head to look directly forward.

Across the traffic light junction, after 100 metres, the road curved to the left. I looked up at the traffic lights, which were still on red, and then looked back at the road ahead. At that moment from around the curve ahead of me there appeared a phalanx of hundreds of cyclists, all wearing multicoloured lycra cycling outfits. They were riding racing bicycles and without exception they were all bent forward, head down. It was obviously a sprint finish, which was to end in front of the grandstands that I had just passed.

I looked at this swarm of racing cyclists who were rapidly approaching the front of my truck. They filled the whole width of the road and a great number of them were heading directly towards my vehicle. "Ooooooooh shit," I thought, gripping the steering wheel tight and bracing myself for the impact as numerous cyclists were about to ride directly into the front of my cab.

With their heads down in racing sprint mode they were not looking ahead to identify any potential obstructions or obstacles. They were straining their bodies to the maximum, purely intent upon winning this stage of the Tour of Rumania. The cyclists would have been racing flat out, reliant upon the fact that the local police would have cleared the road for their final sprint to the finishing line. They would not have for one moment envisaged that a British truck would be barring their way.

As one does in moments of crisis, the Rumanian police officers let off that waft of smell, which indicates that bowels had discharged themselves and that underwear has become heavily soiled. It is colloquially known as "The Smell of Fear". Sitting in the driver's seat of the cab, I had no time to do anything other than to reach out my hand and press the air horn button.

The noise of the air horn, loud and raucous, alerted the racers to the imminent danger that lay ahead of them. Suddenly they looked up and obviously thought "Shiiiii-it" (In Rumanian, of course). They took immediate action to stop from careering into the front of my truck. Those heading directly towards me edged to their right or left, depending where they were positioned in relation to the truck. Some collided with those alongside them and cyclists began to be thrown to the ground, entangled with the riders around them. Men and bikes began to fall like dominoes.

As the swathe of riders continued towards me, the centrally positioned riders pulled away to either side. This forced the riders on the outside to mount the paths either side of the road. Hitting the kerbs acted as an instant braking action and many flew off their bikes, landing sideways beside the road. Others cartwheeled over their own handlebars.

As this catastrophic carnage unravelled in front of my eyes, I casually reached for my cigarette packet. I withdrew a cigarette and lit it. Drawing heavily so as to infuse my lungs with acrid, nicotine-laden smoke, I watched as those riders who had been thrown to the ground, stood up, picked up their bikes and bravely remounted. Unluckily for some of them, riders who were behind them rode into them, knocking them to the ground again. Once more, they remounted and continued towards the finishing line, which lay behind me, out of sight beyond the bend. Most of the bikes had buckled wheels and bent forks by this time.

Once the melee of riders had reduced to a trickle approaching around the distant left-hand bend, I saw that the police officers controlling the junction had begun to take an extremely keen interest in me. Obviously, questions were going to be asked as to why that stage of the Tour de Rumania had turned into a travesty; heavily laden with carnage. I had decided that it was not going to be me who was going to answer those questions and concluded that the better part of valour was discretion.

In other words, I needed to get the f@ck out of there – on the hurry up.

The truck engine was still running. I dropped the clutch, jammed the gear lever into second, let out the clutch and accelerated. The traffic lights were still set at red, but I ignored that basic fact, intent upon making my getaway. There was no other traffic about with which to cause an accident.

Changing up through the gears, I was soon hurtling along at 70mph, passing swathes of corn on the cob and heading for the border at Nadlac, 293 miles away. I drove non-stop to Nadlac, except for when I needed to stop for a piss. To do this I stopped in the middle of a crossroads. Leaving the engine running in case a speedy getaway was required, I opened the driver's door, stood up, leaned out and pissed on to the road. I was paranoid about roaming bands of murdering, robbing rapists and was not taking the chance of being raped by some murderous, robbing Rumanian bum bandit. Piss over, it was back in the driver's seat and full throttle, pedal to the metal, hammer down for Nadlac town.

On the way to Nadlac I passed through the town of Arad, just another dirty dusty insignificant Rumanian town. As you entered Arad there was a restaurant with a large parking area, on the left-hand side of the road.

When I had made my first trip to Rumania for Pro-Motor, two other Pro-Motor drivers, Ronny Hart and Graham (Bugsy) Bertram, had been with me. We had all loaded at Bucharest Exhibition ground and were returning to Britain. I had cartons of Kent cigarettes with which to buy diesel on the black market. Kent, for some strange reason, were the preferred currency for black market activities in Rumania at that time. But Ronny and Bugsy hadn't got any. They decided that they would change up hard currency into Rumanian Lieu and blag it at a petrol station as they had no coupons either.

All of us were on our first trip to Rumania; therefore, we did not know what a litre of diesel cost. They calculated that they would need to change one Deutschmark per litre and both wanted 500 litres. So we found a bank and they changed up 1,000 Dms between them. When we actually went to a filling station it turned out that the black market price for the diesel, paid for in Lieus was only the equivalent of 100 Dms. Therefore, they had 900 Dms' worth of Lieu left over; £360 worth of useless Rumanian Draculas. We could have bought Arad for that.

On the way out of Rumania we stopped at the restaurant in Arad on the Saturday evening and set about eating and drinking 900 Dms' worth of the local currency. The session lasted all weekend.

On the Monday morning we arose to discover that we still had 100 Dms worth of Lieu left. As we left the restaurant parking area there was a little old Rumanian lady dressed in black, signifying that she was a widow. She must have been at least 80 years old. Bugsy stopped his truck and gave her the 100 Dms worth of Lieus. She beamed with joy and crossed herself, overcome with delight. To her it was like winning the jackpot on the Euro Lottery. Then we drove on, heading for the border at Nadlac.

When we stopped just before the border for a cup of tea, Ronny said to me, "I am surprised that he did not have her up in the cab and give her one, in exchange for that money."

"No, that wasn't going to happen," I had replied, adding, "She was far too young; even for him."

Having driven through Arad, I arrived at the border at midnight. I parked the truck on the Hungarian side of the border and went to bed. Before I went to sleep, I reflected upon what had been an exceptionally interesting day. I wondered how many charges of A.B.H., G.B.H. and attempted murder I was wanted for by the Old Bill in Brasov. Also jumping a red light. I decided that it was probably for the best that I never went back to Rumania ever again. Laughing, I fell asleep.

In the morning I drove to Budapest, a distance of 138 miles from Nadlac, passing through Szeged and Kecskemet on the way. I noticed that there had been a lot of new roads built since I had last been there in 1983. It had certainly improved the journey.

In Budapest I made my way to the Aero Hotel, from where I telephoned Croome's office. I was given an address in Nurnberg where I was to load another consignment on the Monday morning. I set out straight away for the Czech border. My plan was to make it to Brno that evening. I knew that Rob and Charlie from Kepstowe were in Brno, site repping at an exhibition that was closing. I was running very short of money and figured that I could draw some from them.

Budapest to Brno was 200 miles. I left Budapest and passed Tata and Gyor on the way to Mosonmagyarovar. Reaching Mosonmagyarovar, the road split so that you either continued west to drive into Austria or turned north to enter Slovakia. I turned north and crossed the border at Rajka, which was the name for the Hungarian side. The Slovak side was named Rusovce.

While I was carrying out the formalities at Rajka, a group of English drivers came into the border office. They were dressed in jeans, shirts and paper thin, cheap, shoddy Turkish, leather bomber jackets. They were all wearing shoes without socks. I asked one of them where they had been and he replied, "The Middle East."

"Really", I said, "and where in the Middle East then?"

"Istanbul," he said, as if it was the furthest that anyone had ever driven.

"That's not even halfway to the Middle East," I said, laughing, adding, "The Middle East starts when you cross the Turkish border heading east or south into Iran, Syria, or Iraq."

"Where you on your way back from, then?" he asked, obviously thinking that I had completed an even more local job than Istanbul.

"Moscow", I replied evenly, in a low key manner.

"Moscow?" he said in disbelief, "Then why are you coming back this way?" he asked, thinking that I was making it up. He knew that the normal route would be much further north than Rajka.

"Because I have brought a load down from the

Moscow Embassy to the Embassy in Bucharest," I said.

"What's Moscow like?" he enquired.

"Better than bleeding Istanbul," I replied, laughing.

The problem that I had at Rajka was that I needed to buy a Czech visa. As I was not returning from a trip where I had come out through Czechoslovakia, I needed one to enter Czecho. Short of hard currency money, in fact down to my last few Deutschmarks, I was not sure that I could afford the cost of the visa. I asked the lad that I was talking to whether they could let me have the few Marks that I needed to buy the visa.

"Sorry mate," he replied. "You ain't one of us. You ain't our problem." With that he walked away laughing. Turning his head to look at me over his shoulder, he called out. "Good luck, mate. Hope that you ain't stuck here more than a few days." He and the rest of the gang laughed at this and then left the customs building.

The Middle East men (laugh!), whose trucks were empty, were through the border quickly. I still had formalities to complete and they were long gone before I left Rajka. However, luckily for me the Czech authorities took a photo of me for the visa and completed the visa document without asking me for any money (a right result). All I now had to do was to make my way to Brno, meet up with Rob and Charlie and sub some money from them. I had more than enough diesel to get to Brno, having topped up in Rumania, so once I was allowed to leave the border I could cruise up the concrete-surfaced motorway from Bratislava to Brno.

Unlike in the 1980s, trucks were now banned from transiting Bratislava, but I took no notice of the ban signs and drove through the city. At one point you passed over a river bridge that had a tower built at one end. On top of the tower there was a restaurant where I had eaten a few times. You had a panoramic view of Bratislava while you ate.

I crossed the river and drove on. On one stretch of the road through the city I saw that the Middle East men had been pulled over by the police. Obviously, for contravening the ban. A police officer stepped out into the road and flagged me to a halt as I passed the other English trucks that were pulled up at the side of the road. I stopped and opened my driver's side door. He asked me what I was doing, driving through Bratislava when there was a truck transit ban. I reached into my paperwork folder and withdrew the document that I had been given at Butova, which stated that I was carrying goods on behalf of the British Government.

At that time, following the loosening of ties with the Soviet Union, the state of Czechoslovakia was in the throes of splitting into two sovereign nations: the Czech Republic and Slovakia. Bratislava was to become the capital of Slovakia. I told the police officer that I had been to the new British Embassy that was to be set up in Bratislava. Therefore, I could not bypass the city as I had been undertaking legitimate business within the city. We spoke in Russian.

He was not too happy at discussing this matter in Russian, but as I explained to him, I did not speak Czech. As a Slovakian, whose language was very similar to Russian, he accepted that the only way that we could communicate was by using the Russian language. Unless, of course, I said, that he spoke English, or German. He didn't. We talked in Russian and he read the document that stated that I was on diplomatic business. Accepting this, he let me continue on my way. He asked me whether the other English drivers were covered by the document. I told him that they were not and that they were nothing to do with me. The Middle East men had gathered around as I spoke to the police officer. They were totally lost as I conversed with the policeman in Russian.

When the policeman indicated that I could go, the English driver who I had been talking to at the border asked me whether I could sort out their problem with the police, seeing I spoke the language. "Sorry mate," I said, putting the truck in gear and pulling away. "I ain't one of you," adding, "I hope that you ain't here more than a couple of days," as I accelerated away. How I laughed, as I drove off.

Fortunately, I found Rob and Charlie in the exhibition hall at Brno. Outside of Brno exhibition grounds there were two hotels; Voronezh 1 and 2. Voronezh 1 had a restaurant and nightclub. Voronezh 2 was merely an accommodation block. Rob and Charlie were staying in Voronezh 1. We arranged to meet in the restaurant of Voronezh 1 for dinner.

We had dinner in the restaurant and then went to the nightclub. At the end of the evening, Rob gave me 500 Deutschmarks to get myself back to the U.K. That did not materialise, but the money came in handy anyway.

We met for breakfast the following morning in Voronezh 1 and they asked me whether I was happy working for them through David Croome. I said not particularly and would much sooner work for them directly. The reply to this was that soon there was the possibility that I could work directly for them but they did not want me to openly leave Croome to start work for them. They did not want it to appear that they had headhunted me. However, should Croome and I fall out with one another then they would be more than happy for me to join their enterprise, subcontracting directly for them.

I took this on board and drove out of Brno feeling a lot happier than when I had entered the city. I was also 500 Dms better off, which would get me to England no problems (Not).

10

The Next Nail in the Coffin

MY relationship with Croome was the same that it had been when I was a driver for him: not very good. I did not like the man and the feeling was mutual. Four years working for him as a driver had been enough. Our relationship was that we tolerated one another.

I left Brno on the motorway north to Prague. There, I took the truck diversion and left the city, heading for Pilsen, the birthplace of pils lager. Once, for a laugh, I had actually driven through the city centre of Prague with a truck. It had been extremely tight. I had passed through sections of the city where I had literally only a fag paper's width either side of the trailer and the level of concentration required to do this without accident had been immense.

I would not recommend that you try that at home. Or in Prague, for that matter.

Reaching Pilsen, I stopped at the brewery and bought two crates of Czech lager beer. I then continued on my way to the Czech–German border at Folmava–Furth im Wald.

The countryside was pleasant and the road dipped

and rose as I passed through a succession of undulating hills. In the small villages, stretches of the road were cobbled and you passed with caution. Occasionally you passed through forestland, where the bright sunshine disappeared until you came out at the other end. Parking areas beside the road denoted picnic spots where crude, wooden seating and tables were provided. As the evening light began to fade, I reached Folmava and the Czech–German border.

Having cleared the Czech side of the border, I drove to the German side. Between the two separate border posts, Czech and German, the road joining them dipped down into a fold in the ground and then back up. This formed a no man's land between the two states. As I drove into the dip I recalled that a German customs officer had been shot dead in this no man's land back in the 1970s. Nobody knew why he had ventured into this area, at night. That he had been shot by a Czechoslovakian soldier was not disputed. Inside the border office of the German customs a framed photograph of the dead officer hung on the wall.

Having spent the night parked at the border I drove to Nurnberg. I found the factory, where I was to load children's nursery furniture. While they were loading the trailer, I was called to the office to answer a telephone call. It was the office boy in Croome's office. He began to give me a bollocking for not having been at the factory first thing in the morning.

I pointed out that I had not been given any instructions as to what time to be there, but he tried to talk me down and said that the goods had to be in

Northampton, the following afternoon. I replied, "No chance mate."

The driving time from Nurnberg to Zeebrugge was ten hours, so that was not possible when adding in the ferry crossing, custom procedures at Dover and driving time to Northampton.

He started to tell me that I would do as I was told, but I interrupted him. Normally extremely calm in the most difficult of circumstances and without changing the tone or inflection of my voice I said, "As you are not listening I'll tell you what, then."

He replied, "What?"

Flatly, I said, "Piss Off," and hung up.

Having completed loading, I drove to the Massa Hypermarket at Alzey on the A61 where I spent the night.

When I arrived at Zeebrugge I discovered there was a large, brown envelope waiting for me. On the front of the envelope, written in black marker pen, was my name and truck number. I opened the envelope and discovered there was a trailer in Zeebrugge destined for the Moscow exhibition complex, V.D.N.K.

Kepstowe had sent the documentation to Dover with the trailer that I was to collect. The driver had given it to P&O; who sent it over to Zeebrugge. I was to drop my trailer, which would ship unaccompanied to Dover. I was then to hook up to the new trailer and make my way back to Moscow.

I handed P&O all the documentation for the trailer that I was dropping off. Shortly afterwards I drove out of the Docks at Zeebrugge, heading east again. I was feeling slightly pissed off, as I had been looking forward to one of the enormous, full English breakfasts that you got on the boat. However, looking on the bright side, I was going back to Moscow.

Croome may have thought that he was getting his revenge but I would have the last laugh.

11

My New Home and a Kebab

THE trip back to Moscow was uneventful. I arrived in Moscow on a Saturday afternoon and called Elena. She travelled down to the Mezh' by Metro to meet me. Instead of going to a restaurant, as I had expected, she said that we would go to her flat where I could now stay whenever I was in Moscow. She wanted me to move in and for us to live together. So, that is what I did, because I wanted that too.

I threw some clothes and my washing gear into a bag and locked the truck. I joined her for the walk up the hill to the Ulitsa 1905 Metro station. It was a beautifully warm sunny afternoon, with clear skies overhead. Elena linked her arm through mine as we walked up the hill. At one point I laughed and she asked me what I was thinking about. I told her that I was not thinking about anything.

What I had been thinking about was David Croome. He must have thought that it was retribution, sending me back to Moscow instead of me going to England as a way of making me pay for not getting the goods from Nurnberg back to England fast enough for his liking. Rather than meting out a punishment he had done me one big favour. Again.

The flat was on the top floor of a nine-storeyed high apartment block in the Leningradski district of northwest Moscow. It was close to the Voikovskaya Metro station. Elena shared the flat with her aunt Vera. The apartment comprised of two bedrooms, a kitchen, bathroom and separate toilet. Vera's bedroom, the larger of the two, was huge and doubled as a sitting room for all of us at times. It also had a balcony that looked out over the enormous open space that was bordered by other apartment blocks. What was to become our room was adequate for our needs. It contained a double bed, coffee table, two armchairs and sideboard. A television set stood upon the sideboard. The kitchen was small but functional. The bathroom was also small but perfectly usable. Elena and I hung our clothes in wardrobe-styled cupboards in the passage. Vera had her own wardrobes.

The open space outside of our apartment block was encompassed by other apartment blocks. They were similar to ours and formed a huge rectangular space. Our apartment block was approximately 500 metres long. It was at the narrow end of the rectangle, as was the opposite block, which faced ours. Along the longer sides of the rectangle, to the left and right as you looked out of our windows, there were two blocks either side. These were as long as our block of flats but divided by a tarmac road that crossed the rectangle of land, separating the blocks on each side.

The whole impression that you gained when looking out of our windows was that you were in a concrete, urban jungle. On the ground floor, way down below our flat, there was a bakery that baked loaves day and night. Next to the bakery there was a chemist's shop. The bakery and the chemist took up half of the ground space of the lower floor. The other half of the ground floor was taken up by other shops, which were mostly vacant.

Elena and I spent the weekend touring the local area so that I could see the lie of the land. We made our way to the Metro station and she demonstrated to me how to buy Metro tokens so that I could use the Metro system on my own. The station was underneath the main Leningradski highway, which ran through this part of the city. *Metro Stansiya Voikovskaya* (Metro Station Voikovskaya) was a transport hub where travellers made onwards connections to buses, trams and trolley buses. All the major Metro stations in Moscow had this function.

While we were walking around the area I was taking note of the road layout for when I wanted to bring my truck home. This knowledge was to prove invaluable over the coming years.

Elena bought twenty Metro tokens for 2 Roubles (4p in English black market rate money). She gave me ten of the small, green tokens to keep for when I travelled alone on the system. We placed a token each in the barrier at the top of the steps leading down to the platform. I discovered that the barriers were not always reliable. In fact, at times you had to be extremely vigilant that you did not get caught. When a train came in heading for central Moscow, we climbed aboard and rode to the city centre. We changed stations at Tverskaya for Pushkinskaya. Tverskaya served line number 2, from Voikovskaya. Pushkinskaya served line number 7, which took you to Ulitsa 1905 Goda, where I needed to get off to reach the Mezh'. We changed to line 7 and rode to Ulitsa 1905 Goda.

Having left the Metro system, we walked down the hill to the Mezh'. Going to my truck, I collected some more of my gear and then we walked back up the hill to 1905 Goda. We travelled back to Voikovskaya and returned to the flat.

The following morning, we left the flat and walked the short distance to the main road, which ran down to the Metro station. Here, we turned right and immediately in front of us were a set of bus stops. I waited with Elena until she caught the bus to her place of work. I then turned round and made my way to the Metro station to travel down to 1905.

Over the coming years I was to use the Metro extensively, down to the point where I used to buy season tickets. I got to know its layout by heart and looked in wonder at the magnificent statues and artwork that they had installed in its stations.

Construction of the Moscow Metro had begun in the early 1930s under the orders of Joseph Stalin. It was intended to be a demonstration of the power and artistic prowess of the Soviet Union. This was the U.S.S.R's largest ever civil construction project and the original system opened in 1935. The bulk of the labour force used to dig and build the network were women.

Outstanding architects and artists were employed to create iconic underground centres, each station having a unique, individual theme. The original stations were designed to reflect different aspects of Soviet life and history. By use of bas-reliefs, friezes, marble and bronze statues, stain glass windows and mosaics, the artists produced underground cultural centres of radiance and beauty. The theme of these individual stations paid homage to historical characters, sport, industry, agriculture and military might. Some stations that were added to the system after the Second World War were themed to show the Soviet military forces who defended Russia and went on to achieve victory against the Nazi invaders.

One major theme of a number of the original stations was the communist revolutions of 1905 and 1917. Huge bronze statues depicted revolutionaries manning the barricades, armed with rifles and other weapons. Many of these statues were of soldiers and sailors who had been instrumental in the revolutions in holding off the Tsarist forces.

All the underground stations were kept spotlessly clean, which was totally contrary to the general state of Moscow, which was dirty, rubbish strewn and highly polluted! Walking through each of the stations, I was amazed at their artistic beauty and unique character. Much of the station lighting was achieved by the use of hundreds of chandeliers, while the highly decorated arched ceilings were supported by ornate pillars and arches.

In contrast to the London and Parisian Underground systems, with their basic, unkempt functional stations, I was enthralled by the magical quality of the Central Moscow stations.

I left the Mezh' and drove to V.D.N.K. (The Science and Technology Park). Having entered the park, I lodged my documents. Returning to my truck, I noticed that there was a German truck parked up near to mine, also a French one. I spoke to their drivers and then to a couple of Russian drivers, who were parked near to us. I asked the Russians whether the kebabs on sale at the kebab stall were fit to eat. They ensured me that they were but to be careful of roadside stalls, where the meat might well be *Sabaka* (Dog)!

Happy in the knowledge that the kebabs here were not dog meat, I walked over to the stall and bought one. The snack was presented on a paper plate, the cubes of meat still on the metal skewer. As I began to eat the kebab, Pete Newlyn and Ronnie Seymour drove into the exhibition ground in their respective trucks. They parked alongside mine.

Noticing my kebab, they both looked across at the kebab stall. The cook was dressed in a white jacket and blue and white checked trousers. The image was spoiled by the massive bloodstains on the front of his jacket. That and the black soot marks that accompanied the bloodstains.

They looked again at my kebab and then once more, at the cook. They shook their heads, in unison. "You aren't seriously going to eat that, are you?" Pete enquired.

"No," said I, adding, "I am going to laugh."

"You are bloody mad," chipped in Ronnie.

Shaking their heads, they walked towards the exhibition hall. I called after them, "You want me to get you one each then, I take it?"

"I would rather eat shit," Ronnie called back.

"Who said you wouldn't be?" I yelled, just as they were about to enter the hall. I could see both of them laughing as they disappeared from sight.

Unfortunately, we did not clear customs and tip our loads that afternoon, so we ended up back at V.D.N.K. the following morning. Once again, my trailer was not cleared but Ronnie and Pete managed to get unloaded. I expect that the kebab seller was bunging the customs, to keep me there longer. I was probably his best customer. That afternoon we drove to the Mezh' and I took the Metro home.

The following morning, I arrived at the Mezh' to discover that Pete and Ronnie were long gone. I made my way to V.D.N.K. and my luck was actually in. The trailer was tipped that afternoon. A telex at the Mezh' comms centre told me to make my way to Siedlce, empty. Arriving at Siedlce I found a telex waiting for me that instructed me to drive to Berlin.

I arrived in Berlin late the following night. By the time that I had contacted his office I knew that Croome was going to try to hold me in Berlin. That would be without payment. It was another punishment. He had left me there for six days previously, which had been retribution for failing to load in Limerick.

However, during those six days I drove all round Berlin, soaking up the sights and had a great time. The best thing was the fact that while I was there, Roger Waters, of Pink Floyd, staged his Berlin "Wall" concert. And guess who went to it.

However, this time I did not intend to sit around in Berlin, so I phoned Kepstowe and asked whether they could load me from anywhere. Fortunately, they had a return load from Poznan Exhibition Ground that one of their trucks was due to pick up and also one from Brno that needed covering. They told me to call back in an hour's time. In that hour, they phoned Croome and told him to send me into Poznan so that their truck could go directly to Brno, where the goods were to be loaded urgently. When I called Croome's office I was told to go back to

Poznan and load from there. However, this information was passed on with very little grace. Phoning Kepstowe to thank them I was treated in a much more civil manner.

12

The Start of the Problems

I left Berlin and drove back to Frankfurt Oder along the poorly surfaced dual carriageway autobahn. Reaching Frankfurt O', the dual carriageway ended at a junction where you could turn off the motorway and enter the town. It was also where you turned off if you wanted to take the road that ran north and south, parallel to the border. Carrying on to the actual border crossing point, I now drove on a single carriageway road, which dropped down a slight hill until it reached the road bridge, that spanned the Oder river. Before reaching the bridge, I came upon the rear of a small queue of vehicles. I had never before been subject to a queue to enter this border. From first using it in 1978, it had always been a quiet place with only a slight amount of traffic transiting it in either direction.

As I was soon to discover, the reason for this and all of the subsequent queues at this and the other German–East European borders was the sudden increase in cross-border traffic. This was generated by the Poles, Czechs and Hungarians realising that they could now travel into the West virtually at will. This allowed them to travel into Germany, predominately to buy consumer goods. They also bought cars, trucks and buses, with which they could return to their own countries. These goods were either for personal or professional use, or to be sold on upon a commercial basis.

One of the problems with this cross-border traffic was that all goods being imported into the old communist states carried an import tax. This had to be paid at the border itself. This procedure took time. Also, as the traffic became heavier, it blocked up these small main border posts while the people were going through their import and duty payment procedures. The eventual result of this was that, with a vast increase in the amount of trucks taking imported goods into Poland plus private importers in their cars, the borders became saturated with traffic.

Unfortunately, the escalation of the traffic happened swiftly. This led to queues of trucks waiting to enter Poland at Frankfurt O' stretching back 25 kilometres along the dual carriageway approach. That was because the head of the queue of trucks was halted at the junction where the road narrowed down. All the other trucks were forced to halt behind it. Cars and coaches, however, were diverted on to a contraflow on the other carriageway. That allowed them to overtake the line of trucks and drive straight to the border. The problem with this segregation was that the car and coach passengers were generally not used to the system and did not complete it quickly. This created congestion behind them, particularly for the trucks queued on the motorway, who could not get into the actual border control area.

Then, there was the problem of the trucks that were carrying imports into Poland. They needed to have paperwork created at the border so that they could carry on to their final destination, under custom control. This again took time and held up the trucks behind them until it was completed. People such as myself, who were normally entering Poland in transit to Russia, could complete our procedures rapidly. We were thwarted by the blockage of the border facility. Therefore, as the border queues at Frankfurt became horrendous, I diverted away from there and began to use other smaller crossing points, which did not suffer from this problem. From then on I would only use Schwedt or Guben.

At Schwedt and Guben there were no freight agents carrying out import documentation, so the trucks that were destined for Poland could only use one of the three major border crossings: Stettin, in the north. Frankfurt, in the centre, or Cottbus, in the south. The only trucks that could use the smaller crossing points were those that were actually transiting Poland. Therefore, I would divert away from the main borders and utilise the smaller crossings. Although this meant a small amount of additional mileage and driving time, the actual saving in time, spent in interminable queues, made it absolutely worth it. I could save anywhere between 12 and 36 hours.

If I was approaching Frankfurt and saw that the queue was a long one, I would drive across to the opposite carriageway and use the contraflow to get to the head of the queue. I would then divert off the main road and from here I could drive north to Schwedt, or south to Guben. Later, I gave up on driving to Frankfurt O' at all and headed directly to the other borders.

Of course, when I was merely leaving Moscow and

travelling into Poland to swap trailers, turn round and go back into Russia, these queues did not bother me. They affected the driver that was bringing the trailer out for me. However, when I had to travel back, at least as far as to Germany, they were a concern. Later, when the traffic heading for Russia increased to an even larger scale than Poland's, I was forced to use the same strategy to enter and exit the Soviet Union: find smaller, underused borders. Originally, this queueing only seriously affected Kukariki, where 48-hour queues became commonplace when entering Belarus. However, that was still in the future and we will come to it later in the narrative.

Having been delayed at the border for a couple of hours, I left and drove on towards Poznan. I spent the night at the Buk Wooden Hut, of course, and drove into Poznan the following morning. I loaded from the exhibition ground and then parked up at the Poznan motel, where I phoned Kepstowe. They told me to drive to Berlin, where I would swap trailers; picking up a refrigerated one that was heading for Aeromar. With this knowledge in mind, I decided that there was no reason to contact Croome, so I didn't bother. I left the motel and drove back to Berlin. Leaving Poland, there was no queue whatsoever. The border post was virtually deserted. Once clear of the border I drove directly to Drei Linden and waited a day for the next trailer. I swapped trailers and headed for Moscow. For a change.

Night-time in Moscow meant dark streets and poor street lighting. Night-time outside of Moscow meant total pitch darkness. It was a dangerous time to drive because many of the Russian trucks, cars and coaches did not use lights at night.

During my time in Russia three Western truck drivers were killed, all as the result of night-time road accidents involving unlit Soviet vehicles. An English driver working for Blue Star – a Dutch company – was killed on the main M1, just to the west of Smolensk. He was involved in a crash with an unlit Russian truck. He did not die at the scene of the accident, but passed away in hospital in Smolensk some days later. My contacts at the Smolensk motel told me all the details. However, as the driver was on his first trip to Russia he was unknown to me.

A German truck driver was killed near Orsha, again involved in an accident with an unlit Russian truck. I saw his vehicle at the roadside following the crash. The cab of his truck had been obliterated in the collision. He died at the scene.

The third was a French driver who was involved in a crash with an unlit, giant earthmover, south of Kiev on the Odessa highway. I later saw his vehicle in a police pound that was situated right next to the road. The truck's cab was totalled. Nobody could have escaped from that carnage alive.

Why so many Sovs drove at night, with no lights on, was a mystery, but in the main was probably due to vehicle faults. Blown fuses or wiring faults were probably to blame. Russian vehicles, with the exception of Sovtransavto trucks, were poorly maintained. There was a general lack of parts in the whole of the country with which to carry out repairs. Unlit vehicles, combined with the pitch darkness, did not help when you were travelling at night.

Another phenomenon was the amount of dust in

the air, which reduced visibility even more. It hung in the air at night, creating a haze in the beam of headlights. As I have said, Russia is an extremely dusty place. In the summer, the roads are strewn with dust, which rises into the air with the wind and the down draft of passing vehicles.

An added night-time hazard was that approaching Russian drivers who were using their lights did not realise the importance of dipping their headlights when other traffic was approaching. You could understand this to a point when you saw how much junk was lying in the roads. This junk had fallen off other vehicles. Some of it was vehicle parts and the rest cargo. Then there were the defective parts that had been replaced in roadside repairs. The Sovs would leave the discarded parts in the actual road and not consider taking them away with them, or moving them on to the verges.

One night, following a Dutch truck into Moscow, I watched as his vehicle suddenly came to an unnatural halt in front of me. He had run over a discarded truck gearbox, which had ripped the oil sump completely off his vehicle.

Autumn 1990 once again signified the start of another phase in my work in Russia. I began to reload commercial loads other than for Xerox from Russia. I had already reloaded exhibition returns from the various exhibition sites; these had included stand fittings and returned show goods. However, now I was reloading consignments for a company called Interunity. Interunity had an office set back off the Sadovaya ring. It was on the opposite side of the road from the American Embassy in Moscow.

Initially, I mainly loaded birthday and Christmas wrapping paper from a company named Kommunar, in Tula, some 200 kilometres south of Moscow on the M2 (not the M2 in Kent. The Russian M2).

Actually, I was to load more than 100 times from Kommunar over the coming years and Interunity always used to ask for me personally when there was a load to be collected from there. They knew that I could drive down to Tula and back easily, within a day. Also, my knowing the locations and procedures there, with regards to Kommunar and the customs, meant that they could leave me to carry out the job on my own. This freed their staff up for other work, rather than having to spend a day out of their office driving to Tula to oversee the operation.

Back in Moscow, after my first trip to Tula, I parked the truck at the Mezh'. I then got the Metro home. I had decided not to take the trailer to our street in case of robbers slashing the tilt cover to see what the load contained. As I walked up the hill to reach home it began to rain, the first rain that had fallen in months. Moscow had been oppressively hot for weeks with temperatures reaching 36C. The rain freshened the air and it was great to walk in it.

When I got back to the flat Elena asked me why I had not brought the truck home. I explained that I did not want thieves slashing the tilt to see what I was carrying. "Micky," she said, in the bored manner of a parent pointing out something obvious to a child, "you know that big building, just round the corner, on the main road leading down to the Metro?"

"Yes," I replied.

"The one that you have just walked past on your way from the Metro." she said.

"Yes," I repeated.

"Well, that is a police academy," she informed me, adding, "and day and night police officers patrol this area, so no one is going to steal from your truck."

"Oh," I replied.

"In future you might as well bring your truck home, rather than park at the Mezh'." she said.

So, in future, I did. When it suited me.

Tula had been an interesting town to visit, because it was the home of the Kalashnikov factory. It was where the AK-47 Kalashnikov assault rifles were produced. When I had first gone there in that autumn of 1990, the town had only just opened up to foreigners. Prior to that, it had been a closed city. Foreigners had not been allowed to enter because of the arms factory. In the Soviet Union there were many closed cities, all of them the home of either factories producing strategic military equipment or secret testing institutions or military units. Many were still closed to foreigners.

Over the years I also loaded other goods for Interunity: consignments of titanium, wooden products, cloth and fabric materials; as well as a consignment of model sailing ships. The ships were handmade and of fantastic quality. During that autumn it also transpired that if I was delivering to Rank Xerox they would reload me with damaged goods, which were to be returned to Venray.

Allegedly, it had been made abundantly clear to David Croome that all Rank Xerox goods were to be transported from Venray to Moscow only on vehicles fitted with air suspension. This was a system where bags of air took the place of parabolic springs, the old method of suspension. Air-ride allowed for a much smoother journey, thereby ensuring that poor road surfaces delivered only a minimum of shock to the truck and the trailer. This meant that less damage would be done to the load. This was especially critical in the case of Rank Xerox, where we were carrying fragile pieces of office equipment over the worst roads in Europe.

My Daf 95 was fitted with parabolic springs on the front steering axle, but the other two axles were air suspension. The Kepstowe trailers that I pulled were air suspension on all axles. None of my loads ever arrived in Klyazma with any damage. I know this because I checked it out with the girls in the Xerox office upstairs at Klyazma. The damage was apparently being caused by Croome using non-air suspension vehicles to carry the goods.

What I did not find out until later was that Xerox had been complaining to Croome about the damage, but, they were not informing Kepstowe, who were unaware. Neither was Croome keeping Kepstowe in the loop. The eventual result of the subterfuge was the demise of the Kepstowe–Croome relationship because, allegedly, Kepstowe lost the highly lucrative Xerox contract due to Croome.

Blissfully unaware of what was going on behind the scenes, I was ploughing back and forward; travelling incessantly between Moscow and whatever European town or city I was told to go to change trailers. Usually, I would leave Moscow and be back within a week at the most.

If the changeover was at Siedlce I could do the

round trip in three days, providing that I did not want too much sleep. Siedlce was not always the change-over point, unfortunately, and I could find myself changing trailers in Berlin, Hannover or even Venray. This meant transiting the German–Polish border. However, as I now avoided Frankfurt O' altogether and used mainly Schwedt to cross between Germany and Poland, this wasn't too bad.

Schwedt also stood on the Oder river. It was situated between Frankfurt Oder and Stettin. Reaching Schwedt, you turned on to a narrow single carriageway road, which led down to the border crossing point. This road was more of a cobbled country lane than a road. The border post was on the German side of the river and both German and Polish customs facilities were located there. They were mainly a collection of single-storeyed buildings and booths that housed the German and Polish customs offices. There was a large building at the end of the complex that housed the offices of the German police. The German police controlled the border security.

It was obvious that the authorities did not want vehicles blocking the border. Therefore, they ensured that you were through and gone in short order. I used Schwedt many times over the next couple of years, crossing not only from Germany into Poland, but also back in the opposite direction.

Leaving the border at Schwedt, you drove over a bridge crossing the River Oder and then drove on through the western Polish countryside. Driving through the Polish towns and villages, you were struck by the fact that you were passing through land that, up until 1945, had been German. The buildings were of the German style, rather than the Polish style. Though when I say the German style, I mean the German style of the pre-Second World War. This was because, over the 44 years that the Soviets had occupied Poland, they had not allowed the Poles to build many new buildings. That is, other than concrete jungle-style apartment blocks when expanding bigger towns or cities.

All of these old towns and villages that I regularly passed through were exactly how they had been when the Soviets captured the areas in 1944 and 1945. Many of these buildings, even in the 1990s, bore the scars and pock marks of the bullets fired when the towns had been captured from the Nazis' control.

Throughout September and into October I ploughed my lonely furrow back and forth from Moscow. No matter where I went to change trailers, either in Poland, Germany or Holland, I always went back to Moscow, either to tip at Xerox, Sofin, or one of the exhibition grounds. However, in mid-October I swapped trailers in Berlin and found that the load that I was to take to Moscow was destined for the All Soviet Television and Radio studios. This was to be my first – but by no means last – foray into the world of the Russian luvvies.

13

It Was News to Me

THE trailer was loaded with the complete studio furniture and technical equipment such as cameras for a new news programme, named Vesti. Most of the equipment had come from Switzerland and I was to deliver it to the studios, at Piatnikskaya Ulitsa in Moscow.

Arriving in Moscow with this highly valuable and high profile cargo, I parked the truck in our street, outside the Joint Venture building, for security. You see, I did take notice of what Elena told me!

The following day I drove to the studios and soon met Arcady, who was the technical director of the All Soviet Television and Radio studios. He was responsible for all aspects of technical equipment at the studios. He spoke flawless English, but found it extremely interesting when I spoke Russian. I also met his assistant, Lyudmila, who would be responsible for arranging the custom clearance for the equipment.

Lyudmila relieved me of my paperwork and informed me that it would take at least three days to complete the clearance. Arcady asked me whether I would be sleeping in the truck while I waited for the customs clearance, or whether I wanted to go to a hotel. "Neither," I replied. "I will be staying at the flat that I share with my Russian girlfriend, in Voikovskaya."

I gave Lyudmila the telephone number for the flat and it was arranged that she would call me, as soon as the custom clearance had been completed. I would then return and unload. I left the studios and discovered that it had started to snow.

I spent three days at the flat, waiting for Lyudmila to call me. During that time I watched a lot of television. In England I hardly ever watched television, but in Moscow I found the television extremely interesting because it helped me to learn Russian. Rather than just hearing words there was the visual element; that helped to explain what was being said. I was working hard at learning Russian. Elena helped me and we spoke only Russian at home.

I was reading my book and progressing with it. In fact, my Russian was becoming very good. I expanded my vocabulary every day and Elena taught me phrases that you would not learn on a course, or from books; mostly Moscow slang and colloquialisms.

Elena and Vera were out working all day, so when I became bored of studying Russian I would leave the flat and walk around the local area. I was soaking up the atmosphere and learning the lie of the land. Sometimes I would stop at the beer stand near the Metro and have a glass of beer. A beer cost 50 Kopeks and I would usually have a Rouble's worth; two. leaning against the Metro station's low wall, while watching the world go by.

You would have thought that when I offered to cook dinner for Elena and Vera, that they would have been delighted seeing that they were working all day, whereas I had nothing to do. However, they rejected the plan. It wasn't the Russian way for a man to be in the kitchen, unless that was where he smoked. So they did not want a cooked dinner ready for them when they got home. Cooking was their job.

This automatically assumed lack of my contributing to the household tasks actually went against the grain. I would have been more than happy and capable of playing my full part. However, traditional Russian culture had developed a society where, within the home, women carried out virtually every task. Male members of the family did not contribute anything to the running of the home. My experiences in Russia taught me that the male population, in the main, were extremely spoilt. This in turn, created an institutionalised laziness among them.

Boris, the dog handler at Klyazma, had told me that a Russian woman would do anything and everything for her husband. In return, the woman demanded repayment for her efforts when they went to bed. Apparently, those repayments were usually quite taxing and exhausting. That was why he had volunteered for so many shifts at Klyazma. To get a rest. His wife doted upon him and did absolutely everything in the home, but the repayments were taking a toll upon him. He was permanently tired and his eyes always looked like piss holes in the snow. Basically he was shagged out. Literally. Fact.

During this enforced three-day break I was also learning a fair amount of information from T.V. documentaries on the All Soviet T.V. network. This, while actually sitting in the flat waiting for that very organisation to call me and let me know that the custom procedures had finished and that I could offload the goods.

On the third morning I received a phone call from Lyudmila, at the studios, informing me that the Russian customs were going to clear the goods that I was delivering for them. She asked me to come to Piatnikskaya Ulitsa as quickly as possible.

As I drove through the city, snow was falling steadily. Not heavy snow, just light falls with small flakes that were drifting and curling through the air. However, it was decidedly beginning to lay upon the paths beside the road.

Arriving at the television studios, I was shown where to position the trailer for offloading. I parked the truck in the street in front of the studio building, as directed.

Within a very short time, a large number of people, both male and female, emerged from the building to unload the equipment. However, these were not your usual *dvorniks*; they were too well dressed. The men wore suits and overcoats. They all had fur hats on their heads. The women, too, were smartly dressed. They had overcoats, mostly fur ones. On their heads they too wore fur hats. All the women wore leather boots, which reached up to the top of their calves.

Suddenly it dawned on me that I recognised a few of the men and women. They were newsreaders who I saw on television on a daily basis. I was amazed. Why would people who were national celebrities be standing around in the snow preparing to unload a trailer full of goods? It would not happen in England. But, of course, this was not England.

The unlikely labour force were newsreaders and production staff from the studio. Delighted to be receiving state of the art, Western technology, in place of their shoddy, Soviet equipment, they were so excited, that they had volunteered to unload the trailer themselves.

The continual snowfall persisted as we unloaded the truck. Small boxes were carried into the building manually. Larger cases were shuttled in by a dilapidated forklift truck, which was continually spewing oil on to the thin, white layer of snow covering the pathway. Eventually we had unloaded all the goods and all the unlikely labour force had retreated back into the T.V. centre.

Arcady led me into the building and took me to what was the actual studio, where the equipment would be used. The cases that we had unloaded were stacked at one end of the room. At the opposite end trestle tables buckled under the weight of a massive buffet and numerous bottles of Soviet champagne and vodka.

A party was beginning for all of those who had unloaded the trailer in celebration of the safe arrival of their new studio. Arcady invited me to join them as thanks for delivering the equipment in pristine condition. I pointed out that I could not drink as I had to drive the truck back across Moscow. In reply, he arranged for me to leave it outside the studios and collect it in the morning. He also organised a taxi to take me home following the party.

An interesting facet of the party was that while mingling I found myself speaking to people that, up until then, I had only ever seen on the television. All the newsreaders spoke English and all took it in turn to talk to me. Mostly, they asked for my view, as a foreigner, on Moscow and wanted me to describe life and conditions in the West. It was extremely surreal. Me, the centre of attention.

The party over, we said our farewells. All the men shook my hand and most of the ladies kissed me, on the cheek. Fortunately, I had shaved that morning. I took my leave and was driven across the city, in the back of a large, yellow Volga taxi.

That evening, when the news came on, I pointed out the newsreaders and said, "I met him," and "I met her."

"And they met you, Micky," Elena said, crossing herself, in the Russian Orthodox Church manner. "God help them," she added.

"Amen," said Vera. And they both crossed themselves.

"Bollocks," I thought to myself, and laughed.

This incident, where I socialised with the influential Soviet/Russian upper strata, was by no means unique during my time in Russia. However, it surprised me that those people were so keen to talk to me. After all, I was merely a British truck driver.

When reflecting upon it later, it struck me that there were two obvious reasons why it should not be taken as abnormal. Firstly, one ethos of Soviet philosophy was that everyone was equal. Therefore, a truck driver was as valuable to society, say, as a newsreader.

Secondly, up until that time, Soviet citizens had not been able to mix with foreigners, or to travel abroad. Therefore, their knowledge and understanding of real life and the true conditions outside their borders had been extremely limited. The new conditions prevalent within the U.S.S.R. now enabled them to be able to speak freely with foreigners. They were, therefore, grasping the opportunity with both hands, so as to improve their knowledge and understanding.

So my first encounter with luvvies in Russia had ended. However, there were more to come, Especially my involvement with Sean Bean in Yalta. In late 1991 he was filming Sharpe's Rifles there.

14

My First Russian Winter Begins

THE Soviet spring of 1990, when I had begun this work for Kepstowe/Croome, had been demonstrably colder than spring in England. And it was long gone. So was the unbelievably hot Russian summer and the following short, wet spell, of autumn. Now, the Russian winter was advancing and rapidly picked up pace.

The light snowfalls, such as the one I had experienced delivering to the T.V. studios, gradually became heavier in nature. Much heavier. Driving conditions became trickier and dangerous. I had some idea as to how bad the Russian winter would get, but found that I was not exactly accurate in my assessment. It eventually became much worse than I had predicted to myself.

I still drove back and forth between Poland and Moscow; Four to five-day round trips. Trip after trip. Week in, week out, with monotonous regularity. But that was what I got paid to do.

October became November and I was still delivering to all my usual destinations, permanently running between Moscow and Poland on this weekly basis. I saw the change in the conditions in the countryside as it progressed week by week.

When driving through the open countryside I noticed how the depth of the snow increased significantly in a short space of time. Initially, the broad open plains of grassland had random patches of white dotted around. This was where the insipidly pale greenery had been covered by light snowfall, which was beginning to lay. Soon, those snowy areas expanded until the whole of the green area had been covered. Then the white covering became deeper, and still more snow fell on top of what was already there. The depth of the snow increased and became a thick blanket covering the land.

The country dwellers lived in small communities dotted among these vast tracts of land. Living far from the urban areas, they were basically peasant farmers (*derevnia*). Self-sufficient, they lived off the land and by their own labour. They did not even have the luxury of the low standard, manufactured, consumer goods that were enjoyed by their urban dwelling fellow citizens. With large areas of Russia being vast open grassland, I was used to seeing the people who lived in the enormous expanse of the Russian countryside driving around with horses and carts throughout the spring and summer. I had witnessed them as they crossed the open country, heading to or from a distant village. As the snow cover in the fields thickened, they removed the wheels from the carts and replaced them with snow runners. They turned their carts into giant sleds. That way, they could still transport their cargoes and themselves across the expansive white wilderness.

By comparison, the large forests and wooded areas, that broke the open countryside remained dark and brooding. The areas of pine trees retained their dark green foliage, supported by black trunks. The deciduous trees had shed their leaves and their gnarled branches pointed out from the trunks, like accusing, skeletal fingers. The black of the trees was a stark contrast to the white landscape. Added to this phenomenon were the snow-laden clouds, which hung in the bleak, drab, dark grey sky. Brooding above this monochrome scene, they hardly moved.

The winter days were short and most of the time I was now driving in the darkness. This brought the problem of the Sovs driving without lights back to the forefront of my mind, especially as the nights in Russia were pitch black. Then, of course, there was the problem of those Sovs that did use their lights driving on permanent full beam. This created another headache when you were night driving.

My mind repeatedly returned to the obvious conclusion that I definitely needed to do something about this state of affairs. I decided that I must have roof-mounted spotlights fitted to the truck. It was a priority and a matter of urgency. As soon as I could get back to the U.K. I would have them fitted at Channel Commercials, my Daf dealers.

In early December 1990, another problem brought about by the onset of winter arose. I was heading for Moscow and had filled the diesel tank at Smolensk. While I was climbing through the ridges that traversed the road linking the two cities the air temperature had dropped to -9C. Suddenly the truck began to lose power and the engine began to misfire. The diesel was waxing up and blocking the fuel filter. This was restricting the flow of diesel to the injector pump significantly. I managed to limp the truck to the next garage and topped the tank with benzene. This solved the problem because the benzene mixed in with the

Figure 1 Parked at Kepstowe's London depot, at the start of a trip to Russia.

Figure 2 The truck at the side of the road, between Sovetsk and Kaliningrad.

Figure 3 Parked in front of St Basil's Cathedral, Red Square, Moscow. One of the few times that I pulled a Croome trailer.

Figure 4 Me, in the cab of the truck when it was brand new. Parked beside a Czech truck at The Mezh', Moscow.

Figure 5 With Margarita at Turku Docks, Finland. The *M.V. Garden* is behind us. Waiting for the red unaccompanied trailer to be unloaded, so as to take it to Moscow.

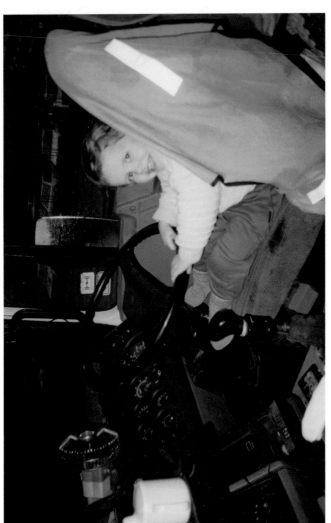

Figure 6 Margarita parking my truck for me in Krasnodar.

Figure 7 Margarita and me in the park at Voikovskaya. The temperature was a bracing -15C.

Figure 8 Inside the G.U.M. department store on Red Square.

Figure 9 Red Square. Directly behind me is Lenin's tomb. Beyond that is the Kremlin Wall and the Kremlin.

Figure 10 Central Moscow. The car on the left is a Lada Zhiguli. The black car is a government Volga.

Figure 11 Elena and Margarita in the park. Despite the snow it was a warm –5C.

Figure 12 The drivers from the Keptowe convoy to Baku for the oil and gas exhibition. I met them near Rostov, in southern Russia. My truck is in the centre of the picture. Among the drivers standing are Pete Newlyn, extreme left; John Mantle, third from right; and Nicky Reynolds, extreme right. The guy in the centre is a Mongolian who drove for Sovtransavto. He acted as guide for the trip and pulled one of the trailers.

Figure 13 In the Caucasus Mountains. Photo: Pete Newlyn

Figure 14 Pete, camel herding in Azerbaijan. Photo: Pete Newlyn

Figure 15 A group photo of the convoy vehicles. Nicky's black Fleetwood Scania in the centre. Photo: Pete Newlyn

Figure 16 The convoy on the road in southern Russia. Photo: Pete Newlyn

diesel and stopped it from waxing. I had been told by Russian drivers that the correct mixture was 20–25% petrol when adding it to diesel. However, continuous use of petrol in a diesel engine over a long period of time can cause damage to the valves, so is not advised but it is a short-term fix. I decided that I needed to provide a permanent solution to this problem as well. Therefore, I would get Channel Commercials to fit a section of Thermoline into the truck diesel system between the tank and the fuel filter.

Thermoline was a length of rubber hose through which a copper strip ran; the hose was inserted into the truck's fuel system between the diesel tank and the fuel filter housing. When you switched on the Thermoline, the copper element heated up. This warmed up the diesel passing through that stretch of hose. It therefore delivered warm, or hot, diesel to the filter. That de-waxed the filter virtually immediately. Shortly, the whole system was warmed and eliminated the problem entirely.

A major priority during the Russian winter was to be able to obtain as much accurate information as you could with regard to the future weather conditions. At that time, in the run up to Christmas and New Year, the temperatures in western Russia fluctuated between 5C and -20C. When I was in Moscow I could get the weather forecast from the T.V. Fortunately, Russian weather forecasts were extremely accurate. I could also see the weather forecast while moving around within the city. The weather report was displayed upon neon signs on top of the buildings. It rolled around and by waiting you could see the forecasts for all the major cities and areas of the U.S.S.R.

However, once I was outside Moscow I could not get the weather forecast, but relied upon my own intuition and what information I was given at service stations, or the motels.

Now that winter had set in I was made aware of the great work that the road-gritting crews did on the main roads throughout the U.S.S.R. I call them gritters because that is what we have in the U.K. However, the Sov crews spread a dark red sand on to the road. No doubt, it was highly toxic and contained chemicals that would be banned from use in Britain. No matter what it was, it was extremely effective. Once spread it turned the ice to water in next to no time. And that water did not refreeze. There were nights when I actually followed the gritting trucks along the roads and did not have the slightest problem at all. In fact, on a few occasions over the years when I was struggling to get traction, gritters going the other way would stop and the driver throw sand under my wheels. Or they would turn around, get in front of me and sand the road, so that I could get going. One thing about the Russians, they would never leave you stuck in atrocious cold weather conditions because they knew too well that the effects could be fatal.

The weather also had a dramatic effect on the view from our apartment windows. Outside the flat blocks, all of the green foliage and grass had disappeared. The foliage had fallen from the trees, while the grass was buried beneath a deep covering of dirty, grey, packed ice. Moving around outside the apartment block left me doing more ice-skating than Torvill and Dean had ever done between them in their lives.

Looking out the windows, it was like a scene from a Lowry painting; the dark-clad Russians walking through the monochrome landscape outside of the apartment blocks.

Personal protection against the ever-decreasing temperatures was also a priority. I had taken to wearing thermal underwear, heavy shirts and warmer coats against the harsh temperatures. I bought these locally in Moscow. I still wore jeans and my high length, low-heeled boots. However, I had now also taken to wearing a fur hat, a rather fine one made from blonde raccoon. It was the mutt's nuts, no doubt about it.

Dressed as I was I could have been taken for an average Russian, no problem, which was fine. In Moscow, people who travelled or walked on their own did not chat freely with strangers. You only spoke if you were stopping to buy something, such as a Metro token or flowers, etc. Therefore, if you dressed like a Muscovite (*Moskvitch* = male Muscovite, *Moskvitchka* = female Muscovite) and did not talk to anybody, you were easily taken for a local and you were left alone. I found this to be a good thing. Moscow was an extremely violent city.

Obviously, another factor to be taken into account now that it was winter was the exceptionally poor standard of driving in Russia. With the exception of their international truck drivers, in Sovtransavto, who were of a high calibre, and their long distance internal truck drivers, the rest were absolutely rubbish.

When you drove out on the super slabs between Moscow and the other major cities you encountered hardly any other vehicles. It was possible to cruise along the long straight highways for mile after mile and not see another vehicle in front of you, or behind you. It was like being in your own little driving world.

It was as if the ultra-wide highways had been constructed purely for your own personal entertainment.

However, driving in Moscow was worse than in any other city that I had been in. The standard of their average drivers was pathetically poor. The Russians did not have a clue. Showing scant regard for the laws of the road and a total lack of cognitive skills, they turned every adverse situation on the road into a nightmare. Their lane discipline was virtually non-existent and their attitude extremely selfish. Coupled with their absolute lack of courtesy and consideration for any other road users or pedestrians, driving in the city was a difficult task at any time of the year. However, during the winter period the task became much worse.

Having driven there, throughout the spring, summer and autumn of 1990, I was well aware of the very low standard of driving within the city. However, what amazed me was the total lack of preparedness of their vehicles for the winter conditions. That, coupled to their complete inability to adapt their driving so as to drive safely in the atrocious weather. Every day that I was driving there, whether in Moscow or on the open roads, I saw uncountable numbers of vehicles broken down at the roadside, obvious casualties of the bitingly cold weather. They were frozen up or overheated. Then there were the trashed vehicles that were littered around as the result of road accidents. Many of the accidents I actually witnessed as they took place. Most were the result of driving too fast for the conditions. Over-braking was another contributing factor. You would have thought that as these conditions reoccurred every winter, the Russians would be able to cope with them and drive in them safely. But, unfortunately they could not.

One impressive thing about Moscow's actual road network during the winter was the level of preparedness by the authorities to keep the roads open and the traffic flowing; even though the ordinary drivers seemed to be aiming for the opposite. During the snow season, October to April, you would see fleets of gritters, snowploughs and snow shovels waiting at strategic points around the city. As soon as it snowed they would spring into action. If the snow was heavy, the ploughs would move along, side by side, ploughing the snow to the side of the road. Sweeper trucks, working in concert with the ploughs, would sweep the snow on to other trucks, which had conveyor belts for moving it up and into their tipper bodies. In operation, these teams were awesome and did a fantastic job of keeping the main roads clear of snow and ice. And they worked 24 hours a day.

Another thing that the deeply intensifying winter conditions also signalled was that soon it would be 1991. The New Year was nearly upon us.

In the U.S.S.R. December 25th had no relevance whatsoever. They did not celebrate the birth of Christ upon that date. In fact, their Christmas Day was held on 7th January. This was apparently a more accurate interpretation of the date upon which he was really born. It was the date acknowledged by the Orthodox Church. Russian Christmas though was a religious celebration and not a commercial celebration.

Russian New Year's Eve is when their version of Father Christmas (*Jaja Marozhe*) brought the children their presents. It is also a major celebration for the adults. The evening is usually spent eating and drinking. At midnight, the New Year is toasted in and then it is common to consume a full meal. The early hours of New Year's Day are then spent continuing to drink and telephoning family and friends, to wish them, "Happy New Year" (*S'novum Godum*).

As with May Day, the Russians take a number of days off following the celebration. It is a long national holiday, during which time commercial entities do not operate.

However, during the period that is our Christmas, Russia was still working as normal. Therefore, so was I. This meant that I was in Moscow for the New Year and experienced the celebrations. The festivities, as far as Elena and I were concerned, began early. We socialised with our small circle of friends in the run up to the main event.

Firstly, we travelled outside of Moscow one evening with our friends Volodin and Larissa. They took us to an exclusive restaurant outside the city limits, the Russian House. Here, fine Russian cuisine was served, but at a price way beyond the means of the vast majority of Russians. However, for me the cost was only what I would spend for eating at a good restaurant in England.

Another evening we visited our friends Yuri and Svetlana, who lived on Gorky Street, between Pushkin Square and Red Square. Both extremely talented artists, Svetlana painted, while Yuri created masterpieces in leather.

Unfortunately, Yuri suffered from bouts of depression, during which he became rampantly alcoholic. Once he began drinking he would drink until he fell asleep and then start drinking again as soon as he woke up, be that day or night. The drinking sessions could go on for weeks until, suddenly, one day he would just stop.

When we visited them, he was in his normal mode and we all had a highly pleasant evening.

New Year's Eve morning, Elena and I were watching the news on T.V. One of the female newsreaders that I had met at the studio, was reading it.

I said to Elena, "Did I tell you, that I have met her?"

Elena replied, "Yes Mickey, I know. You tell me every time that she comes on T.V."

"Yes, Elena," I said, continuing mock seriously, "But I have actually met her."

Elena looked at me for a short while, shrugged her shoulders and shook her head. The look upon her face one of complete disbelief and exasperation.

"*Hoy doorak,*" she said, continuing to shake her head and leaving the room.

I found out later that *hoy doorak* meant "f@cking idiot".

Not a bad assessment, I would have said, on reflection. The woman reading the news was not all that bright. I know. I had met her. As I told everyone who would listen.

We were spending New Year's Eve at the apartment of our friends Kostya and his partner, Little Elena, seeing in the New Year and then spending the night there. Little Elena, as I called her, was a short lady, whereas my Elena was tall.

In preparation for this New Year's party we went shopping in the afternoon on our way to their flat. We arrived loaded down with foodstuff, alcohol and with a large bunch of flowers for Little Elena. This was normal behaviour, in Russia, when you were guests.

The evening was spent eating snacks, drinking and dancing. The music for the dancing was provided by the All Soviet Television and Radio New Year's Eve spectacular on the T.V. At midnight we ate a roast pork dinner washed down with endless glasses of alcohol. Kostya had provided bottles of cola for me to water down the raw vodka when we drank the succession of toasts.

Having eaten, the girls took it in turns to telephone family and friends to wish them "*S'novum Godum*". After toasting in the British New Year, which was at 3am Moscow time, we went to bed.

The flat only had one bedroom, so Elena and I slept on a settee bed in the living room. Elena fell asleep straight away, but before I drifted off I thought briefly about the changes that had occurred in my life during the previous year.

15

Taking Stock

PURPOSEFULLY, I left Moscow on 2nd January. Elena had the whole week off as the Russians took the 1st to the 4th January, as holiday. I left her at our flat and made my way out of the building into a flurry of snow. The weather was slightly cold, -10C, but the truck started first time, although she did blow a few large clouds of blue, grey exhaust smoke for a while, in protest.

Once I was clear of the city I cruised along the M1 and headed for Brest. I was en route for Berlin, where I was to collect a trailer loaded for an exhibition at Krasnaya Presnaya. My hope was that I could get to Berlin, swap trailers and get back to Moscow in time for 7th January. If I could, Elena was going to take me to a Russian Orthodox Church where we would attend the Christmas Day service.

While I was driving through Russia, Belarus and Poland, I noticed that there was hardly any traffic. Obviously, a direct consequence of the New Year holiday.

On the way from Moscow to Brest hardly any snow fell. Although the temperature was low, -5C to -12C, the road surfaces were fine. The gritting crews had not taken the holiday period off by the look of it. But, it appeared that the G.A.I. had. There was no sign of them at the roadsides.

The chance to cruise along the road at a constantly high speed without being bothered by the police, weather conditions, or other traffic allowed me to take stock of how the Russian adventure was developing up to that point.

The performance indicators basically fell into three categories: the truck's aptitude for the task at hand; the financial situation; and my improvement regarding learning the Russian language.

With regards to the truck's performance, I was extremely satisfied with my Daf 95. Considering that it was basically West European spec', as opposed to being perfectly set up for Russia, then it was handling the situation amazingly well.

Yes, there was the diesel waxing issue, but that was not the fault of the truck. That was the fault of the temperatures and the poor standard of diesel. That problem could be overcome once I returned to England and had the Thermoline system fitted.

Again; the night vision problem. The addition of top spotlights would greatly assist that.

No. The truck was handling the conditions perfectly well, so far. Not one breakdown.

Regarding the financial situation, I was making very good money out of these operations. Of course, I was working extremely hard, but the rewards were worth it. I could see that, provided I maintained the work level, then I could carry on making money, which had to be a good thing.

Finally, the matter of learning Russian. As with the other two subjects, this was going extremely well.

I am not for one moment suggesting that learning Russian is simple. However, learning the basics of the Russian language is. In Russian, as opposed to English, you do not use, A, an, or the.

Although they have the verb, "to be" [*bit*], it is not broken down. So, there is no use of am, are, or is, either.

In English; where we would say, for example, "I am an Englishman," in Russian you would merely say, "I Englishman." Or, as another example, in English we would say, "I am a driver." or "I am the driver." For both of those, the Russians would say, simply, "I driver."

So, to be able to talk simple Russian, you merely have to know the personal pronouns. I = ya. You = tee, etc. Then, a few nouns, such as *voditilee* = driver; *rabotnik* = worker; *graseevee* = handsome. Then you can speak Russian, straight away.

Another big advantage is that, unlike in English where we have a multitude of verb forms, the Russians only have three: past, present and future. This again simplifies matters greatly at the beginning.

However, to be fair, once you get further into learning Russian, then you discover that they have a vast myriad of word endings that we do not have in English. But, that is much further into your experience. To begin with, you can speak away quite easily.

By January 1991, having spent a very large number of hours learning Russian, I was more than content with the standard that I had reached up to that point. I could communicate well and hold ever more complicated conversations with most Soviets that I met. All in all, I was highly pleased.

If only my English had been that good.

In learning Russian, I discovered that they had different words for types of snow. Firstly, of course, you learnt *shnee-yek*. This meant snow. But they did not stop there. There was *bolshoy shnee-yek*. Big snow. Then you had *nee bolshoy shnee-yek*. Not big snow. And, of course, *mokree shnee-yek*. Wet snow. I encountered all these types of snow during my time in Russia. And many more!

In so far as the weather, conditions heading West to Berlin were definitely in my favour. The return journey was completely the opposite. Snow, at first just light flurries that began between Poznan and Warsaw, increased in intensity. Having passed Siedlce, I was driving almost continually through heavy blizzards.

Looking out through the windscreen, you saw the snow coming at you from all angles. This proved to be extremely disorientating. Added to which was the gloom. And no, I didn't have Viktor from Femtech with me!

The gloom was the oppressive, grey half-light of the daytime hours. Staring into this hour after hour was highly tiring. Your eyes seemed to be being sucked out as you tried to see through the swirling, dancing flakes that obscured the road. Then, as day turned to night, the blackness out of which the whiteness of the snowflakes were driven towards the truck made the act of driving even more fatiguing.

These terrible conditions saw me not reach Moscow until the evening of 7th January. I had missed the Christmas church service. However, it had been a good try. Driving to Berlin and back, I had been at the wheel 18 hours per day. I had been working on four hours' sleep per night and had managed Moscow to Berlin and back in five days, purely because I had wanted to attend the church service. In better conditions, I knew that it would have been possible to complete the trip on time. A brave attempt, or an extremely stupid one? I never was too sure.

16

Beer-Flavoured Ice Lollies

THE next morning I drove to Krasnaya Presnaya; the exhibition was for consumer products. By the afternoon the custom procedure was completed and my trailer had been unloaded.

Rob and Charlie from Kepstowe were on site, acting as site reps. This entailed them liaising with customers and ensuring that the goods were delivered to the correct trade stands to the client's satisfaction.

When the goods from my trailer were unloaded, I saw that there was a consignment of canned beer for one of the stands. Six pallets worth, to be precise. The pallets were delivered to the stand by the exhibition hall crew. A British salesman from the company displaying the goods began to check the cases and prepare to arrange them on their display racks.

Rob, Charlie and I were standing by my truck when the salesman approached us. He was extremely perturbed. He had opened a few of the cases to discover that, due to the extremely low temperatures, the beer in the cases had frozen. In doing so it had expanded and large nobs of ice had pushed up through the ring pull openings of the cans. What he basically had now was six pallets of frozen, beer-flavoured lollies.

Obviously, there was no suggestion that this predicament was my fault. The goods had been loaded on a tilt trailer, when they should have been transported in a fridge. That way, the temperature could have been set at above freezing to protect the consignment. However, the goods had arrived on site unfit for purpose. They could not be used for display purposes and therefore needed replacing. They needed replacing, rather urgently. Rob, Charlie and the salesman disappeared rapidly, heading for the freight agent's office to telephone England. I looked around and said out loud, "Was it something I said?"

There were six days until the exhibition opened. Fortunately, there was an Aeromar trailer that was already loaded sitting in Wandsworth. The driver had been due to leave the following day. Kepstowe arranged for the company that was exhibiting the goods to deliver another six pallets of the beer to Wandsworth, where it was immediately loaded on to the trailer. However, they could not contact their driver, to ask him to come in straight away and ship out directly. So, they came up with a plan.

They arranged for a subcontractor to bring the trailer out as far as Poznan. They then instructed me to drive to Poznan, swap trailers and return to Moscow with the Aeromar trailer. However, I had to be back in Moscow within four days so that the goods could be unloaded and displayed upon the exhibition stand before the trade fair opened. Personally, I was totally underwhelmed by their plan.

Rob insisted that I pull out of K.P. and head immediately for Poland, without any delay. Urgency being the order of the day. Of course, displaying my usual professional attitude to the job, I did no more than leave the exhibition grounds and drive directly to our flat, in Voikovskaya. I was having a good night's sleep, before I attempted this trip.

The following morning, I left Moscow. The temperature was a warm -5C but there was no snow falling, thankfully. The roads were clear of ice and the traffic was minimal. I cruised along the wide road, putting in a good 15-hour driving shift. That night I reached Kukariki and crossed the border before parking for the night. The next day I made Poznan and waited for the Aeromar trailer to arrive.The trailer turned up on the Thursday evening. The subbie had made good time and, thankfully, Frankfurt Oder had been relatively quiet. I really needed to be back at Krasnaya Presnaya by the Sunday morning. So, I set out immediately and drove to Siedlce.

The following morning, I left early and went to the border. Kukariki was quiet. Just a few trucks heading in to Belarus. The border procedure was completed swiftly and I was soon driving away from there. The time was 3pm.

Up to that point everything was looking good, but once I entered Belarus the skies darkened ominously. Soon, light flakes of snow began to drift down, blown through the air by the light breeze. The sky became darker and the flakes became bigger.

"Bleeding great," I thought, knowing what was coming.

By the time that I had reached the M1, I was driving into a perpetual blizzard. The all-encompassing, dark grey, half-light, reduced my visibility to around 20 metres. It would have been foolhardy to drive quickly, so I crawled along through the blinding snowstorm. Mile after tedious mile with absolutely no respite. I had two options available to me: either park up and wait for the snowstorm to subside, or keep going. I decided upon the latter. I reasoned that if I parked up and the blizzard did not decrease, then I would have lost a lot of time for nothing. So, I kept going. Slowly. Snow was laying on the carriageway.

It was just after midnight when I arrived at the motorway service area near Minsk. The blizzard had not abated at all. From Brest to Minsk I had coped with this massively heavy snowfall. However, it had taken nine hours to cover a distance that should have taken four. I pulled on to the service area, parked the truck and went to bed. Exhausted.

When I woke six hours later it was still snowing. I filled the diesel tank and pulled out on to the motorway. Fortunately, while I had slept, the snow ploughs and gritters had been working. The road surface was ice free, although snow was drifting on to the road again. It formed large patches of white upon the bland concrete.

From Minsk, Moscow was a nine-and-a-half-hour drive away. That day, it took 19 hours. The snow at first light once more turned to a blizzard. When I reached the end of the motorway at Borisov the snowflakes were the size of footballs. As the Belarus plain ended, I began to climb the first of the three massive ridges that stood between me and Moscow. The incline brought you through a large area of forestation. Trees packed close together lined the roadside. The snow, driving towards me, was funnelled through this natural chamber. This increased the intensity of what I was driving into. The wall of trees restricted the light and my vision.

Once clear of Smolensk, the countryside was more open and I was not driving through dense forests. Visibility increased and the snow began to lessen in intensity. By the time that I arrived in Moscow, in the early hours of the Sunday morning, it had stopped completely. I made my way to the K.P. exhibition ground and parked up. Job done.

Unloading the six pallets later that morning, I was regaled by Rob, Charlie and the salesman about the brilliant time that they had enjoyed the preceding evening. Relaxing, pissing it up and eating well.

I could have done with finding three of those frozen beer cans. And I know exactly where they would have bloody well ended up.

17

Gorbachev's Alcohol Policy

MIKAEL Gorbachev, the leader of the U.S.S.R. was teetotal. It was his strongly held belief that alcohol was creating many problems within the Soviet Union and destroying the fabric of life. He therefore decreed that any person found to be intoxicated in public would be arrested. This was, though, with the exception of foreigners. Foreigners were to be treated with respect.

However, his police force interpreted this command as an excuse to inflict unwarranted violence upon those Russians who were discovered to be drunk in a public place. I witnessed this for myself at Voikovskaya Metro station. As I was climbing the stairs from the platform to the entrance way, I was aware of a police officer leaning against the wall, next to the wide set of entrance doors. Suddenly, a Russian male, who was obviously the worse for alcohol, blundered through the aluminium-framed glass door. The police officer did no more than swing his night stick and deliver a blow to the drunk's face with the whole of his strength. The drunk was knocked backwards and collapsed to the floor, unconscious. The policeman called for back-up on his radio and two other officers arrived. They dragged the man away and outside the station I watched them throw him bodily into the rear of a Ulaz police jeep.

When I related this incident to Elena she informed me that the drunk would have been taken to a police station and thrown into a cell. If it was his first arrest for drunkenness he would be released the following morning, after having been hosed down fully clothed. For a second offence he would have been hosed down and then taken to court. The court would sentence him to a period of detox. For any subsequent offence he would be taken directly from the scene of his arrest to the detox centre. She assured me that the regime in the detox centres was extremely brutal. I did not doubt it. After all, this was the second incident of police brutality that I had witnessed at first hand. They did not piss about. Not if they could inflict some gratuitous violence.

Despite the fact that foreigners were to be treated with respect, if they were discovered to be drunk, they could face problems. Johnny Dicks was set upon by four members of the police in Yaroslavl. They discovered him wandering back to his truck late at night. He had enjoyed a session in a local hotel, but the Yaroslavl police soon put paid to his enjoyment.

Mistaking him for a drunken Russian in the darkness of an unlit street, one of the officers hit him. John did no more than to hit the officer back, dropping him to the ground and breaking his jaw. Unfortunately, this particular officer was the head of police in Yaroslavl. His fellow officers, out of retribution, set about John with alacrity. And their nightsticks.

Beaten to a pulp, John was then thrown into a

police car and driven to the local police station. At the station the beating continued. Eventually, the police went through John's pockets and discovered his passport. The beating stopped.

A doctor was called. The doctor, among other things, put ten stitches into John's lacerated top lip, fifteen into his bottom lip and all without an anaesthetic. John was then put back, gently, into the police car and driven to his truck. Here, they ensured that he made it safely into the truck's cab and then left him. No doubt the thinking was that the beating could then not be linked to the police. Not, however, that John was liable to make a formal complaint. To whom would he have complained? The head of the Yaroslavl Police? That would not have been much of a conversation. John with his mutilated lips and the police commander, with the broken jaw, that John had given him.

I met up with John in Berlin five days after the assault. He took his shirt off and showed me his upper torso. There was not one square inch of normal, coloured skin. He had literally been beaten black and blue.

The Russian people called their police officers, "*chi–niks*", which was slang for teapots. The Russians said, jokingly, that their police officers existed on a diet of tea and bread. This was because the officers were supposed to be teetotal, so that they were not being hypocritical in their treatment – or rather mistreatment – of drunks. However, I had heard the police called other things as well.

I had heard myself call them other things.

18

Around the Houses, to Orsha Hill

THE morning after witnessing the incident with the drunk in the Metro station, I set off for Poland. At Siedlce, I received instructions to drive to Berlin where my next trailer would meet me. I pushed on to Berlin and then had a three-day wait for the trailer. When it eventually arrived, I discovered that it was loaded for Borispol, Dnepropetrovsk and Zaporozhye in Ukraine. After Zaporozhye, which was in the deep south-east of Ukraine, I had two further deliveries to make. To Vitebsk in Belarus and then Pskov in Russia. As Vitebsk was north of Orsha and Pskov further north from there, I thought that it would have been better to have delivered to them first and then headed into Ukraine. However, the loading order had apparently been dictated by when the goods were actually wanted on site.

I took over this new trailer and set off back, through Schwedt, to Kukariki. From Kukariki I drove to Borispol, where the first delivery turned out to be spare parts for a food production line. The line had been installed by a British company named A.P.V. Baker. Knowing Borispol from my Femtech adventures, I knew where the airport was for the custom procedure and this consignment was dispatched rapidly. I then headed east, towards Poltava. It was obvious that Ukraine was in the grip of winter. Deep snow covered the open ground and I drove through flurries of freshly falling snow. At Poltava I stopped the night at the Sovinteravtoservice hotel. I then drove on to Dnepropetrovsk. Arriving at Dnepr', I found the factory, which was described as a tractor manufacturing plant.

It was not.

Entering the factory grounds, the following morning, I discovered a high security control arrangement for all vehicles entering and exiting the site. Not what you would normally expect at a tractor factory. That was because the, so-called, tractor factory actually produced battle tanks for the Soviet Army and was not only highly sensitive, but also extremely top secret.

I knew that the Russian word for Spy was *spion*. But, despite the fact that I would have found it amusing to say, "*ya spion* [I am a spy]," I thought it better not to under the circumstances. Firstly, if they beat you to a pulp in Russia for merely being pissed, what would they do to you if they thought that you were from MI5. And secondly, I did not fancy Siberia in January.

My consignment for Dnepr' consisted of four enormous wooden crates, which would need to be offloaded through the roof of the trailer due to their size. The factory managers had arranged a mobile crane to lift the cases from the trailer. Once I had positioned the truck where they wanted to unload it, next to a four-storeyed building, they then explained to me that these cases were to be swung into a window on the fourth floor. They had a crew of men on the fourth floor who were going to catch these cases when the crane swung them through the window opening.

I did not say, "You're having a f@cking laugh," but believe me I definitely thought it.

The contents of the cases was a computer system, the value of which was in excess of £2 million. If this little escapade went tits up I could see me being landed with an insurance claim for that amount. I therefore suggested to the managers that they unload all of the cases on to the ground, first. Then I would close the trailer and drive away. This would give them more space to work with the crane.

Fortunately, they agreed with me. I am very convincing. However, after having unloaded and before driving away I ensured that my delivery note was duly signed to state that the goods had been safely delivered and were in perfect condition upon delivery. Leaving them to pick up the pieces, if that became necessary, I headed off further south towards Zaporozhye.

Zaporozhye is a heavily industrialised city and gives its name to a small, tinny little car that is produced in one of the city's two car factories. The car is better known by Russians as a Zap. I was delivering safety equipment to one of the five gigantic steel works within the city.

When I entered the steel works, I saw that the supposed road that I had to use was, in fact, nothing more than a strip of compressed ice. The ice was at a depth of at least a foot in its thinnest section. I also noticed that the main production buildings were situated to the right of the road that I was driving on. To the left of the roadway there stood an enormous railway marshalling yard. The two were linked by a long succession of concrete bridges that passed above the roadway I was negotiating. I had a passenger in the cab, a foreman, who was going to direct me to the unloading point.

As we passed under the first set of bridges, we came to a stretch where there was a gap of some 50 metres between the initial set and the subsequent set. The ground to the right was banked. In the banking there was a side turning. Pointing to the turning, my passenger said, "*Na prava, too-da.* [Go right, there]." I began to make the turn and as I did so he suddenly instructed me, "*Nee-yet. Preeyama!* [No. Straight on!]" I looked across the cab towards him for confirmation of which way to travel. He was pointing straight ahead. I straightened the steering wheel and looked directly ahead. It was then that I realised that the road in front of us sloped upwards and that the next set of bridges were lower than the first. Much lower. Too low.

I braked immediately but it had no effect. The truck merely slid forward on the compressed ice. It slid under the first bridge with a loud scraping noise as the roof of the trailer came into contact with the underside of the bridge span. The harsh, awful noise reverberated within the enclosed space. The truck came to a halt with the trailer wedged below the bridge. I looked across the cab, to the passenger seat, but it was empty. My guide had gone. He had bailed out, obviously thinking that it was probably not just the underside of the bridge that was going to be hit.

The steel mill's manager arranged for one of their massive Ural six-wheel trucks to help to remove the trailer from beneath the bridge. It was dragged out backwards, screaming and protesting (or was that me?). Once it had been released, I carried out the delivery. By the time that I had finished at the mill, it was early evening. I could have parked there for the night, but decided that I just wanted to get away from the place. Before leaving Zap' I had inspected the damage to the trailer. By rights it should not have been sealed by the customs because it was in an unfit condition. However, they had resealed it and I was not going to argue.

So I drove back to Dnepr, through a blizzard and stopped the night at a police post. From there I had to make my way to Vitebsk. The direct route was to go back to Kiev and take the Leningrad highway north. Vitebsk lay beside the highway, north of Orsha. However, I had decided that I was going to drive to Vitebsk via Moscow. It would mean driving 200 miles further than going via Kiev, but I considered it worth it because I would take a couple of days off at home in Moscow.

After two days off in Moscow, I headed for Vitebsk. Arriving there in the evening, I parked in the security park at the Sovinter' hotel in the town centre. When I awoke the following morning, I could hear that there were a large number of people gathered around the truck. Pulling the curtain back, slightly, I saw that I was surrounded by three police cars and a police van. There were also about twenty of Vitebsk's finest ranged around the vehicle, armed to the hilt.

With the truck's curtains still pulled around, I dressed quickly, turned on the ignition and cued the cassette player. As I threw the curtains back, the Rolling Stones' *Start Me Up* blared out at full volume. The police officers spun around in alarm to find me sitting there, casually smoking a Marlboro. Having had the element of surprise, I had taken them completely off guard.

The police took me to the office of the company that was importing the goods. Having studied the paperwork, the employee at the main office vouched that I had a genuine reason to be in Vitebsk and was delivering to them. The police then left.

At that moment in time just across the nearby border in Lithuania, the ethnic Lithuanians were agitating for total separation from the Soviet Union. Russian forces were using live ammunition to quell the demonstrations and rioting. Many Lithuanians were killed during this period. The Vitebsk police were paranoid that a British truck was so close to what was going on, perhaps suspecting that I was carrying arms for the protesters, or that I might witness some of the atrocities if I were heading into Lithuania. No, doubt had I have been I would have found that I could not proceed.

I was driven back to my truck by another employee, who then led me out of town, to the site of the factory. Once within the confines of the factory compound, I was advised to park my truck inside one of the huge factory buildings. Inside the massive hall I discovered that it was actually heated. That was probably for the best, because outside the temperature was dropping alarmingly and was already down to -20C. I was then taken to meet the Russian management and the English crew who were installing the production line in this factory.

An indicator of life in provincial Russia was that, due to it being the day that the weekly cargo flight from Moscow arrived, all the town's custom officers were at the airport. Therefore, I could not unload until the following day. As a recompense, I was allocated a room at the local hotel, actually the only provincial hotel that I stayed at that was on a par with Smolensk, Minsk, or one of the better Moscow hotels. I was taken there on the bus that ferried the British workers back and forth. The next day, I returned on the bus and eventually the goods were unloaded. But by this time it was 5pm and the factory manager suggested that, as it was snowing heavily outside, I stay that night at the hotel and leave for my last drop, at Pskov, early the following morning.

Although it was snowing, the temperature had risen to -15C, so upon arrival at the hotel, I parked the truck and switched it off. Watching the usually precise weather forecast on the T.V. I was informed that the overnight temperature would be -12C and the next morning it would be up to a tropical -10C. Therefore, with no fear for the truck, I left it switched off and went to bed.

Imagine my horror then the following morning when I left the hotel building and walked into an icy cold blast from the strong wind. Before I had even seen my temperature gauges on the dash of the cab I knew full well that the outside temperature was nowhere near as high as -10C. Once inside the cab I looked at the gauges, which informed me that it was, in fact, -30C. Of course, the oil in the sump had frozen so that it had the consistency of tarmac. There was no way that the truck was going to start.

The hotel receptionist phoned the factory, who sent the shuttle bus over and we got my truck started. But by then it was late afternoon and snow was bucketing down. I left the truck in the car park with the engine running all night and took a hotel room. I drove to Pskov the following morning.

During the first couple of months of the year in western Russia there is a dip in the temperatures. They go down to around -30 to -35C. This spell generally lasts for approximately a week. Then they begin to rise again. I had hit that low spell. On the way to Pskov I attempted to buy petrol from every garage that I passed, but none of them would sell me any. Due to the cold weather, the tankers were not running and the garages were saving the petrol for their regular clientele. I offered all sorts of inducements, but and for probably the only time that I was in Russia, I could not bribe anyone. I found it reprehensible that in a nation as corrupt as the Soviet Union, I could not corrupt anybody. Bloody communists!

What this meant, in essence, was that the fuel mix that I had in the running tank was not sufficiently strong enough for these severe temperatures. I needed to get petrol, urgently. Fortunately, despite the truck waxing up, I managed to limp into Pskov and found the factory straight away. Again, I was admitted to the factory and the truck was parked inside a large, empty, heated building. Once more I was taken to a large hotel, in Pskov centre, with the British crew working in this factory. However, as it was Friday, I had to stay there for the weekend. The British had interpreters, who they had hired at their first site in Borispol and taken with them to Vitebsk and Pskov. I was in the restaurant having a meal with a male and female from the interpreter's team. The local band were playing and suddenly the girl turned to me and apologised for the fact that they were playing Jewish music. She bemoaned the fact that much of the music produced within the U.S.S.R. was Jewish. Surprised, I merely shrugged and said that it did not matter. I was also surprised at the vehemence of her attack.

On the Monday morning I returned to the factory. Having told the interpreters that I needed to access petrol, I was shown to the office of the factory's head engineer. The two female interpreters who took me there had been taking the piss out of two of the British workers in Russian. I had been listening to it. When we arrived at the head engineer's office he introduced himself to me in Russian. One of the interpreters translated this into English for my benefit. She introduced the head engineer as Sergei Mikhailovich. Speaking in Russian, I said, "*Priviet Sergei Mikhailovich. Meenya Zavoot Mick. Pah – Russkie Misha. Pa – Engleski Mick. Kak dilla?* [Hello Sergei Mikhailovich. My name is Mick. In Russian it is Mish. In English Mick. How do you do?]." I noticed that the two interpreters had made a hasty exit, obviously realising that I had understood fully what they had been saying earlier about the English guys.

The head engineer organised for the drivers of the company's petrol driven trucks to drain off some of their fuel, which went into my truck's tank. The mixture was then, probably, around five to one. Still not really enough, but better than nothing.

I completed unloading that afternoon and left Pskov. By the time that I arrived at Vitebsk that evening the temperature was at -30C and I was struggling to keep going. I drove to the hotel and parked the truck in the car park, leaving the engine running all night. Booking into the hotel, I paid for my room and went to the restaurant, where I had dinner.

I was asked by Tony, the manager of the British

crew, why I had returned. I explained the situation and he suggested that I drive out to the factory in the morning and ask for help in locating petrol. The next morning, I drove to the factory but when I met the factory manager he would not offer any assistance whatsoever. I noticed Tony in the background laughing.

Feeling pissed off with the manager's attitude I left the factory and began to make my way the 60 miles to Orsha. Reaching the M1, I turned right heading for Brest. Soon I came across the hill at Orsha.

The hill was a kilometre long, steady, steep incline. I was on a short stretch of dual carriageway, which ended at the top of the hill. I looked at it with foreboding as I approached. I was not confident that the truck would produce enough power with the waxing fuel filter to manage the ascent successfully. I looked around. The landscape was one complete blanket of deep, white, snow. The only building in sight lay miles away, surrounded by that sheet of whiteness. I was isolated in the centre of this bleak wilderness. I knew that over the summit of the hill lay a fuel station. It was only a couple of kilometres from the top of the hill. I had filled there many times and knew that the ladies at the garage would sell me petrol. I just had to make it to the fuel station and I would be fine. That was all. Make it to the fuel station.

It was not snowing, but drifting snow was being blown along the carriageway by the extremely strong, gale force Siberian wind that was driving in from behind me. I looked at my temperature gauges, which informed me that the outside temperature was -42C. Getting that far, from Vitebsk had been a struggle. I had driven slowly, limping along and had not attempted to use high revs. As soon as the truck had started to miss regularly I had allowed it to come to a gradual stop. It would maintain idling speed while halted and the filter would begin to clear a little. Once the idle was regular and smooth I would set out again. But this hill was going to force me to increase the amount of revs that I expected from the engine to obtain the power needed to get over the summit. I was not sure that the truck would be capable of this. However, I could not sit at the bottom of the slope indefinitely hoping for a miracle. There was no way that the temperature was suddenly going to rise to -20C, or higher. Far from it. It was more likely to go lower, particularly as the day came to an end. There was only one thing for it: take my chance and see what happened.

I drove at the hill and at first I thought that I was going to make it. But, about 200 metres from the top of the hill, she ran out of power and would go no further. She came to a halt and stalled. Painstakingly slowly, I reversed the truck back down the slope, bump starting it and made another attempt. After an hour and three more tries, I was climbing the hill and this time got to within 100 metres of the top, when the truck gave up the ghost again. I had decided that if this attempt was unsuccessful, then the only thing for it was to climb out of the cab, expose myself to the Arctic temperatures and change the fuel filter.

I had decided to leave the engine running up until the last possible moment. Having ensured that my clothing was fully done up, I put a scarf around my neck and pulled my fur hat down tight on my head. I ensured that my ears were fully covered by the bottom of the hat. Putting rigger gloves on my hands, I climbed out of the cab. Having grabbed the tools and spare filter from the tool locker behind the driver's door I went round to the nearside and jacked the cab over to gain access to the filter housing. The cold was beginning to bite as I worked feverishly to remove the old filter from its mounting. Once it was loose, I turned off the engine. Now I had to work quickly. I removed the old filter completely and replaced it with the new one.

However, while removing the old filter, which was full of diesel, I almost dropped it. It slanted over and cold, icy, water-laden fuel poured on to the glove, covering my left hand. I thought no more about it and continued with my task. Once the new filter was fitted and tight, I primed it with fuel by manually bringing up diesel using the hand operated lift pump.

Racing round to the driver's side, I climbed up on to the step of the cab and turned the ignition key. As I did so I levered myself into position and jammed my foot down hard on the accelerator pedal. On the third attempt, the engine fired, but only spasmodically. I started it again and it began to idle. I went back to the filter, racing against time and the freezing cold. I bled the fuel filter so as to get all the air out of the system.

The truck by now was idling smoothly. I dropped the cab back down and went to the tool locker. I was placing the tools back into the locker when I noticed that I had absolutely no feeling whatsoever in my left hand. The fuel that had poured on to the glove had become icy cold due to the high water content. I now faced a serious dilemma. Here I was, in the middle of nowhere, my hand encased in a virtual block of ice. This situation could produce frostbite in the hand and the more far-reaching consequences could be gangrene, or even hypothermia if I could not get the problem dealt with. Things looked extremely bleak.

Having closed the tool locker, I climbed up into the cab and closed the driver's door. The heater was merely blowing cold air as the truck had not yet warmed up. I ripped the glove from my hand and placed the hand between my thighs, hoping to heat it. The hand was completely numb. I had absolutely no feeling in it at all and this lack of any sensation was spreading into my wrist. This was serious. Very serious.

I looked out, over the white wasteland to my right and wondered whether I should try to make my way to the isolated cottage about 2 miles away. I could see that they had smoke billowing out of the chimney. That meant a fire and warmth. But, that 2 miles was covered in at least knee-deep snow and maybe an even higher layer. It would be a difficult and possibly highly dangerous route to take if I attempted to make it to the house.

As I weighed up my options, another truck drove up and parked beside mine. The driver, a Danish man, having noticed my warning hazard lights flashing, had realised that I had problems. Within minutes I was sitting on the passenger seat, in his warm cab. He had taken my frozen hand between his and was massaging the hand vigorously. He was attempting to stimulate the circulation so that blood flowed into the icy hand again. Still I had no sensation in it. Suddenly, the blood and sensation returned to the hand. It was like receiving a 20,000–volt electric shock. The pain was excruciating. I ripped my hand from between his and shoved it between my thighs. I squeezed my legs tight upon the hand and rocked back and forth, moaning with pain. After a few minutes the pain had subsided until it was no more than a very heavy throbbing.

I returned to my truck, where the heater system was now blowing warm air. We then drove to the nearby fuel station, and the *babushkis* in the garage sold me the vital petrol that I needed. The Dane drove with me to Minsk, accompanying me to the motel even though he did not need to. He was heading directly for Kukariki. We shook hands and parted company, never to see one another again. As he drove away, I realised that in the middle of all of that trauma we had not even asked one another's name. We were just two anonymous individuals who had been brought together fleetingly, in the face of severe adversity.

I spent two nights at the Minsk motel. I had taken a room and slept there rather than in the cab. I needed to warm myself up.

When I left the motel to drive to Poland the temperature was a more reasonable -20C. Crossing into Poland, I received instructions to load at Stettin in the extreme north-west of the country. I loaded there and then made my way to Michendorf, where I swapped trailers once again. The Croome driver collecting the damaged trailer from me took one look at it and asked, "Is that legal?"

"Only if you don't get caught," I replied, laughing.

"Thanks very much Mick," he said, ironically, "I am going to look a right prat when I get to Zeebrugge and try to tell the other drivers that I did not do this. No one is going to believe me."

"I believe you," I said, convincingly. But there again, I was actually a very convincing person.

19

Fighting in the Street

THE next few weeks were taken up with repetitively driving to Poland, changing trailers and returning to Moscow, spending my days rolling up and down the M1 and spending my nights at Smolensk, Minsk, or Siedlce. By now I knew the road like the back of my hand and I was well known at all the motels and most of the diesel stops.

One cold, snowy, Sunday, March afternoon, Elena and I met our friends, Volodin and Larissa, at the Aragvi restaurant. This was located in a cellar situated in a small square, just off of Moscow's Gorki Street. We spent that whole Sunday afternoon enjoying fine Georgian food, wine and brandy. Leaving the restaurant at 6pm, I went ahead up to the street, while the others retrieved their coats from the cloakroom. In the street, I was attacked by three men, who stole my wallet. However, I fought back, fuelled by anger and adrenaline; breaking the nose of one of them in the process. He was arrested by the police at the scene and they recovered my wallet, which was in his coat pocket. However, the other two men had escaped, but they were not unharmed. During the attack, I had sustained an extremely serious cut to my left temple.

Elena, Larissa, Volodin and I were taken by police van to a police station some 500 metres away along Gorki Street. Here we were to make statements. While the others made theirs, I was placed in an office where a policeman attempted to take mine. It was a complete waste of time. The effect of my concussion meant that I could not understand even basic Russian, nor could I manage to speak any German. I was having difficulty even managing to speak English. There was not one officer in the police station who could speak English anyway. They would not allow Elena to translate for me as she was a potential witness if the case came to court.

Eventually, the officer in charge of the station told Volodin that I needed to make a statement at the British Embassy, which was to be translated into Russian. Volodin was to then deliver it to the police station. We were then, after two hours at the station, unceremoniously shown out into the cold night air. However, my wallet, containing more than £600 in various currencies, stayed at the station as evidence. Up to that point I had received no first aid whatsoever for my cut temple, which was still bleeding profusely.

Volodin, having retrieved his car from the Aragvi square, drove us through the city to a hospital in the Moscow suburbs, roughly a mile north of Voikovskaya. We entered the large building and Volodin strode across the dark, dank, reception area, to the main counter. Here, he flashed a warrant cardholder and the receptionist ran off up an adjacent corridor. She returned shortly and signalled for us to go to an office at the end of the corridor. Elena and Larissa remained in reception while Volodin and I entered the office. Inside the room that we entered we discovered two men seated around a desk. One was probably in his 50s, he was the doctor. The other was late 20s, he was the assistant. They were both drinking vodka from dirty glasses. As wildly disorientated as I had now become with concussion, I noticed immediately that the doctor was cross-eyed. Extremely cross-eyed.

I looked around the dirty room. Paper and used bandages littered the floor. Cobwebs hung from the ceiling and the light shades. Dilapidated furniture was strewn around. A smeared, glass-fronted cabinet held more vodka bottles and a few, extra, dirty glasses. "And I thought that the N.H.S. was bad," I joked, to myself.

The doctor asked Volodin whether I was from the Mafia. Apparently, Mafia members were brought to the hospital to be patched up following altercations. So that the doctor was not obliged to inform the police, as the law insisted, the Mafia usually provided him with at least a couple of bottles of champagne, so as to assist his diagnosis. Volodin went out to the boot of his car and returned with two bottles. I required diagnosing. And a drink.

We were actually into the second bottle before the doctor instructed his assistant to see to my wound. The blood that was leaking from the cut beside my eye had been overlooked while we sat there drinking. Nobody, not even me, was particularly bothered. I was sitting on the examining couch, swigging champagne from a dirty glass, while the assistant examined my cut head. Taking a dirty piece of rag from a filthy enamel kidney bowl, he wiped the wound ineffectually. He then smeared the cut with a dob of Vaseline jelly before wrapping a length of bandage round and round my head. By the time that he had finished, I looked like Rambo, on a bad hair day. Referring to the vodka bottles in the glass cabinet, Volodin said, "You have enough vodka then, doctor."

"Anaesthetic," the doctor replied flatly.

"Who for?" Volodin enquired.

"Well, not for the F@cking patients," Doctor Zhivago replied. He obviously self-medicated, so he wasn't all bad.

Eventually we left the room after shaking hands with the two men. The doctor looked me straight in the eye, or maybe not, as we parted company.

We drove back to the flat and all went up in the lift. Vera, upon seeing the state of me went ballistic. Not at me, but at the others for allowing this to happen to me. When she had calmed down, she asked me whether there was anything that I wanted. I asked for champagne, which was provided cold from the fridge. Not like that tepid crap that we had drunk at the hospital.

The following morning, I drove the truck to Klyazma, accompanied by Elena. She had taken time off work to help me. My head was splitting and I was not 100% as I drove through the Moscow rush hour.

At Klyazma, while the trailer was unloaded, I took Elena up to meet Marina and the other Xerox ladies. While I sat drinking a cup of tea, Elena and Marina were deep in conversation together. When I had finished the tea, Marina took us across the compound to what was the medical centre for the army unit. We entered the building to find a spotless room, full of up to date modern equipment. The army major/ doctor examined my head and redressed it properly. I now had a normal sticking plaster over the eye, rather than my off white, dirty bandana. The major informed Elena that I was to rest for at least a week. We returned to Voikovskaya and I went to bed. While I slept, Elena phoned Kepstowe and informed them what had happened. They said for me to rest for the week and then to contact them. They would tell Croome.

The following day we went together to the British Embassy so that I could make my statement for the Russian police. Although having told the embassy staff that all of my money had been stolen, they insisted that I pay £50 for the statement and translation. The argument that ensued was straight forward. I insisted that I could not pay as all of my money had been stolen and I was potless. They insisted that I pay £50 out of money that I did not have or no statement. Stalemate.

Then Elena asked whether we could pay in Roubles, because she had plenty in her handbag. They grudgingly agreed and charged me 50 Roubles, which had actually cost me £1 on the black market. They then carried out the statement and translation service. I paid Elena back as soon as I had money again, which was the next day.

The day after the embassy fiasco, we travelled to the Rank Xerox head office on Ogorodnaya Sloboda. Marina had arranged for me to draw $1,000 so as to have enough money to run the truck. I told them that I would repay it as soon as I returned to Moscow. But, their money was safe, because they could recoup it from Kepstowe if need be. And Kepstowe could have it stopped from my account with Croome.

That evening Kepstowe rang me and told me that Croome insisted that I left Moscow the following day. That was against the doctor's orders and I was still not feeling too great. I agreed, but insisted on my part that I return to the U.K. for medical checks to my injury, and also to have the spotlights and Thermoline fitted. Kepstowe agreed without any hesitation whatsoever. I then phoned Croome.

At first, Croome told me to drive to Berlin and wait for a trailer to come out. I would then return to Moscow with it. A disagreement ensued but at the end of it he said that he would load me from Germany for the U.K.

I also insisted that I had enough time off to be able to get the vehicle serviced by Channel Commercials. Another disagreement began but I insisted again that it was going to happen. I then phoned Channel Commercials and arranged for the truck to be serviced and my spotlights and Thermoline to be fitted. I could not guarantee them exactly when I would get to Ashford but they said that they would order the parts in ready and fit them as and when I arrived.

Elena told me to be very careful travelling to the U.K. and back. I replied that I was always careful.

"No, you is not," she stated, "You go to the Aragvi and you is bugged."

"Are mugged," I corrected her.

"Bugged, mugged," she retorted, "It is you that got it.'

I did not bother to correct her again. I would not have got anywhere.

The reason why Elena and, in fact, many Russians could not get "am", "are" and "is" correct is because, as I have previously said, they did not have them in their own language. So, of course, when they spoke in English with British people, the Brits found it highly amusing that the Russians confused the words.

As I developed my Russian, I took special care to pronounce my words properly and picked up the Russian accent with the Moscow dialect. Not only did this allow me to be better understood when speaking Russian, but it allowed me to do a good impression of Elena and her curious use of "is", etc. Actually, the other English drivers, when I was quoting something that Elena had said, would insist that I put on the accent and used her exact words. This parody gave them a really good laugh.

20

The Snow Must Go On

THE following morning, I climbed into the truck and headed west. It would be the first time in nine months that the truck had been back in the U.K., as opposed to back in the U.S.S.R. When I reached Siedlce, I found a telex instructing me to drive to Rothenbach, in Germany, where I was to load children's nursery equipment.

As Rothenbach was near Nurnberg, I drove to Berlin and then headed south, past Leipzig. I arrived in Rothenbach during the evening. Parking in the town, I went to a local pub for dinner. While eating in the restaurant, I was invited to join the few regulars sitting at the *Stammtisch,* a table that is reserved for honoured guests, or regular, long-term ones. During the conversation they asked me where I had come from. I told them and they said that it must be extremely cold there. I told them the tale of Orsha Hill. When I finished the story, one of the regulars, an old man in his 70s, informed me that in 1941 he had been serving in the German Army and had been shot through the neck. Where? On the hill, at Orsha.

★

The next day, I loaded the nursery goods and drove to Zeebrugge. Back in England, I tipped the nursery ware in London and dropped my trailer off in Wandsworth. Then I went to Tooting Hospital. From there I made my way to Ashford, Kent, where I turned up at Channel's premises. The next morning they began work on the truck. While I was waiting, I telephoned Kepstowe. They informed me there was a loaded trailer in Croome's yard that I was to take to Krasnaya Presnaya for an exhibition.

They also told me that I would be staying in Moscow as they had eight exhibition trailers going into the city, which I would shunt to the trade fair. I was to swap trailers with each driver as they arrived and allow them to turn around straight away and head back to the U.K. This not only suited me, but I knew that it would suit the subcontractors as well. Everyone a winner.

The work upon my truck was completed at 7pm. From Ashford I drove to Croome's yard. Disappointingly, I had missed David, who had gone home by that time. He only expected drivers to work 25 hours a day. He saw no need to do it himself. I picked up the trailer and was given the paperwork for it by Croome's night watchman, Charlie Parsley. An old hand of the Middle East, Charlie had driven overland to Karachi on one trip.

Crossing the Channel that night, I set out for Moscow the following morning.

Spring was fully in force throughout Western Europe, but winter still held Russia in its grip. The same old scenes of seas of snow, cold weather and icy roads. As I reached the Russian police post between Orsha and

Smolensk, on my way back to Moscow, a policeman emerged from the post and stopped me. It was a pitch black night and bitterly cold. He slid his foot back and forward, on the ground and said "*Osterozhnia, Marozhe* [Be careful, it's icy]." I thanked him for the warning and told him that I was parking there anyway.

In the morning, I set out for Moscow. No more than two kilometres down the road, there were two Russian trucks, laying on their sides. They had crashed during the night presumably as the result of the icy conditions. The police were in attendance, blue lights flashing wanly in the weak sunlight. The driver of each truck was laid out at the side of the road beside his truck. Both were stone cold dead. A sombre warning not to take the weather conditions for granted. Unfortunately, I was to come across many, many more, dead bodies during my time in Russia. Some the result of road accidents and some the result of the freezing Russian weather. None of them made a pretty sight.

Passing the scene of the accident, I continued on my way to Smolensk, where I filled up with diesel. I then continued on to Moscow. And here was where I got my first chance to test out the Thermoline system. Climbing up over the ridges past Smolensk, the temperature was down to -10C. Suddenly, the truck began to misfire and lose power. I immediately flicked the Thermoline switch down to activate the system. I travelled approximately 50 metres with the engine still missing and then the engine suddenly surged. She picked up to full power and the truck soared along the road as smoothly as silk.

The Thermoline had been a sound investment. Over all of the coming winters it proved its worth, time and time again. I never ever had to add petrol to the diesel again.

In Moscow I delivered the trailer load of goods to K.P. Once I had finished work, I drove to the Xerox Head Quarters and repaid them the money that I had borrowed.

21

When One Door Shuts, Another Slams

I was in Moscow for two weeks, shunting the trailers to and from the exhibition sites. Then I loaded returns, from Klyazma. The broken goods were for return to Venray.

En route for Venray, I stopped at Siedlce. There was a long fax waiting for me in the Hettman telling me that I was to tip the returns in Venray and reload from there for Klyazma. Also, as my Soviet visa was running out, Kepstowe had renewed it and the new visa was being sent out to Berlin by DHL. I was to collect the visa from Berlin on my way back to Moscow. I sent a reply acknowledging these instructions and then set out for the West.

Once again, the May Day holiday was nearly upon us and this trip was going to coincide with that. However, Croome was insistent that I tip before the holiday. I tipped and loaded at Venray, on Thursday, 25th April 1991. While I was loading, a Croome truck turned up. He too was running to Klyazma, so we decided to go together. That evening we drove to Dortmund and stopped for the night. The next day we set out for Berlin. I wanted to get there, collect my visa that day and get into Poland that night. However, once we passed Hannover, the autobahn ground to a halt. It was complete gridlock. The stationary traffic was caused by the sheer volume of traffic heading for Berlin and it was stop-start traffic all the way to the German capital. We arrived in Berlin that night and went to a pub.

The following morning, I took the Croome driver with me. We drove to the D.H.L. office but it was closed. I then went to Tegel airport's D.H.L. office. They informed me that my package was at the city centre office, so I drove back there. However, it was now 9am and the office was still closed. As I waited, the Croome driver went to a phone box.

Suddenly, I saw movement through the office window. I went to the door and shortly afterwards, with my visa safely in my pocket, I was driving back to Drei Linden to collect my trailer. The Croome driver told me that he had phoned Croome's office and they wanted me to ring them, when I got to Drei Linden. When I made the call I was accused of deliberately taking my time getting to Berlin, which was why I could not collect my visa. This, apparently, was so that I could spend the May Day holiday in Moscow. I was told to leave the trailer there and drive back to the U.K. I would not be paid for the journey from Venray to Berlin and back. Also, the Channel crossing would be at my expense. When I pointed out that I actually had my visa, I was told to get on my way to Moscow immediately. However, I refused, saying that as I was not going to get paid, why would I want to go all of the way to Moscow for nothing. I was then told that I would get paid, but I demanded that they put that in writing on a telex to be sent to Siedlce. No telex, then the trailer would stay there. Then I hung up.

As we drove to the Polish border, I thought about the situation that had just occurred. For some reason, the other driver had obviously not told them about the traffic on the autobahn the previous day. However, he had told them, as he thought, that I could not get my visa until the Monday. This may have had something to do with the fact that he had met a German girl in the pub the previous evening. She had told him that if he was there on the Saturday night, then he could go to her place and they could listen to music (I presume that is a German phrase for "The sound of bed springs").

Whatever. But Croome's plan had been that I go back to the U.K. and he would stay in Berlin to look after the unattended trailer with its valuable cargo. Suddenly, everything made sense.

So from then on I made his life unbearable. Knowing that he was bone idle, I drove him to the point of complete exhaustion and way beyond. Not wanting to show him Schwedt, we queued in a 15-mile queue at Frankfurt Oder. I would not let him sleep during the wait. Once through the border, we parked up for a sleep, but I only took four hours and then got him up to start off again. He wanted to stop the night at Siedlce but I forced him to drive to Kukariki.

As soon as we entered the Soviet Union we drove into a blizzard, which continued all the way to Moscow. I would not stop, except for another four-hour sleep. And, as I pointed out to him, if I got to Moscow and tipped before May Day but he did not then his boss was going to want to know why he hadn't. When we arrived at Klyazma, his eyes were like piss holes in the snow and he could hardly stand up for exhaustion. On the other hand, I was reasonably fresh. But that was because I worked like that most of the time and it was normal for me.

Once we had both tipped at Klyazma, he drove to the Mezh' to sleep, while I drove home. The following morning I received a phone call from him explaining to me how, the previous evening, he had sold a pair of ripped jeans to a Russian guy. When the bloke had returned asking for his money back, the Croome driver claimed to have seen him off with a knife. So he was going to leave Moscow straight away in case the Russian returned tooled up. The story would possibly have been convincing had I have not heard him use it at least twice before. Both times he had left a group of Croome's drivers drinking in Moscow and set off back alone, no doubt having phoned Croome and grassed up his so-called mates. Still, once a lying bastard, always a lying bastard, eh?

I spent a leisurely five days in Moscow, during which time Kepstowe called the flat. They told me to load a consignment of shoes from the Bata factory in Petrovskoye, a suburb of northern Moscow, once I had finished my well-deserved break. It was an Interunity load. I loaded the consignment and headed out of Moscow.

Back in England, I tipped the shoes in Northampton and then ran to Sheppey for the inevitable showdown with David Croome. The meeting was terse. David stated that there was no longer any work available through him as he could not make any money by using me. He handed me a cheque for the money that he owed me. He then asked me what I was going to do now that he could no longer supply me with work.

I replied that I was going to go and see Kepstowe. "I would rather that you did not," he said. "Because you would be taking work away from me."

I replied, "I thought that you just said that you cannot make any money out of using me anyway?"

"I am going to call Kepstowe and tell them that I do not want them to use you," he stated.

"Do what you like," I replied, standing up and walking casually out of his office.

I drove from Croome's yard to Sheerness to put his cheque in the bank, but, before I paid the cheque in, I stepped into a phone box. Remembering what David had said about him not wanting me to approach Kepstowe for work, I lifted the receiver and dialled Kepstowe's office.

22

A Hard Day's Night and Day and Night

APPARENTLY Croome must have telephoned Kepstowe Freight as soon as I had left his office. He told them, so it was reported to me, that "under no circumstances" did he want me working for them. They replied that they would consider his request (for request, I think that they meant demand).

I held a meeting with Kepstowe the next day. At the conclusion of the meeting I was asked what I would do if they did not employ me as a subcontractor. I replied that I had a few companies in Holland who were extremely keen to get me to work for them, so naturally I would go to Holland and take up one of the offers. It did not matter to me if I did not come back to England. Just as long as I was running to Moscow.

Kepstowe considered what Croome and I had said to them, and the following day I was leaving Wandsworth, pulling a Kepstowe trailer bound for Moscow.

I spent the next two months running mainly between London and Moscow. Therefore, I was not at home in Moscow as often as I had been on the Poland shunts. However, for Elena and I this was better than had I been unable to obtain work to Russia at all. And to be fair to them, Kepstowe worked things so that I would stay in Moscow shunting where possible. So I would take over other people's trailers and let them leave with my empty ones. This suited almost everybody.

At the end of July 1991, American president George Bush visited Moscow to hold a summit meeting with Mikhail Gorbachev, the leader of the Soviet Union. Tonnes of cameras, lighting and sound equipment had been shipped from the States to Schiphol airport in Holland by the American T.V. companies. This equipment was then shipped on to Moscow, in the back of four trailers, by me and three other owner-drivers. We then waited in Moscow for a few days so that we were on site when the summit ended. Then we were tasked with taking the American T.V. companies' equipment from Moscow back to Schiphol airport, from where it would be flown back to the States. However, from the pull down of the equipment to its delivery time at Schiphol we were going to be on an extremely tight schedule to meet the deadline for the return flights to America.

So, it really was not a good time to be ill. But, unfortunately, that is what I was.

Gorbachev and Bush were holding a final press conference at the Kremlin on the Wednesday afternoon. As soon as the conference ended, the camera equipment would be loaded. Three of the trailers had to be in Schiphol on the Saturday morning to catch an afternoon flight. The fourth needed to be at the airport early on the Sunday morning. Because I was ill,

I was allocated the last trailer. The other three drivers loaded my trailer for me and then set out for Holland early on the Wednesday evening.

I left Moscow at 7am Dutch time on the Friday morning, but in reality I was still not well enough to drive. I had 48 hours to cover the 1,285 miles to Amsterdam and be there for 7am, on the Sunday morning. The first day's shift I drove to Siedlce, only stopping to fill up at Smolensk and for the border crossing. Fortunately, the border was extremely quiet. I completed the border procedure and then drove on to Siedlce, where I parked up, at 2am, on the Saturday morning. I slept for six hours and then set out for the border at Swieco–Frankfurt Oder. I crossed Poland with the minimum of stops and arrived at the border to find that my luck was in. It was empty. Clearing the border, quickly, I drove to Berlin and realised that time was so tight that I had better not take a sleep break for fear of missing my deadline.

I pushed on and drove past Hannover and Osnabruck intending to cross into Holland at Bad Bentheim. I arrived at the border at 1am on the Sunday morning. Luckily, the German customs did not question why I had turned up long after the German truck driving ban had started. I crossed the border and drove to Schiphol. I found the unloading site and stopped the truck. It was 3am on the Sunday. I had covered the 1,285 miles in 44 hours. But, I was totally exhausted. I lay on top of the cab's bunk and immediately fell asleep.

I was awoken at 7am by loud, continuous banging, on the door of the cab. I got up to find a young man and woman standing there. They were from the freight agents office and wanted my paperwork. Having got it, they went to their office to arrange customs clearance, for the flight. Thirty minutes later they returned and told me to back on to an unloading door in the front of the warehouse. After another 30 minutes the trailer was empty, my paperwork returned. I drove off of the bay, parked and went back to bed.

That evening, I was collected from my truck by the young couple. They took me to their flat for a shower and then to a very expensive Chinese restaurant for dinner. At the restaurant, I was introduced to Susie, an American woman. Susie had been in overall charge of the news equipment movement. She offered me the opportunity to work as a subcontractor for her company, moving equipment from Schiphol to any destination in Europe where the American news media needed to cover events. She offered to fly me to the States to meet her bosses and discuss it. It was a tempting offer. A very tempting offer.

On the Monday morning I spoke to Kepstowe, who sent me to load from Venray. But this load was for Hemel Hempstead, not Klyazma. I spent more than a week in the U.K. and then loaded an Aeromar fridge for Moscow. With my paperwork for the load I was given a roll of new designs for Interunity to pass to Kommunar at Tula. This turned out to be more important than it seemed. I shipped out of Dover on the 14th of August. This was significant because the 15th was my birthday.

Arriving in Moscow on the Sunday afternoon, I parked the truck with the fridge trailer at the Mezh' and went home to the flat.

Elena and Vera were waiting for me and we had a small party to celebrate my birthday. They had bought me presents, among which was a small axe and knife set in a leather holster, from Vera. The axe was about 10 inches long and the blade was razor sharp, as was the knife. I did not realise it at the time but the following day I would use the axe for real in self-defence. Having finished our little party, we went to bed and I slept very well. I think that had I known what the next few days were to bring I would probably not have slept at all.

23

Left, Right at the Centre of History

THE following morning Elena switched on the television. However, instead of the usual morning news programme, the screen was blank and they were playing Tchaikovsky's Swan Lake. Elena kept saying to me, "This is a bad day for my country Micky." She did not say why, but just kept repeating it. I saw her off to work and then went to the Mezh', from where I drove to Aeromar.

On the way to Aeromar, I crossed over the M.K.A.D. and on the left-hand side of the road I saw a column of Russian tanks parked one behind the other, facing in the direction of the centre of the city. The crews were at rest, sitting atop their turrets, casually smoking and drinking tea. I drove past the line of forty or so armoured vehicles and carried on to Aeromar.

At Aeromar, everything appeared normal. Everyone went about their work. I had reversed the trailer on to the loading bay for the cargo to be discharged. Then I was called to the manager's office. There was a phone call for me from Kepstowe. Lifting the receiver, I discovered that it was Mark Hughes on the line. The conversation was very strange, right from the outset.

Mark: Micky. Are you all right?

Me: Yeah.

Mark: Are you sure?

Me: Yeah.

Mark: There's been a coup.

Me: Where?

Mark: There.

Me: What, in Moscow?

Mark: Yes. The men in grey suits are back (a reference to the old communist leadership).

Me: Bugger me!

Mark: No thanks.

I should not have said "bugger me", Mark was, after all, gay. However, he then told me that as soon as the trailer was tipped to leave Aeromar and drive directly to the border and get out of the country. I reminded him that I had the new designs for Interunity–Kommunar in the cab. He told me to drive into Moscow, give them to Interunity and then head straight for the border. If I came across any problems entering Moscow then I was to abandon the idea and throw the designs out of the window on the road to Brest.

I hung up the phone and then told miserable Bob the news. When I left his office he was on the phone to American Airlines, trying to book a seat on the first available flight to the States. Well, probably two seats, considering the size of his arse.

Driving into Moscow and passing the column of tanks again, I realised that this was big. Very big. A coup in Moscow. This was real life history being made. And I was there. Right in the middle of it. Then I decided that I was not going to leave Moscow. I was going to stay with Elena and I was going to be part of it. Here I was, right in the middle of a major world event. Bugger driving to Brest!

I drove in to Moscow on Leningradski and then turned on to the Garden Ring, anticlockwise. I passed the American Embassy, went up on to a bridge, crossed over the ring road and came down the other side. I parked against the kerb, took the designs and left the cab. Interunity's office was behind the line of buildings, to my right.

At Interunity's office, I met Zoya, who took the designs from me. She kept saying, "This is a bad day, for my country," over and over again. Maybe it was, but probably not as bad a day as it would be for me if Kepstowe found out what my real intentions were.

When I got back to my truck, I was surprised. At that point of the Garden Ring, there were 16 lanes of traffic, eight in each direction. When I had gone to Interunity the traffic had been moving freely. Now, every lane was jam-packed with gridlocked traffic. "No point sitting in this." I thought to myself. I decided that I would go and buy some badges.

I collected Soviet enamel lapel badges, I had probably about 100 pinned up in the cab. They were small works of art. Every Soviet city and town had its own, depicting a local scene of interest or monument. Then there were communist party badges, sporting event badges, space travel badges, etc. Not only did I collect them for me, my brother sold them at boot fairs. I decided that while I let the traffic clear, I would get some more.

I knew that there was a shop up on Kallinina, where I had crossed over the Garden Ring. So, I went there. I spent 30 minutes in the shop and then stepped outside carrying two plastic bags brimmed full of badges. Back in the street, I noticed that people were lining the path on either side of the road. Coming along the street there was a mobile crane. Seated on top of the crane's jib was Boris Yeltsin, who had just become president of the Russian Federation. He was shouting through a loud hailer and people were leaving the paths to follow the crane. They were going to the White House.

I had been very tempted to follow them, but instead returned to my truck. The traffic was still totally grid-locked and now people were climbing from their cars and arguing with one another, even coming to blows as they lost their tempers. I sat in my truck cab parked against the kerb and laughed to myself. But I did not laugh for long.

A large man who was standing on the pavement approached the cab. He was obviously pissed. He began to shout and swear at me, railing off about for-eigners causing problems in his country. Fortunately, I had placed Vera's axe set in my work bag that morning and I now got it out. The man stepped towards the truck, screaming and shouting. I pulled the axe out of the holster. I did not like his level of aggression. The Russian then put his foot on the bottom step of the truck and grabbed hold of my mirror arm with one hand. He pulled himself up and his face was level with mine. There was wild anger, in his eyes. I lifted the axe in the air and turned it so that the flat side was downwards. He drew his free hand back and formed a fist, ready to punch me. I brought the axe down with full force and smashed it against his fingers, which were holding the mirror arm. His intention had been to seriously assault me and I had to prevent that at all costs. If his actions had drawn a crowd I could have received a severe beating or worse.

Even over the noise of all of the chaos in the roadway, I heard the snapping noises as his fingers were broken. His wild, angry eyes widened alarmingly and then his broken hand lost its grip on the mirror arm. He fell away from the truck and crashed to the pavement. He lay there motionless. A few passers-by glanced at him, but nobody came to his assistance. Just then the traffic ahead moved. I started the truck and pulled away from the kerb.

I needed to make the junction 200 metres ahead and turn left, across all the traffic. That would take me towards the Mezh'. Keeping an eye on my attacker, who was still laying on the ground, bit by bit I edged forwards until I was at the junction. The police there helped me to cross the road and I was gone. Speeding up, I headed for 1905. No, not the year, although it might as well have been.

At 1905 I came across another problem. The police were not allowing traffic to turn left and head down to the Krasnaya Presnaya embankment because they could get to the White House that way. They were diverting all traffic back the way that I had come, straight into the gridlock. I ignored the police and turned right, which would take me towards home. I could park there. No problem. However, there was a problem. On the way, police diverted me off into a housing estate. I knew that this was not a through road. I was driving towards an angry mob, who were blocking the street. They were carrying communist banners and would not be too pleased with any foreigner that fell into their hands. Once again I found myself in imminent danger.

Luckily, I just had room to spin the truck without side-swiping the parked cars. Not that I was too bothered about that. I drove back to the main road, but had to turn left. The police were still blocking the right turn that I had wanted to take. I was heading back towards the Mezh' again.

I came back to 1905, but turned away, right, to avoid the police, who had formed a cordon on the far side of the junction. By going round the block I came out nearer the Mezh' but once again the police were blocking the junction, preventing you from turning right. One officer, without thinking, went to my passenger side (to talk to the driver, obviously) and the other stepped on to the pavement. I shot forwards, turned right and drove down to the Mezh'. Job jobbed.

I parked by the hotel. There were four Dutch trucks parked there as well. One was my great friend Arri' from Pickford's B.V., but he was leaving. He asked me to go with him, but I declined the offer. I was staying.

The other three were from a Dutch company delivering to Moscow for the first time. Therefore, it was their first trip to Moscow and they were bricking it. They had driven straight into the middle of an armed coup. In fact, the older of the three drivers, Pete, later had a nervous breakdown caused by this experience.

Just as I parked up, two police cars escorted a Czecho–Freight truck to the parking place. When the driver emerged from his cab, I could see that he had received a severe beating somewhere in the city. His face was very badly cut and he could hardly walk. The police took him into the hotel. I followed them in and sent a telex to Kepstowe saying that I was trapped in

Moscow. I then walked to the Metro, thinking how lucky I was that I had avoided the Czech driver's fate.

Later, at home, I received a phone call from Rob at Kepstowe asking me what I thought that I was doing. Blaming the Interunity designs, I said that I was trapped in the city but would escape as soon as I could. I then told Elena and Vera what I had seen in town and also on C.N.N., which was showing in the Mezh' communication centre. I had seen tanks in Red Square. Tanks outside the White House, with Yeltsin on top of one and the chaos on the Garden Ring, of which I had been a part. My truck was in some of the shots at the Garden Ring and also outside the Mezh', as the camera at the White House panned along the river bank. Well, at least my truck was becoming world famous.

The next morning, I went back to the Mezh'. People on the Metro were even more subdued than normal. It was deathly quiet, the atmosphere heavily tense with fear and uncertainty. From the Mezh' I walked to the White House.

Elena had told me not to go there. She said it would be dangerous. She had also told me that when I went there, I was not to take a camera. She knew that I would not heed her advice. No camera because people in the massive crowd might think that I was spying on them. When this was all over, the authorities would be looking for those who had taken part. So, no camera.

The crowd at the White House had grown bigger and bigger ever since Yeltsin had first led them there, riding on top of the crane. It was the anti-coup protestors' stronghold. They would defend it against the coup leader's tanks. Vera had gone there to join the protest. So had my friends Volodin and Kostya. Elena had called them "the other three idiots". I, presumably was the main idiot.

I walked to the White House and carried out a complete circle of the building. I noticed that there were absolutely thousands of protesters guarding the building. They were cheering and singing in defiance. I also noticed that they had derailed trolley buses to provide some defence against the expected tank attack. The tanks outside the building were unmanned. Their crews had joined the protest and abandoned them. At the back of the building there was an enormous lawn. Here, thousands listened to political speeches in support of democracy. I listened to some of them, mingling in the massive crowd. Then, I walked back to the Metro and went home.

The city was tense. There was an atmosphere of uncertainty and fear in the air. It was generally rumoured that the tanks would go in that night. There could be absolute carnage around the White House. Vera, Kostya and Volodin were staying there overnight. Elena was alarmed for their safety. When we went to bed, I could not sleep. At 2am, I heard the sound of many tanks driving down Leningradski. I hoped that Vera and the two boys would be all right.

The next morning, I left Elena at the flat to travel to the Mezh'. I was going to leave Moscow if possible. I could not stay there forever. Before I went, I promised Elena that if the coup had succeeded, then no matter how long it took, I would return. She waved me goodbye, as I stepped into the lift. I could see that she was crying.

The city was now deadly quiet. There was hardly anybody on the streets. Only a few vehicles were using the roads. You would have thought that a nuclear bomb had gone off and that the few of us above surface were the only survivors. At the Mezh' I went to the comms room and watched as C.N.N. showed pictures of people disabling tanks. They jammed large pieces of concrete into the vehicle tracks as the tanks drove by. Or, they had a tarpaulin sheet laying on the ground. As the tank reached it, a man either side would lift it, blinding the crew by covering their observation hatches. I noticed that the shots had been taken during the night and were being rerun on a continual loop. I also recognised where the pictures had been taken. On the Garden Ring, near the American Embassy.

I went out to my truck, started it and then drove out of Moscow. The streets were deserted. The pavements were empty. It was a ghost town. Reaching the outskirts of the city and the road to Smolensk, I got out of the cab and took one long look at Moscow. Climbing back into the cab I drove away, vowing to return.

24

Back to the Future

THE basic story of the coup was that a group of eight hard line Communist Party bosses were not happy about Gorbachev withdrawing the Russian Army from occupying the Eastern European satellite nations. It was also organised to stop Gorbachev's plan of giving sovereignty to first Kazakhstan and then all of the other Soviet republics. They envisaged that these were the first steps in the break-up of the U.S.S.R., the end of communism in Russia and the loss of their personal power. They had Gorbachev and his wife Raisa placed under house arrest at their holiday home by the Black Sea. They then tried to seize power in Moscow.

Having left Moscow, I headed for Minsk, where I parked for the night at the motel. When I got there I was told by Sergei, the duty spiv, that the coup had failed and was over. Gorbachev had flown back to Moscow and taken back control of the country.

So I knew that everything was O.K. and I would be returning to Moscow soon. Life did not look so bad.

★

At the Kremlin, in Moscow, it was business as usual. Gorbachev immediately spoke to the Western leaders. He told them that if they did not help him, financially, then there would be another coup and he would lose power. If that happened and the communists won, there would be a return to the Cold War and the threat to peace. This of course, would cost the West a fortune for rearmament. There then began a massive drive by the West to supply Russia with goods. This was to convince the Russian people that Gorbachev was improving their lives, then they would not want a return to communism.

Kepstowe Freight drew up plans to ensure that they benefited from this upsurge in trade. They increased the number of vehicles that they were running and took on more subcontractors to carry the goods. They also began to send unaccompanied trailers by ship to Turku in Finland. These trailers were collected by Finnish and Sovtransavto trucks and delivered in Russia. This upsurge in Kepstowe's operations meant that I benefited directly as it guaranteed me consistent work.

Happy with the news Sergei had given me in Minsk that things were back to normal, I went to Poland and loaded frozen strawberries at Torun. Although the strawberries were destined for England, I had to divert to Hamburg on the way back. Here, the company that was selling the strawberries took samples from the load to check them for radiation. Poland was contaminated by the nuclear fallout from the Chernobyl nuclear accident of 1986. Satisfied that the radiation level was low enough for human consumption, they sent me onward to deliver the cargo in Great Yarmouth.

After tipping the strawberries in Great Yarmouth, I dropped the fridge trailer off at the rental company in Slough. In exchange, I collected a tilt trailer that Kepstowe loaded for Kiev and Moscow. As soon as it was loaded I set off for Ukraine. I arrived in Kiev, where I was delivering the part consignment to a new customer. I parked at my usual spot outside the library. Once again, the Ukrainian nationalists were demonstrating in support of independence at Kreshatik Square. Their blue and yellow flags, the colours of the Ukrainian flag, were waving everywhere.

The next morning, I drove to the customer's warehouse in the suburbs of Kiev. Here I met Mark, an English, ex-City of London trader who had set up a business importing cosmetics into Ukraine. Up until this time it had been impossible for average Ukrainian women to purchase these items. He was bringing in the kind of products that you would buy in a pound shop back home. I delivered his freight and then drove off, heading for Moscow.

Arriving at our apartment block, I rode up in the lift and rang the doorbell of our flat. Elena opened the door and I said "*Vot Ya* [here I am]," seeing myself as the dashing hero returning, as I had promised. She looked at me for a moment and then burst out laughing.

And they say that romance is dead, eh?

After a couple of days in Moscow, I set out for London, where I discovered that my next trip was once more to Ukraine. However, it was not just to Ukraine, it was for five destinations within Ukraine: Kiev, Poltava, Jolty Voda, Dnepropetrovsk and

Nikolayev. Once again I headed for Kiev, but only got as far as Kukariki when the whole trip came to a shuddering halt.

Firstly, I had to endure a 36-hour queue to actually get into the border. Once inside, I discovered that Jolty Voda, Nikolayev and even Dnepropetrovsk were all closed cities. As far as the Soviet authorities were concerned, I could not go to any of them.

I spent five tedious days stuck on the border while they deliberated the situation. Then they came up with a solution. I would deliver to Kiev and then go to Poltava, where I would unload the goods for Dnepropetrovsk and Jolty Voda as well. Then I would go to Odessa and be escorted by the K.G.B. to Nikolayev.

The goods for Kiev were cheap deodorants for Mark's business. I tipped them and then went to Poltava, where I was kept waiting around for another five days until I could unload. What I could not understand was why I could not go to Dnepropetrovsk. The goods were for the tractor factory and I had already delivered there.

Having been warned that I would be sitting around, I did no more than to book in to the Sovinter' hotel. The receptionist wanted me to pay in hard currency, however, I told her that I only had Roubles. Paying in Roubles, I saved myself £80. When I unloaded the goods, the people from Dnepropetrovsk, who had been forced to travel to Poltava to collect their consignment, criticised me for refusing to go to their factory. The staff at Poltava told them that it had not been my decision, but I do not think that Dnepr' believed it. Having unloaded in Poltava, I drove the 500 miles to Odessa, over the course of the following two days. At Odessa, I parked at an industrial estate where I was to meet my K.G.B. escort.

The escort, a K.G.B. major, arrived in a red Lada Zhiguli. We set out for Nikolayev straight away. At the entrance to Nikolayev I was pulled over by the local police, who wanted to stop me from entering the city. However, the major drove back and ordered them to let me pass. We drove into the city and stopped outside of the Okean shipyard. The shipyard built warships for the Soviet Navy. That was why Nikolayev was a closed city. While waiting in front of the shipyard to unload, the whole of the Nikolayev English language translation team was paraded and I was introduced to each of them. I passed along the line, shaking hands and chatting to each one. I felt like a dignitary, meeting the teams, before a cup final.

Once the goods had been unloaded, I followed my escort back out of the city and we drove back to Odessa. I stopped the night at the industrial estate and it was arranged that he would take me into Odessa the next morning to make a phone call.

At the arranged time he had not arrived. Nor had he, an hour later. So, I drove into the city myself and found the P.T.T. office. My next move was meant to be to reload wine from Moldova for the U.K. However, when I contacted the exporter in Moldova they informed me that the consignment would not be ready for two weeks. I must admit that the thought of sitting in Moldova for a fortnight after all of the wasted time on this trip filled me with about as much excitement as the thought of pulling out my own fingernails. I needed to phone Kepstowe, but the waiting time for a call to London would be two days. So

I left the P.T.T. What I needed was to find a hotel with immediate phone access to the U.K. Outside the P.T.T. I met my K.G.B. escort, who was looking for me. Having explained my problem to him, he took me to a hotel and I telephoned London. They told me to drive to Moscow, where they had an exhibition load that I could collect.

I parted company with my escort, but not before he had sold me two cartons of Marlboro and changed $50 into Roubles. So much for the K.G.B. being guardians of the state's moral standards.

Arriving back in Moscow, I made my way home. Elena and I sat in the edge of the bed, talking about what had happened during the previous four weeks, while I had been away from Moscow. Then, she suddenly pointed down to the area of my groin and pronounced, "*Mi-Yi-Kee*. He is a '*ooligan!*"

I did not understand what she meant and looked at her quizzically. Slowly and deliberately she said, "Mickee, I is pregnant!"

Automatically I replied, questioningly, "You are pregnant?" but she thought that I was correcting her English.

"OK," she said, "I are pregnant."

"I am pregnant," I responded, correcting her again.

"No Mickee," she said, "You is not pregnant, I are pregnant."

I looked into her face and said, "That is fantastic. I am so pleased."

She asked, "You don't mind?" A worried look upon her face.

"Of course not," I replied, smiling widely.

★

We spent the next two days arranging for Elena to travel to England for a holiday. We went to the British Embassy, where we organised her visa. This took two days.

In order to obtain the visa, I had to supply an invitation letter, stating that I would cover all of her costs and accommodation in England. I also had to convince the jobsworth of an immigration officer that we were not going to the U.K. to get married. I achieved that by pointing out that I was still married in England. When we left the embassy, Elena called her a "*Dura hoy apparatchik* [Stupid f@cking pen pusher]." I agreed.

We also went to the Aeroflot offices and booked her flights. She would fly to the U.K. on the 14th December and back to Moscow on 27th. I then phoned Kepstowe and told Rob that I planned to finish work by 13th December to meet Elena when she arrived at Heathrow.

So, holiday arranged, successfully. Having spent a few days in Moscow, I returned to England.

Reporting to Kepstowe's office, I was summoned by the managing director, Neil Richardson. He was not going to allow me to finish on the 13th December and wanted me to work right up to Christmas so his drivers could start their Christmas break early. However, I convinced him that I should have the time off that I wanted. As I pointed out, I had worked all summer without a break, while his drivers had taken their summer holidays. Also, that I wanted Elena to meet my family before she had our baby. Then there was the point that I would return to Moscow by the New Year holiday, meaning that they had a truck already in Moscow to cover any reload. When I left his office, we were both satisfied with the outcome of the conversation. Well, I was.

To the immense delight of the rest of the Kepstowe office staff, my next load was going to bring me back into contact with the world of the "luvvies". When Rob told me that I was going to be a "luvvie" again, they all fell about laughing and then started to take the mickey.

Of course, I rose above it all and would not bite. Well, except to tell them to "piss off!" Rob also told me that Kepstowe had finalised details to open an office and warehouse facility in Moscow, in the New Year.

"If you are doing that well, does that mean that there is more money in it for me?" I asked.

Rob leaned back in his chair and laughed. He laughed long and hard.

"That's a no then, I take it?" I said.

The next load was to Yalta in the Crimea. I was to deliver for Thames Television, who were shooting the Sharpe's Rifles series. On the way, I had to deliver a small consignment to Mark in Kiev. In addition, I was to be accompanied to Yalta by a small, four-wheeled truck. This was, in fact, a catering wagon.

25

Going on Location

HAVING crossed the Channel, I parked in Zeebrugge and slept. I awoke to find the catering wagon standing in front of my truck. The driver, who I nicknamed Magnet, introduced himself. We set out for Yalta straight away. Well, straight away, after he had made us both some bacon sandwiches in the back of the cook wagon. It turned out that his truck was well-stocked with food.

We drove through Belgium, Holland and Germany, crossing into Poland at Schwedt. Once in Poland, as both of our vehicles were right-hand drive, we had problems overtaking slower moving vehicles. But, I would go out when I saw that it was safe and he would follow me. If I kept my left-hand indicator on, it meant that he was OK to keep coming. If I put my right-hand one on, it meant get back in quickly. If there was a vehicle heading towards us, I would stay out until he was safely in and then I would move back to the right. I was acting as a block for him. We crossed Poland and then came to the back of a 36-hour queue for Kukariki. When I told him, he asked me how I knew that it would be that long. "Experience mate," I replied. "Bitter experience."

It was actually 35 hours. Not a bad guess. It snowed heavily as we waited in the queue. Having completed the border procedure, we slept. Magnet had been amazed when I started talking Russian to the border staff. We left the border and drove to Kiev, where we parked outside the library. My truck was in front of his. During the night I woke up. I threw the curtains back and saw that the street in front of me was deserted. I thought that I was still in the queue at Kukariki. I started the truck and drove off. It was only after I had gone about 100 metres that I realised where I was. I turned around and went back and parked behind Magnet's vehicle. Then I went back to bed.

Obviously, the queues were getting to me and I had to do something about it.

In the morning we drove to Mark's warehouse and then stood in the back of the cook wagon, where we had bacon and egg sandwiches for breakfast. As we were eating, Mark appeared and said, "Bloody hell Mick, what have you got here?" I told him that I had won the lottery and bought the truck, which Magnet drove for me and did the cooking. Mark almost believed me, but I spoiled it by laughing. Magnet, for his part, was getting upset. He wanted to be in Yalta with his workmates and when we found out that I could not tip that day, he was annoyed. The following day, when they told me that I still could not tip, he decided that he was going to go on ahead on his own. I watched him drive out of the industrial estate and I must admit that I was not sorry to see him go.

I had named him Magnet because when we had first met I had told him to keep as close to the back of my trailer as possible. He had taken me at my word. In fact, he had followed so close behind me that when I touched my brake pedal his brake lights came on. During the days that we were together in Kiev I had renamed him "That Whinging Twat".

Eventually, the Ukrainian customs cleared the trailer and Mark's consignment was unloaded. I left Kiev and headed to Poltava, where I stopped for the night. The next day I drove to Yalta, a 450-mile journey. On the way I passed Dnepropetrovsk and Zaporozhye. Crossing on to the Crimea peninsula, I found myself driving over a range of hills that over-looked Yalta. These were the Heights of Yalta, which were described in the Crimean War stories.

When I arrived at Yalta, I found the location that I required. It was set up on the top of the cliffs to the west of Yalta, overlooking the Black Sea. The build-ings were luxurious and set in a manicured landscape. This was a retreat for the Soviet elite. Here they holi-dayed, away from the rigours of running the Soviet Union.

The receptionist on duty in the main building gave me a room key and told me that I could use all the amenities on site. The film crew were away up country shooting and would not be back for three days. I therefore had another wait on my hands. However, unlike Kiev, where the temperature had been hovering around zero, in Yalta, it was 20C. A more enjoyable break this time.

I discovered Magnet working in the main restau-rant building. On his own, after leaving me in Kiev, he had crossed the Ukraine. Near to Kharkov he had come across a tragic scene. He had passed a barricade that the police were clearing from the road. Beside the barricade were two dead people. They had been shot. The Russian police did not cover dead bodies. I had seen many instances where, if there had been a road accident resulting in fatalities, they just laid the corpses beside the road in the open. This was a practice that I was used to from trucking extensively in Yugoslavia during the '70s and '80s. In both countries the attitude to bodies indicated just how cheaply life was regarded. I could tell that Magnet had been seriously affected psychologically by the sight. I also discovered that later, after I had left Yalta, he had suffered a broken ankle and been flown back to the U.K. Not a good trip.

I spent the three days eating well, drinking well and sleeping well. On the fourth day the crew returned from location and I was able to hand in my paperwork so that the customs procedures could be instigated. There was a Russian crew from Mosfilm who were handling the location logistics. They arranged the customs attendance for the following day. After having taken my papers, they told me that the English crew and actors were upstairs having a party.

As I joined them, I was given a bottle of red wine and told to help myself to the buffet. I did. While enjoying the party, I was spoken to by some of the actors. They did not know who I was and thought that I was another actor who had flown in to play a part. They were intrigued when I told them that I had driven the truck out from England. As the little drinking session went on, I spoke to Sean Bean. He asked me if I liked football. He himself is a passionate Sheffield United fan. When I said that I did, he invited me to watch some football videos in the crew bar that evening. So, after dinner, I joined him and the other main actors and we watched tapes of Match of the Day that he had flown out to him every week. Sean and I were sitting next to each other. While we watched the football we talked and I found him to be a very nice guy. He explained how he got into acting having gone to amateur dramatics as a hobby when he first started work. He had really enjoyed it and decided to take it up seriously. We had a great evening in the bar.

The next day, the trailer was unloaded. Once the trailer was empty I set off, heading for Dnepropetrovsk. There was a new contract for goods to be loaded from Dnepropetrovsk and I was to collect the first load. I found the factory late that evening and as I arrived it began to snow. I was not surprised. The temperature in Dnepropetrovsk was 4C.

The load that I was collecting was a full trailer of zinc watering cans and buckets. The Englishman who was importing the items to the U.K. was named Rob. He, like Mark, in Kiev, was an ex-City trader. He had a Ukrainian girl, named Julia, acting as his translator. They eventually married and I was in Dnepr' a couple of weeks before the wedding. I was invited to it, but by the time of the ceremony, I was long gone. Over the following years, I loaded many times from Dnepropetrovsk for Rob. Fortunately, I did not have to go to the tractor factory ever again. Good job. They did not like me any more after the Poltava fiasco, but the women working in the zinc factory liked me. They liked to talk to me about life in England.

Once loaded with watering cans and buckets, I left Dnepr' and headed for Kukariki. I was lucky because I had one of Kepstowe's new trailers, which had a

1,000 litre diesel tank underneath the chassis. I was lucky because at that time there was a diesel shortage in Ukraine. This had been caused by the Russians, who had turned off the supply because of a political dispute. I was also lucky because I was friends with Julia, who worked at the fuel station at Borispol. I gave her little presents and she gave me diesel. So, as I left Dnepr', I was feeling lucky that I did not have to scratch around to find fuel. I had a 700-mile journey across Ukraine ahead of me through potential snowstorms. That was enough to think about without worrying about diesel.

I drove through Ukraine and eventually reached Siedlce, where I swapped trailers. Then I drove to Moscow, tipped and reloaded and set off back to the U.K. I was going back for my Christmas break and Elena's first trip to England.

But before I could start my break, I had to deliver my load of wrapping paper from Tula to the importers premises in Bristol. So I found myself rocking and rolling down the M4. At Bristol I parked outside the importer's warehouse. The next morning when the staff arrived for work the trailer was opened and they discovered that, despite numerous phone calls, Kommunar had sent birthday wrapping paper instead of Christmas paper. Just at Christmas, when they were desperate for as much Christmas paper as they could lay their hands on. I heard the quaint old West Country saying "Four Farks Ache" a number of times.

It was decided that I would take the load to another of their warehouses in a different part of the city. Pulling out of their yard, I had to turn right and climb a very steep hill. I was halfway across the road, when a milk float came rocketing down the hill towards me.

The milkman had obviously knocked it out of gear to get his speed up. The float was coming towards me at at least 40 mph if not 50. Luckily, I got the trailer clear of the other lane just as the float sped past my tractor unit. I heard the long drawn out, Bristolian scream of "Cnuuuuu-ut" as the float careered past and I could physically smell the tang of fear that was coming from the milkman's undergarments. They would need a good industrial strength cleansing if they were ever to be worn again. I decided that this foul-mouthed outburst and unnecessary screaming by the milkman, was merely attention seeking.

26

"And it's Goodbye From Him!"

HAVING tipped the load at Bristol, I returned to London. I dropped the trailer off at Slough and went to Kepstowe's. Here, we reconciled the money that I was owed by them. With a cheque, to pay into the bank, I left and drove to Brighton. I parked the tractor unit in a parking area on the edge of the town, where it would stay for a week. I did not need it while Elena and I stayed with my brother, Chris, and his wife, Jane. The following day, Chris drove me to Heathrow in his car. As we were driving on the M25 we ran into fog, which got progressively worse. By the time we reached the airport you could not see your hand in front of your face. Arriving in the terminal, we discovered that all flights had been cancelled. All incoming flights were being diverted, but Aeroflot did not know where Elena's flight was. They could not even tell us if it had left Moscow.

Chris asked, "How can they lose a bloody great plane?"

I didn't know, but they obviously had.

Reliably informed by B.A.A. information that the plane would not land at Heathrow that day, we returned to Chris' house in Brighton. That evening,

Elena rang us to inform us that her plane had actually landed in Brussels and that all the passengers were being put up, free of charge, in a luxury hotel. The flight would fly to Heathrow the next morning. So, the following day we returned to Heathrow and this time we successfully collected her from arrivals.

Elena and I spent a week with Chris and Jane before driving to Great Yarmouth in my truck. We drove to my mother's shop, where we stayed with her and my stepfather over Christmas. As part of the Christmas celebrations we were looking forward to The Two Ronnies on the T.V. Their catchphrase at the end of the show being, of course, "And it's goodnight from me and it's goodnight from him".

On Christmas Day afternoon, when the news came on the B.B.C. we were amazed to see pictures of Mikael Gorbachev beamed live from the Kremlin in Moscow. Gorbachev announced calmly that the Soviet Union was dissolved with immediate effect and no longer existed. He also announced that he resigned with immediate effect as secretary general of the Soviet Union. We sat there confused and shocked, especially Elena. She had arrived in Great Yarmouth as a Soviet citizen. Now, following Gorbachev's pronouncement, she was a Russian citizen, only.

Still, as I said; "That's Great Yarmouth, for you."

On Boxing Day, we drove to Stanwell Moor, near Heathrow. This was where Kepstowe's Pete Newlyn lived. We stopped the night with Pete and then he drove us to the airport. Having seen Elena off, at departures, I drove my truck to Kepstowe's, where there was a tilt trailer waiting for me destined for Moscow. The plan now was that I would drive to Moscow and that Elena and I would spend New Year's Eve with Kostya and Elena, as we had done the previous year. I hooked up my truck to the trailer. The paperwork and my money were in the back of the trailer, so I retrieved them. Then I set out for Dover.

My plan for getting to Moscow in time for the New Year celebrations was simple. To get to Berlin on the 28th. Siedlce on the 29th. Smolensk on the 30th and to arrive in Moscow on New Year's Eve afternoon. But we all know about plans.

On the first day, instead of making Berlin, I hit heavy snowfall in Germany. This persisted all the way to Hannover, where I called it a night. On the second day, the snow was even worse and with interminable delays on the Berlin ring road I only made it as far as the border at Frankfurt Oder. Having cleared the border, I parked up to sleep. I was unwilling to drive into Poland at night because of the black ice situation.

Leaving the border the following morning, I soon came across the scene of a fatal accident. An unmarked Dutch truck, which had left the border during the early hours, had crashed. As I slowly passed the scene, I could see that the driver was still behind the wheel of the truck. He was quite clearly dead.

The Polish police, in attendance at the scene, were in no obvious hurry to remove his body and they would not allow me to stop. I may have been able to help out and contact his company from Poznan.

I pushed on, crossing Poland. However, the snow that had stopped during the night picked up again between Poznan and Warsaw. I battled on, but only made it to Siedlce. I left there the following morning, crossed into the ex-Soviet Union and struggled towards Moscow.

At midnight Moscow time, I was passing the police post at Orsha. No New Year's Eve party for me.

The police officer on duty pulled me over, but only to wish me a Happy New Year. The policeman at the Russian post just up the road did the same. However, he also warned me that the road ahead was very icy. The gritting crews were not working. I went on to the restaurant, just past the police post, and parked for the night.

When I had gone to bed I had switched off the truck. In the morning I discovered that overnight the temperature had plummeted from -5C to -18C. The truck only just managed to start, but with the Thermoline switched on the faltering diesel flow increased to its normal rate and the truck ran well again. I pulled off the restaurant parking area and headed for Moscow. Now that it was too late, the snow had stopped falling.

Arriving in Moscow, I drove to the flat. Here I had to unload the clothes that Elena had bought in Brighton as well as my gear. There were also the baby provisions that I had bought. As I had decided that our baby, when it came, would have all the benefits of English products, I was spending my downtime in London trawling Mothercare and Boots. I was amassing baby milk, bottles, sterilising equipment, nappies, etc. Of course, as soon as I began to unload everything from the cab of the truck, it began to snow. I certainly hoped that, when it came, the baby would appreciate the effort that I had made upon its behalf.

Elena and I spent the extended New Year holiday together and then I tipped the trailer at V.D.N.K. Having reloaded from Tula, I set out for England. However, I still remembered the night in Kiev where

I had jumped up and driven off, imagining that I was still in the queue at the border. Therefore, instead of making for Kukariki, I drove to another Belarus–Polish border, near Grodno. I had not used Grodno before, but wanted to test it out. I wanted to see whether it would be a quicker crossing than Kukariki, where you now had to queue for more than 24 hours to leave Belarus and enter Poland.

Leaving Moscow, I drove to Minsk, where I spent the night; not at the motel, which was on the south-west outskirts of the city, but at a police post on the western edge. The next day I drove to Grodno. Having passed through the town, I soon came to the border complex.

Set in a dip in the ground, it appeared that the site was in a bowl. Strangely, the Sovinteravtoservice office was not situated within the complex alongside the custom buildings and gantries. It was at the side of the road outside. You carried out the Sovinter' procedure before you were admitted through the main gate. Another peculiarity was that the border was only open for truck traffic during daylight hours. This was due to the fact that, although the border complex had full, electrical power, the Sovinter' wooden hut did not. Therefore, they could not process trucks in the dark. Having learned the process at the border and completed the formalities, I drove out into Poland.

The first major town in Poland after crossing at Grodno was Bialystok. While transiting the town I passed a motel. Stopping, I checked it out and discovered that they had a telex as well as direct international telephone facilities. It was ideal as a replacement for the Hetmann motel at Siedlce. From Bialystok I drove to Warsaw. Entering Warsaw from the north-east, I transited the centre of the city and emerged in the west. Satisfied with the route to and from Grodno and knowing where I could make contact with both London and Moscow, I drove westward, heading for England.

27

The Full 1,790 Miles

MOSCOW to London, via Grodno, was a total distance of 1,790 miles and for the first five months of 1992, I was trekking back and forwards, along that route. Occasionally, I changed trailers in Poland, but usually I drove all the way back to the U.K. I think that this was because Kepstowe, aware that the baby was coming, wanted to ensure that I could stock up with supplies ready for the birth. Once the baby was born they kept me in Moscow and on shunts to Poland for most of the time. This was to give me as much time at home with my new child as was possible. Kepstowe treated me well and I repaid them by working hard upon their behalf.

Besides seeing me clocking up thousands of miles, the beginning of 1992 also saw Kepstowe open the Moscow office at Octopus. This was situated in the south-east of the city, in an area known as Aviamotornaya.

Octopus, who were a German–Russian Joint Venture, owned an office and warehouse complex. Kepstowe rented an office and use of the warehouse. Importantly, the warehouse was heated, which proved critical during the winter. Temperature-sensitive cargo, such as Kodak's printing chemicals, could be kept from freezing during the periods of bitterly cold weather. The opening of the office meant that Kepstowe vehicles no longer needed to park at the Mezh'.

The parking along the Krasnaya Presnaya embankment was becoming crowded as more trucks were engaged running freight from the west into Moscow. This intensified when the east European trucks that had always previously parked outside the Ukraina hotel on the opposite west bank of the river were banned from that area. They moved across to the Mezh'–Krasnaya Presnaya part of the embankment, swamping the area.

Their incursion on to the east bank caused the end of the parking there because they began to behave exactly as they had done outside the Ukraina; using the locality as a toilet, leaving piles of rubbish, worn vehicle tyres and parts strewn about, and running their engines day and night. This had caused the residents of the Kutovsky area on the opposite river bank to complain to the authorities and those residents were important people; politicians, top brass from the military and foreign diplomats.

Once settled on the Krasnaya Presnaya embankment and not having learned their lesson, they did the same thing. Complaints from those running the Mezh' and the exhibition ground then led to parking on the K.P. embankment being banned. That was with the exception of trucks attending the exhibitions.

As everybody then looked for somewhere else to park, the Kepstowe trucks and the subbies had Octopus available to them. I parked either at Octopus, or at home, whichever suited what I was doing.

The office at Octopus was run by Mark Hughes, who had moved out from London permanently. He was assisted by Paul, a New Zealander, who had been driving a seven-and-a-half tonner for Kepstowe in the U.K. They were joined by Marina, from Klyazma. They had poached her from Xerox.

The Kepstowe fleet of vehicles had increased from four to seven and they now had a host of new subbies running for them, through Alan Johnson. In addition, they were beginning to ship more unaccompanied trailers from Harwich to Turku, in Finland, which were then brought to Moscow by either Finnish trucks, or Sovtransavto vehicles. Kepstowe were doing well out of the boom in the Russian market and consequently so was I.

As I lived in the city, the lack of amenities that struck the other drivers did not affect me. Parking at Octopus, they were miles from the city centre and therefore it was difficult to take advantage of the city night spots. Sometimes Mark and Paul used to run them into the city if they wanted to go, but they then had to get a taxi back. On the other hand, I used to go out socialising with Elena separately from this ex-pat community. Occasionally we would meet them in town, but as her pregnancy developed these occasions became few and far between.

The boom in Russia actually spawned some new places to go to for an evening. There was the opening of an Irish bar, on Kallinina, and an American bar, near to the Mezh'. The Irish bar was on the first floor over the top of a Russian supermarket. The owners were the Irish company that ran the duty free shop at Sheremetyevo. They were given permission to open it as long as they provided a supermarket for Russians.

This was the ground floor establishment, where you could pay in Roubles. The bar upstairs was part of a hard currency shop. To be honest, it was like drinking in Tesco, but with less atmosphere.

In comparison, the Texan Bar was a free-standing wooden shack. That is to say, that it was free standing until it burnt to the ground. The Americans who owned the Texas Bar, in a show of outrage and bravado, defied the Russian Mafia and would not pay protection money. Not long afterwards they had nothing to protect anyway. The bar was torched.

In early March 1992, I left Moscow in the company of Pete Newlyn and Mike Mudie. Pete was driving his Kepstowe truck and Mike, who had since left Croome, was now an owner-driver, running an old Volvo F12. We headed into Russia to the town of Tambov. We were delivering equipment for a dust free room to a telephone factory.

While unloading at the factory we noticed that a vast crowd of people, who were meant to be working, merely spent their time standing around and watching our activities. Mike and I had to strip our trailers so that our goods could be unloaded through the roof by a mobile crane.

The Russian office worker who they had allocated to us as an interpreter spoke less English than I spoke Russian. However, she explained that because in Russia there had to be full employment, everybody within the town and surrounding area had a job at the factory. This led to massive overmanning. Basically there were three people for every job. So they took it in turns to do the job. I wondered whether that would catch on in England? However, this overstaffing problem was going to contribute to some serious problems within the ex-Soviet Union soon afterwards.

Back in Moscow after the Tambov trip, Micky Packham and I loaded exhibition returns from Krasnaya Presnaya. We set off westwards and I introduced him to the border at Grodno.

Although when we arrived there was a short queue of trucks, it was nothing like the mayhem at Kukariki. We queued for six hours and were then at the front. He was impressed. However, we did not get into the border that night and went in first thing in the morning. However, when the truck control officer inspected our trucks, it was a disaster. He discovered that the customs at Moscow had not crimped the seals correctly. The departure office number was illegible. He presented us with two alternatives. Return to Moscow, a trip of 620 miles, each way, or drive to Brest and go through Kukariki. A distance of 390 miles. We chose to go to Kukariki, but knew that we would be going to join the back of a minimum 24-hour queue.

He could have merely opened the trailers, checked the goods and resealed the trailers. We could have then driven directly into Poland. But he was too lazy to do his job properly. Before we left Grodno, Micky managed to get himself banned from the Grodno border.

Having completely ruined our trip, the officer, who spoke a little English and kept using the phrase "Stand by gents," when he meant "Wait here", wished us a cheery but very false "Goodbye gents. Have a good trip."

I presume that it was the officer's false sarcastic

cheerfulness linked to his insincere sneering smile that annoyed my mate so much. He really wound Mick up and my colleague did no more than go extremely red in the face and scream "F@ck off" at him, at the top of his voice.

This got him banned because the officer, though obviously not knowing that you said, "Wait here" instead of "Stand by gents", definitely understood "F@ck off". I, who had said nothing, was not banned. I mean, I had only laughed (For about ten minutes solid).

We drove to Brest and, as predicted, came to the back of a 24-hour queue. We queued throughout the night, catnapping over the wheel as the queue slowly moved forwards. In the morning, we were sitting in Mick's truck, tired but laughing and joking.

He had his C.B. on and suddenly we picked up the voice of a Welsh lad named Martin, who was a ham radio operator broadcasting from Swansea. Mick talked to him for a while, but the boy was not too quick on the uptake. Having been told time and again that we were British truck drivers sitting on the ex-Soviet–Poland border, he kept thinking that we were bus drivers, for some reason. When Martin ended the transmission and having been told, many times, that we were truck drivers, he said to Micky, "So tell me Mick, while you are sitting on the border in the queue for so long what happens to your passengers?"

"What passengers?" Micky asked, mystified.

"The passengers from your bus," Martin replied.

Micky's face went as red as a post box and he screamed into the mic, "F@ck off, you F@cking stupid Cnut!"

Well dear reader, having lived an extremely sheltered life, I can assure you that I was both shocked and appalled. And also rendered helpless, with uncontrollable laughter.

By mid-June, with Grodno having become almost as bad as Kukariki. I had now shifted my border crossing point to Kaliningrad. This was the main town and seaport in what was an outpost of the Russian Federation, situated on the Baltic Sea. Much further West than Grodno, I had to drive through Lithuania to get there. This added another 100 miles to my trip each way. However, this border was deserted every time that I used it. No queues at all. I could pass through it in less than thirty minutes. The time saved was immense.

With my baby due any day in Moscow, I set out for England accompanied by Pete Newlyn and two drivers, who were both named Kevin. The two Kevs were double-driving a truck for Euro-Movement. I led them to Kaliningrad and we crossed the border into Poland at Bagrationovsk. Having crossed the border we stopped at the first Polish town, Bartoszyce. There we bought strawberries in a local shop. We were going to have strawberries with Russian champagne that evening, for a treat.

Pete and I set off again, but the two Kevs left a while after us. Having driven through a wooded area I heard Pete, who was following me, shout over the C.B. that a Polish van had cut him up overtaking on a blind bend in the woods. When the van came up behind me I kept weaving across the road so that he could not pass. Pete came up from the rear, got alongside the van and then threw his truck over to the right. The Polish van driver, with nowhere to go, had to take to the fields. There was a massive cloud of dust as he went cross-country. He had just managed to get his van back on to the road when the Kevs passed him. Having heard on the C.B. what had happened, they did no more than cut him up themselves. Once again he took up rallycross with his van, raising another massive cloud of dust and debris into the air. Hopefully that taught him his lesson, but I doubt it.

Having left Poland, we were crossing Germany and pulled on to Herford Services to phone Kepstowe and have some lunch. Pete went into the phone box and was talking to Rob. As he was finishing the call, I asked him to ask Rob what I was doing next. He came off the phone and said, "Rob says that you will probably be getting pissed because you have had a little, baby daughter, in Moscow." He then very warmly and genuinely congratulated me. I was ecstatic.

When we arrived in Dover there were instructions for me to leave my trailer there, so that I did not lose time with custom clearance. I drove straight to London and picked up another trailer that was waiting for me. Within no time I was back on the road to Dover and then onwards to Russia.

When I arrived in Moscow, Elena and our baby, Margarita, were still in the hospital. New mothers were kept in for seven days at that time. However, I could not go to the hospital. Vera explained to me that in Russian maternity hospitals men were not allowed on the premises. Giving birth was women's work and for women only. If you wanted to see your baby, you had to stand outside and hope that your wife could get to a window with your child. You could then see them, but from a great distance. I wondered what they would have thought of fathers being present at the birth, which happened in England. But I did not have to go to the hospital, or to wait too long. I had got back to Moscow the night before they were coming home.

The next morning, I drove to Octopus, where I was told to drop the trailer off and get home, as soon as possible. The Kepstowe staff at Octopus gave me a card and presents for my daughter. I did as I was told and got home just before Vera returned from collecting Elena and Margarita by taxi. For the first time, I held my tiny little baby daughter in my arms. She was beautiful.

At Octopus, Mark had told me to take the next two weeks off so that I could be at home with my new baby and Elena. We spent the fortnight organising feeds and changing nappies, all the fun things that you do with a new baby. We were also visited by numerous guests and had minor, little parties. At the end of the two weeks, I went back to work, expecting to be sent back and forwards to England. However, Kepstowe had now arranged my work so that I either remained in Moscow shunting trailers, or travelled only as far as Poland, normally to change over at Siedlce. This was a bit awkward because I was not using Kukariki. I returned to using Grodno, where the traffic that had been building up towards the level at Kukariki had virtually disappeared. This was due in part to the extra diesel cost used bypassing Kukariki that the East Europeans did not want to pay and partly because the Grodno border was not open at night for trucks. From Grodno I would drive down to Warsaw and then on to Siedlce. Having changed trailers, I would then drive back to Grodno. I was going nowhere near Kukariki, where the queues were getting even worse; 48 hours minimum going in and 36 hours coming back out.

I spent the rest of 1992 not trucking any further west from Moscow than Poland. That was except for once and I was perfectly happy. So was Elena and I think that Margarita was, too. Well, she smiled a lot, but that may have just been wind!

I did make one trip to England, in October, to set up the truck for the coming winter. I had new tyres fitted all round and brand new batteries. The truck was also serviced. This was all carried out by Channel Commercials and was part of the terrific service that they gave me over my time trucking Russia. Nothing was too much trouble for them.

Also, while on this trip, I met up with a friend of mine, John Marshall. John told me that if I wanted to take a holiday and bring Elena and Margarita to England, he would drive my truck for me. That way the truck would still be earning. However, I think it was really because he fancied making a trip to Moscow, but didn't want to risk his own truck to do it.

Before 1992 ended, we had Margarita christened in a Russian Orthodox Church in the north of Moscow. Her godparents were little Elena and Kostya. At the same time, they had their newborn son, Anton, christened and Elena and I were his godparents. The ceremony was quite interesting, with a main priest and a choir of young trainee priests. They did not sing hymns, as is the case in Western churches. They sang chants, with intricate harmonies. The church itself was fascinating, with walls covered in icons; the ancient, religious paintings. The ceilings were highly decorated, with religious friezes.

28

None of My Business, Either

THE year 1992 was a fascinating time because the Russians went ahead with some very interesting reforms to drive the country towards capitalism. The West had supplied Russia with billions of U.S. dollars in finance, so that they could set up a viable banking system. Yeltsin decreed that all businesses were now no longer state owned. They passed instead into the hands of the company directors. Under the Soviet system, companies did not have to make a profit. Now, freed from state control, they did. A theory that most of the directors did not comprehend.

Locally, the Mayor of Moscow, Yuri Lushkov, announced that all legal tenants of the capital's properties now owned those properties. Basically, this was everybody because up until that time every property within the country was state owned. The flat that we lived in, therefore, fell into Vera's ownership because she was the legal tenant.

With the privatisation of all the Soviet businesses came the issue of a 50 Rouble voucher to every Russian citizen. They could invest this in any business that they wanted. Margarita received one too, even though she was only a few months old. I suggested to

Vera and Elena that they invest in a major company, such as Sovtransavto or Aeroflot. But instead, they invested in a company that promised an annual interest rate of more than 20%. It was, of course, a scam. Within a short while, the company closed and those running it disappeared with all the depositor's money. This was to become a depressingly regular occurrence as Russians were routinely conned out of their money by such scams.

One of these scams was perpetrated by a company called A.O. M&M. They set up a major scheme, advertising on T.V and in the papers. They guaranteed to pay investors 20% per month on their investment. Hundreds of thousands of people invested with them. If you put in 100 Roubles say, then a month later you could get 120 Roubles back. Or, leave it in and each month it would increase at 20%. I knew that this company could not be investing that money anywhere themselves that would give them back enough of a return for them to do this. They were paying out the initial investors from the money that they received when new investors joined the scheme. It was unsustainable. After a year or so, the Russian government closed down the company just as it was about to go bust. However, thousands of Russian people took to the streets to protest over the closure. They did not understand that it could not continue to make them money.

The company directors fled abroad with the loot. All except for one who was left behind to take the blame. However, he stood for parliament and with the popularity of A. O. M&M behind him was elected. As a member of parliament he was immune from prosecution and therefore got away with it.

A. O. M&M's T.V. advertisements showed that by investing with them you could end up with a fur coat, a Rolls-Royce and a flat in Paris. The only people who ended up with those were the board of directors of M&M.

This Gangster Capitalism was endemic. Some of the newly privatised companies swindled their employees. They set up a second company and sold their products to it instead of their original customers, but they sold to their puppet company at a fraction of the price paid by their real customers. Then, the puppet company sold the goods to the original customer at the real price. The directors of the manufacturing company pocketed the profit.

However, they told the employees that as they were not getting so much money for the product, the staff would have to work for nothing, or lose their jobs. Many employees did, with the promise of pay when the market improved.

Some Russians went into business with Western companies, which invested money into the product. The Russian company then got rid of the Western company and kept their money. The Russian government introduced a 60% import tax. This greatly increased the price of any imports. However, they failed to set up a realistic income tax regime. Under the communist system, as the state was paying everyone's wages, they had not needed to collect income tax. This left a vacuum in state finances and they were soon unable to afford to pay the wages of state employees, such as teachers, or to pay people's pensions.

It was in these circumstances that Russian friends of mine asked whether I intended to set up a business or invest in Russia. Taking the actions of the Mafia into account as well, I told them no. I had my own trucking business that was registered in Britain and I paid British tax. That was enough for me. Russia's Gangster Capitalism was of no interest to me whatsoever. Neither did I want to apply for Russian citizenship for myself, which Elena had suggested. However, even without Russian citizenship I voted in three elections in Moscow.

I was not entitled to do so, obviously, being English. However, I did not allow that small legality to stop me. We voted in a local school hall. It was very similar to the voting centres in England; people sitting at a desk handing out voting slips as you registered; a row of curtained booths, in which to mark your ballot paper; a large metal box where you placed the ballot paper once you had completed it. The place was as drab as any polling station I had used in England.

One election was for the *Duma*, the Russian parliament, and the other two were for local councillors. On the first occasion, Elena took me along to see how voting was carried out in Moscow and then for a joke allowed me to mark her ballot paper, while we were in the voting booth. I then posted the voting slip into the ballot box. On the other two occasions I think that she just could not be bothered herself and once she obtained her ballot paper left it up to me entirely. Well, by then I knew the system. The strange thing was that no one seemed to object, probably because vote rigging is rife in Russia anyway.

So in my own inimitable way, I probably helped to launch the political career of a member of the *Duma*; or wrecked the careers of some aspiring Russian politicians.

There was that old joke about the communist one state, one party, Soviet Union, that, "The first Conservative member of Parliament for Moscow South East has just taken his seat. It is in a prison cell in a Gulag prison camp in Siberia".

That may have been where I would have ended up had some sharp-eyed apparatchik discovered that I was voting illegally in their elections, although I could have voted legally if I had have become a Soviet citizen as Elena had suggested. However, the drawback to that was that I would have to renounce my British citizenship. She could not for the life of her understand why I laughed so uproariously when she proposed that.

Then again, I almost achieved Russian citizenship one night at Bryansk.

I had stopped at a kiosk in the centre of the town to buy some cigarettes. The guy behind the counter then asked me whether I wanted to buy a Russian passport. Just like that. No preamble. I considered the proposition. Obviously, it had been stolen for a start.

What was in it for me? As far as I could see, nothing. Well, nothing other than a long jail term if I was caught with it. And that was highly likely because standing beside me there were two uniformed police officers, drinking vodka while on duty.

The kiosk worker showed me the passport. The photograph looked nothing like me. The age was wrong. And the original holder was a woman. This bloke behind the kiosk counter was probably the world's worst criminal. Or – and much more likely – a complete and utter f@cking idiot!

29

Paying the Bill

I spent Christmas '92 and New Year '92–93 in Moscow. I had to work on Christmas Day unloading a trailer at Sofin's depot. Monday, the 28th, which was a Bank Holiday in the U.K. saw me reloading from Kommunar's at Tula. Then, I was finished until Monday, 4th January. New Year's Eve, we spent in the flat. Elena cooked a roast dinner, which we ate at midnight while watching the fantastic firework display. From our flat, looking eastwards across the north of Moscow, we could see the displays from four of the launching sites. We toasted in the New Year and then Elena began the marathon task of phoning all her friends, to wish them "*S'novum Godum*".

The New Year holiday over, I was soon back at work. Having the office in Octopus running my operation, I was much better informed as to what I would be doing and when. This gave me the opportunity to plan ahead regarding social activities and work. For example, when I was going to do a shunt to Poland this was normally planned so that I left Moscow on a Monday. Then, all things being equal, I could be back in Moscow on the Friday. I would then have the weekend off and start again on Monday, tipping and shunting for the week. My shunting in Moscow did not confine me to that city alone. I began to run to destinations such as Razan, Orel, Voronezh and Tver. This meant that I made the acquaintance of a much wider number of police officers.

As my truck was one of only a few right-hand drive that ran to Russia, the police were at a bit of a loss. When they stopped my vehicle they automatically went to the nearside and would bang on the cab door. I sat on the opposite side and eventually would shout to them, "*Droogee strana* [Other side]." They would walk around the truck and if I was sat with the door open, would look into the cab, see where the steering wheel was positioned and ask why the truck had the steering column on that side. I would tell them that my boss (*nachalnik*) had done it because he did not like me and wanted to make things difficult for me. That was basically true. I was my boss and I had bought a right-hand drive truck.

Now I would not say that the Russian Old Bill were not too bright. They weren't, but I would not say it. They kept making the mistake about which side the steering wheel was on. One, seeing the column on the right, but unable to see across the cab, thought that I had a steering wheel either side and then chose which side to drive. Another was banging away at the passenger door and when I had finally convinced him to come round to the driver's door, asked me where the driver was. I told him that the driver was on the bunk, fast asleep and that the truck actually drove itself. He believed me.

Then, of course, there was the situation with the fines, for minor or spurious speeding offences. Although, I hardly ever got stopped by then, I did get the occasional tug for *boostera bee-yadesh* (speeding). The line of living in Moscow still continued to work and, of course, by then, it was true. So, I paid the minimal fines, with them thinking that I was paid low Russian wages. One day, driving near Minsk, I was stopped by the police and shown a newspaper headline. This stated that Belarus was going to double the amount of fines imposed upon foreign drivers. So, the fine for speeding would go from 10 Deutschmarks, (£4), to 20 Deutschmarks, (£8). He then fined me 2 Roubles, which was 4p.

One day I was speeding along the motorway between Borisov and Minsk when I was caught by a roadside radar trap. I decided not to stop as it was a chilly day and I did not want to stand out in the cold arguing the toss with the Old Bill. So, I floored the accelerator and increased the speed from 60 to 70mph. The Old Bill jumped into their beaten up Lada Zhiguli, flicked on the blue lights and gave hot pursuit. Hot being the right description.

Flying along, I could see their blue light, which was basically flickering as opposed to flashing, way back behind me. They were not catching me but were keeping pace. Eventually, I got bored and pulled over. I waited a while for them to arrive and when they did the car pulled to a halt, with steam and smoke billowing out of it. They had flogged it to death. You could hear from the bag of nails sound that the engine was producing that the car had completely had it.

For all of their effort they relieved me of 4p for speeding and 4p for not stopping for them.

I wonder how much the new engine for their car cost the Belarus Police. More than 8p probably.

Over my time in Russia and the ex-Soviet Union

I had quite a few laughs with the Russian police, or rather at their expense. However, there was one area where they were not funny. That was in the case of road accidents. Basically, if you were a foreigner and you were involved in an accident, then you were automatically to blame. That meant that you then paid cash for the damage. Virtually no one had motor insurance.

If the Old Bill became involved, you also paid them a fine, which went straight into their pocket. I was involved in two minor accidents in Moscow. One was where, in gridlocked traffic, a car beside me tried to pull to its right and crashed into my nearside wheel. He probably had not seen my small vehicle, sitting, beside him. The other was when an idiot turned across me at a junction, where I was turning right. Both accidents were not my fault. In the first one, I was sat there with my handbrake on not moving. He had moved and he had hit me. The second one was caused by the half-wit, who was in the lane to my left, steering across me and hitting my truck. In both accidents I paid out; $50 a time. The reason was that on both occasions there were police in the vicinity and they were making their way towards the scene. Rather than pay them as well, I coughed up and was then away before they could get their greedy, grubby little fingers, on the cash in my wallet.

As I have said, Yeltsin's policies, ill thought out and disastrous, had left the country unable to afford to pay its government employees. This, no doubt included the police. They therefore obviously decided to abuse their position and power to supplement their wages, or lack of them. But basically, all they were doing was continuing their tradition of corruption. Whether they were better off or not, I do not know. But, I did all I could to ensure they were not any better off at my expense.

The level of corruption, within the whole of the country was illustrated by the activities of the police. If the people responsible for law and order were that bent then it was obviously prevalent at all levels. My understanding of this was that everything was intertwined: the government with the police; the government with the armed forces, etc. Just one complete system of endemic corruption.

30

1993 and all That

TWO immediate disasters occurred during the beginning of 1993. Firstly, on a trip to Poland to swap trailers the truck bringing my new trailer out to me broke down on the stretch of motorway between Poznan and Warsaw. I drove to the services where it was parked. There was heavy snowfall, at the time. The broken down truck belonged to my friend, Fred Stanton, a haulier from the Isle of Sheppey. The truck had developed an engine fault and would not build up any air. Despite the fact that the engine was on its last legs, the driver was continuing to run it to warm his cab. Absolute madness. The second was when I almost broke my arm fitting a trailer up for loading in Moscow.

The Poland incident saw me having to climb under Stanton's tractor unit to manually wind off the brakes, which had seized on. While doing this I was laying in deep, wet snow and was obviously highly amused. The driver did absolutely nothing to assist me and it was by pure chance that my Dutch friend, Arri', who drove for Pickford's B.V, turned up and helped me. We had to tow the tractor from underneath the trailer that I was collecting and then move it back, out of the way of traffic using the service area. As I say, Fred's driver did nothing to help us himself, but I know that he was sacked, upon his return to England.

Unfortunately, Arri' was also sacked on his return to Holland. His manager sacked him for not getting to Moscow in time for his delivery booking. The manager did not have the benefit of seeing how appalling the weather was, as Arri' and I struggled through blizzards to get to Moscow. And having taken him via Grodno we had actually saved somewhere around 40 hours of queueing at Kukariki anyway. Still, that is managers for you. However, that incident highlighted to me how lucky I was to be working for Kepstowe and not hauling for Dutch companies. Dutch companies paid well, but they definitely wanted their kilogram of flesh all right.

The incident with my arm occurred when I drove to the new Bata shoes premises in the east of Moscow. I was leaving the trailer at their site, so they could load it as and when they were ready. I had dropped the trailer and was actually in the back of it putting the roof bars back into place, so that the floor space was clear for loading. Unfortunately, one of the bars would not go into the rubber slots that held it in place. I climbed up and was swinging on the bar, so that my weight forced it down into its receptacle. The temperature at the time was -15C and there were large slabs of ice on the trailer decking. Dropping from the bar, I skidded on a slab of ice and fell backwards, landing on my left arm. The pain was unbelievable and I thought that I had broken it. I then had to drive the truck back across Moscow, through rush hour traffic, to reach home. Then, I could get Elena to take me to the hospital.

The drive across Moscow had been one of excruciating agony. Every pothole that the truck went over sent waves of extreme pain through my arm. As luck would have it, when I arrived at the flat, Vera was at home to babysit Margarita.

When Elena and I finally got to the hospital, I was in uncontrollable agony. I therefore did not appreciate the delay that was caused by the woman receptionist, who could not get her head around my name while she was registering me. It ended up that I was registered as *Mikael, Petrovich, Tvemlov.* This then became one of my aliases. Eventually, I was shown into a consulting room, where once again I found a doctor and his assistant. I was sent for an X-ray. Two old ladies were the radiographers. I was seated by a couch with my arm on the couch ready for the photo to be taken. The X-ray machine had probably been in use since the turn of the century; the 17th century. It was just about clapped out. When the women took the shot, it rumbled, crackled, hissed and reverberated, before finally dying, with a long drawn out wheeze.

The doctor looked at the subsequent X-ray and decided that nothing was broken, other than the X-ray machine, that is. This meant they were not going to plaster the arm. Instead, the assistant took me to another filthy, cobwebbed room, where he spread a substance that looked like marmite and smelled like dog shit all over my left wrist. He then bandaged it tightly, cutting the circulation. With no painkillers or liquid anaesthetic this time, Elena and I soon found ourselves back outside the dingy premises. The doctor had told Elena that I should return in a week's time so they could see how it was progressing. I told Elena that I was not going back to the hospital under any circumstances whatsoever. We then returned to the flat with my arm still agonisingly painful. I got Elena to remove the bandage and wash off all the dog shit that Tonto, the doctor's assistant, had applied to my wrist. I then got her to put on a new bandage and not put it on tightly. The last part of my medical strategy was to self-medicate with a full bottle of Stolichnaya vodka. This produced the desired effect and I went to sleep.

Once I was over this traumatic experience of having what I considered to have been dog shit smeared liberally upon my arm, I returned to work. The first job was to drive to Kineshma, some 250 miles north of Moscow. I was to load rolls of material for Interunity. Gennie and Zoya from Interunity drove there in their Lada to supervise the loading and organise the customs procedure. Having to spend the night there, we were taken to a shabby, filthy hovel, which was described as a hotel. Gennie spent the evening getting pissed on cheap vodka and admitted to me that he was a major in the K.G.B. I was not surprised. All J.V's had K.G.B. on the staff to spy on the goings on. Having loaded the rolls, the next day, I returned to Moscow.

My next trip was another first time to a new destination. I had to head down the M4, south-east of Moscow, to Voronezh. Here I was to load machine tools. I was accompanied on this and subsequent trips by the exporter. He was named Yuri and used to ride in my cab.

Voronezh was 325 miles (520 kilometres) from Moscow and, believe me, it was a good day's work to complete the return trip in a day. But that is what we did. I ran to Voronezh, accompanied by Yuri, probably about 30 times, between early '93 and mid-'95. What was handy was that Yuri lived in a flat close to Voikovskaya metro station. Therefore, I would park the truck at home overnight. We would then set out together from Voikovskaya at 6am and be back in Moscow late that night. The following day I would take the trailer down to Octopus for the customs clearance. A very good arrangement, because I made good money from it.

My arrangement with Kepstowe was different to that of the other subbies. They were paid a round trip rate, from London to Moscow and back. If I travelled from Moscow to London and back, I was paid that same rate. However, if the subbies were sent on extra mileage, say to tip or load outside Moscow, then they were paid a flat rate of 50p per mile. I would get 50p per kilometre in England, if, for example I ran to Bristol and back, to tip wrapping paper. But, when I was shunting in Moscow, I was paid £150 per day, which covered mileage, up to 200 kilometres, in that day. Every kilometre that I drove over the 200 basic, was paid at 50p. On top of this I was paid £10 for starting before the office at Octopus opened in the morning and £10 for finishing after it had closed in the evening. I also got £15 per night out for every night that I was away from Moscow. So, the trip to Voronezh paid me £590 and my diesel bill for the trip was a staggering £3, at £1 per 100 litres. A subbie who made the same trip would receive £325.

Yuri was an interesting character and somewhat of a mystery to me. He had lived and worked in England for the Soviet government during the Cold War. He had been engaged in some kind of engineering project in Wolverhampton. He could not have done that without being either a member of the K.G.B. or being extremely highly vetted by the K.G.B. The fact that he spoke very good English was a bit of a clue. I, of course, was therefore extremely careful as to what I said to him, particularly about my little misdemeanours within his country. In fact, the only time that I did not watch my tongue was one time when we were driving along and discussing restaurants, both in England and Russia. Yuri said to me, "Of course, the quality of food in Russia is far superior to that in England." I turned and looked across the cab at him, in amazement. I opened my mouth and said, "F@ck off, Yuri" and laughed!

In that winter of 1993, I carried out many trips outside Moscow, to either tip or reload trailers. Generally, this entailed me returning home late at night. Either I took the truck and trailer home, or I went to Octopus. Depending upon the time and other considerations, such as the weather. I would either drop the trailer there and drive home in the tractor unit, or I would leave the whole rig there and go home by Metro. This meant that I saw normal Moscow nightlife, first-hand, from varying aspects.

One of the first things to strike you about nocturnal Moscow was that the level of road traffic dropped and it was easier to drive around than during the daytime. This did not mean that the standard of the Russians' driving improved, far from it! This was probably because more of them had been drinking alcohol by then, as opposed to during the daytime.

So, it was also of no surprise to me that there was a large amount of people on the streets at night, who had been imbibing heavily, staggering along the footpaths and in the actual road. A source of minor amusement, but also of concern. I had seen a documentary on Russian T.V. about alcoholism within Russia. This was part of the new trend in what was the old Soviet media. They were aiming to tell the truth, rather than peddle government propaganda. The documentary indicated that in Russia as a whole, more than 80% of the population were what we would describe in Britain as chronically alcohol dependent. A staggering figure. Like the staggering figures on the pavements every night.

As Gorbachev's old laws about public displays of drunkenness had been repealed, the police did not interfere with or attack drunks any more. They were allowed to just get on with it. Should they collapse on the path, or in the street, they were left where they lay, an extremely dangerous state of affairs. That was typical of the Russian attitude and mentality, which seemed to be all or nothing.

Around Moscow, Portakabin-style buildings had appeared outside all the Metro stations. These were, in fact, kiosks, which served food, alcohol, music CDs and most consumer products. Most of the products on sale had been imported. Among these kiosks, there was usually at least one selling draught Russian beer, which was actually quite good and quite cheap. The kiosks then became a gathering point for the local alcoholics. Besides drinking, they would sing and dance along with the music that was blaring out from the music kiosks' speakers. Therefore, they produced a form of street entertainment. Not much of an entertainment, but some form of it.

31

Casualties of the New Society

THE *Pee-yenisti* (drunks) were a common sight around the kiosks and at night laying around, unconscious, on the street, tram tracks and pavements. Many of them were casualties of the gangster capitalism that was prevailing in Russia. As all property had been privatised, other than strategic government buildings, a housing market was becoming established. People who were chronic alcoholics had found themselves owning their own flat. These flats had a value. And that value was identified by the Mafia.

They would approach the owner and wave a large wad of Rouble notes in front of their face. The alcoholic, seeing more money than they could have ever envisaged, was talked into taking that money in exchange for signing over their flat. Instantly they found themselves homeless. The amount of money that had been offered them was nowhere near the true value of the property. Therefore, they could not buy a replacement home. The city council no longer owned any property so would not rehouse them. They found themselves living on the street, but at least they had plenty of money to buy alcohol. Well, at least in the short term, until the money ran out.

The most innocent of the victims were, of course, the children of the newly dispossessed. They were forced to live with their parents on the streets. That was, for as long as the money lasted. Then, unable to feed the children, the alcoholics generally abandoned them. These kids were then picked up by the authorities and placed into children's homes. A bleak outcome.

Most of the alcoholics took to living in the local parks. These areas of greenery, like everything in the ex-Soviet Union, could hardly be described as immaculate. However, they provided some relief for the local residents from the highly polluted urban environment. The drunks, however, prevented the locals from enjoying the amenities by their drunken behaviour. They also resorted to crime to pay for their alcohol. Then, of course, there was also their aggressive begging. Although we had an enclave of alcoholics in the park at Voikovskaya, they rarely attempted to interfere with the mothers and young children who used it. This was because one of Elena's friends was a policewoman on maternity leave. Her husband was a serving policeman. Through their contacts, the alcoholics were visited by the police and instructed as to their behaviour. Any alcoholic who did not toe the line received a savage beating from the police. Grudgingly, the drunks learned their lesson.

Other casualties of the new society were journalists and financiers. The journalists had thought that the new society meant that they could investigate wrongdoing and corruption with the same amount of freedom as their Western counterparts. They soon discovered that they could not. Vested interests, who did not want their nefarious schemes investigating, arranged for the journalists to be killed. These killings took the form of either car bombings, or shootings. The same fate awaited financiers who did not give loans to the Mafia or other powerful individuals. Their fates were usually sealed with a car bombing. The new post-Soviet society was extremely violent and brutal. It was exactly what I had described in 1990 when I had named it "The Wild, Wild East".

The year 1993 was when Elena and I had to decide upon our long-term future. We had to take into account the social climate within both Britain and Russia and decide where we wanted Margarita to grow up. By the end of October, we had definitely decided.

32

All Aboard the Skylark

IN February '93 I went to the British Embassy in
Moscow in order to get a new passport. My old
one actually expired in April '93 and I was told that I
could renew it when I returned to London. However,
that was not the answer I wanted and I was prepared
for it.

I knew that in England they were now only issuing
the new red E.U. passports, and I did not want one. I
wanted the traditional black passport. So, I informed
the embassy that, unfortunately, due to my work, I
would not be returning to England for the next three
months. Therefore, my passport would expire and
I would have trouble with the Russian authorities.
This, of course, meant that the British Consulate in
Moscow would have trouble because it would have
to deal with the problem. And, as I pointed out, I
could be pulled anywhere in Russia where I was with
the truck and detained. This would mean consulate
staff having to travel there to solve the problem. They
did not want that at all, so, they issued me a brand
new black passport, which was actually one of the
very last ever issued.

With this new passport safely stowed within my

passport wallet, I was, of course, free to continue plying my trade in the Russian wilderness. Kepstowe kept me working from Moscow, either shunting or running back and forwards to Poland, up until Margi' was a year old. It came, therefore, as a bit of a shock to the system when, just after her first birthday, I was sent back all the way to London. However, this gave me the chance to stock up with English clothes for all three of us. So, I had a major spend-up. I need not have actually bothered. This trip signified the beginning of a series of trips between Moscow and London as once again Kepstowe changed direction. My direction.

As with everything, I took the positives from the situation. I was able to shop in England. I was earning good money and I was able to arrange for Elena and Margi' to come to England in late September for a month's holiday. Kepstowe were happy for me to take this at that time as all of their drivers would have had their holidays by then. I was also not going to return to England for Christmas, which left Octopus covered during the holidays. In addition, they were quite happy for John Marshall to drive my truck and they would provide him with work while I was off. Therefore, they were not losing the use of my vehicle. All round, everyone was happy, particularly John as it was arranged that he would definitely go to Moscow. However, he may not have been quite so happy if he had known what would actually happen when he got there. But we will come to that, in good time.

I began to run back and forwards, but the immediate drawback to the situation was that I was away from Elena and Margarita. Of course, as a truck driver, you accept this. It is all part of the lifestyle, but neither

Elena nor I was overly happy with the enforced sepa-
rations. However, we had to get on with it. One big
change that had occurred while I was on my enforced
exile in Eastern Europe and Russia was that, instead
of shipping everything out overland, Kepstowe were
now sending trucks out by boat to Finland. They then
ran down into Russia, passing through Leningrad, on
the way to Moscow. The boat journey took three
days, but that was better than spending three sleepless
days queueing at borders. The queue for Kukariki had
now become at least 48 hours.

The boat, the M.V. *Garden*, sailed from Harwich,
leaving in the early hours of Saturday morning. It
docked in Turku, Finland, on Tuesday morning and
then returned to Harwich, where it arrived on Friday
evening. On its way it stopped at Wilhelmshaven, in
Germany. Arriving in Harwich, on a Friday evening,
I booked in with the shipping agent and handed him
my customs documentation for the load. He would
then produce that to the customs for me. I would
have expected to be instructed to return to my cab
and wait. Instead, I was told to make my way to the
pub over the road from the dock gate. Then, when
the boat was ready for loading I would be called from
there.

In the pub, I found Micky Packham and Pete
Newlyn, who had received similar instructions. As the
evening progressed, Alan Bremner and Steve Clarke
joined us. They were two of the other subbies. At
2am, on the Saturday morning, a docker came to the
pub and called us across to load on to the ship. As by
this time none of us were capable, the dockers drove
our trucks on for us. We, in turn, once safely aboard,

threw our bags into our cabins and went down to the bottom of the boat, where we discovered the bar. We went to bed at about 5 am.

The routine aboard ship on that trip and most of the subsequent ones was that we would get up on Saturday afternoon. Then we would go to the driver's lounge, where we could watch videos. While there, we would take it in turns to go to the bar and bring back a case of Finnish beer. At teatime we would go to the galley and eat. Then we would spend the evening and well into the following morning drinking in the bar, laughing and joking. On Sunday afternoon we would get up again and repeat the whole performance. Monday was much the same except that, as we were getting off the boat early the next morning, the evening session was subdued and we went to bed early. My bar bill per crossing was generally £35. There was a book where you marked down what you had and settled up on Monday night. It was a good system and we did not abuse it. Tuesday was the only day that I managed to get to breakfast and I never had lunch on the boat.

On the Tuesday morning, we would drive off the ship and head for Moscow, an 800-odd mile trip. Driving via Helsinki, crossing the border at Vaalimaa, we would pass through Leningrad and drive the remaining 500 miles to Moscow. We generally arrived in Moscow on Wednesday evening. That was provided that it was not winter. In winter we were generally lucky to arrive in Moscow on Thursday night. The other boys got to Moscow and unloaded before the weekend. They would then set off back to the U.K. via Poland. Usually, I would be kept in Moscow and be home for the weekend.

In early August however, I shipped out from Dover, as opposed to Harwich. This was because I was on my way to Odessa. Going via Turku would have been pointless because of the mileage and crossing at Grodno was not worth it either. On this trip I was running with Mike Mudie. We were both going to Odessa with cargoes of baby milk powder. The milk was actually destined for Kazakhstan. Why we did not take it there directly ourselves I do not know. From Odessa, it was being shipped by rail. We crossed into Belarus, at Kukariki, following a 40-hour queue to enter the border. From there we drove the 650 miles to Odessa.

Mike had just returned to England from Odessa when we set out on this trip. Therefore, I had asked him what the diesel situation had been like while he was down there in south-west Ukraine. Knowing the current situation regarding the availability of fuel was important. It varied considerably. One time you could pay in Roubles, another they would only accept hard currency, and then there would be shortages; a whole range of variances for which you wanted to be prepared. Mike had assured me that they were only taking hard currency, so I did not change any money into Roubles at the border. I had some, but not much. I would top up again when we got to Moscow, which was where we were going, after Odessa.

When we reached the bottom south-west corner of Ukraine, I needed diesel and pulled on to a service area. I approached the main building and talked to the people on duty. They told me that I could pay in Roubles, if I wanted to. So, Mike's information had been wrong. But, there again, I spoke to them in Russian and he would not have when he was there the previous trip. It was cheaper to pay in Roubles than in hard currency. The hard currency rate was normally four to five times more than paying in Roubles. So, I ended up getting 25 litres for £1, instead of 100 litres. Not an overall massive amount of difference, so I was not too sorry.

At that time, the Ukrainian government had not yet introduced its own currency. The Rouble was therefore still in use. However, one of Boris Yeltsin's actions within Russia had been to stop the use of hard currency for purchasing goods. He had stated that it was not right for Russians to be unable to buy goods in their own country because they were not available for Roubles. This had put a stop to all the duty free shops' activities within the city and ended the two-tier system operated by McDonald's and Pizza Hut, etc. It did not put an end to the use of hard currency for buying fuel; the petrol station managements were making a lot more money than by accepting Roubles.

Another thing that had ended had been Sovinteravto' trying to make us buy diesel coupons. Nowhere would take them. Following the privatisation of businesses in 1992, the petrol stations had passed into the hands of the station managers. They presumably took the view that they no longer wanted to accept coupons, either from foreign truck drivers, or from Russian companies. This was a form of credit and at that time there were no credit facilities being offered by banks. Therefore, they did not see why they should offer credit. They were not paid until the coupons were redeemed by Sovinter' or the newly privatised Russian companies. As many companies were failing and going bankrupt, allowing them credit was taking a huge risk. Therefore, we no longer bought coupons on the border, but merely paid cash at the pumps.

Having tipped at the docks in Odessa, we went to the hotel and phoned London. We were told that we were to head for Moscow, where we would backload from an exhibition. It was two days away from my 43rd birthday and I wanted to get home to celebrate it. We had driven all the way to Odessa at an unbearable – for me – 50mph. Mike had not wanted to push his old truck any harder than that. However, I told Mike that on the way to Moscow I was not hanging around as he dawdled along. We therefore set out from Odessa and that night parked in a lay-by near Gomel.

The following morning, we hammered it again and soon came across a 10 kilometre stretch of newly laid tarmac. This had a gravel mixed top coat. Slowing, from 65mph to 60mph I thrashed the truck over this new surface. The traffic coming the other way was delighted, tooting their horns, waving to me and swerving all over the place as I screamed past. When we were on a banked section, one car actually drove down the embankment and then along it, trying to avoid being peppered with my gravel buckshot. He failed miserably and I could hear the sound of his car being struck by hundreds of stones as I roared past. Mike, who was following behind, had dropped back to a safe distance to avoid flying stones. However, when we discussed the incident later, he was not amused by it. Still, you will always get people who have no sense of humour.

Think about it seriously. Had those Belarus motorists been that upset then they would have chased after me so as to demonstrate their annoyance, surely. There again, I had form for being chased by a Lada Zhiguli, in Belarus. The police one. These poor motorists probably did not want to blow their engines attempting to stop me. Wise choice, I would say.

We made it into Moscow that afternoon and Mike followed me to the flat. He knew Elena, having met her a few times before. We introduced him to Margarita and he loved her. He stayed for a cup of coffee and something to eat, then left to drive to Octopus. That evening, Elena, Vera and myself held a small celebration for my birthday. Nothing elaborate.

33

Man the Barricades

JUST after my birthday, a British theatre company brought a production to Moscow, which was put on at the Malie theatre, near to the Bolshoi. The trailer containing the scenery for the show had been brought out to Octopus by one of the subbies. He had then picked up a trailer that I had loaded and headed off west. I was to tip the trailer at the Malie theatre on the Friday night and reload it on the Sunday morning. The production was taking place on the Saturday. It was part of a general "British Luvvies Week" at Moscow's culture spots.

Due to the fact that trucks were not allowed into central Moscow during the daytime, Monday to Saturday, I could not go to the Malie until after 6pm on the Friday evening. The Malie stage crew then had to unload the freight during the evening and get set up for the Saturday night performance. I drove into the city centre, where the trailer was unloaded. I then took the truck home, ready to drive down on the Sunday morning. This simplified things for me as to reach the Malie from home I simply drove straight down Leningradski into central Moscow.

On the Sunday morning, I drove down to the

theatre and parked the trailer near to the stage door, where it was to be reloaded. This meant that I was at the Red Square end of the building and could see where the communists were holding their weekly, Sunday rally. There were tens of thousands of them, waiving bold red banners, decorated with communist slogans, or carrying large pictures of Lenin and Stalin.

An old lady, who must have been at least 70, approached me. She asked me, in Russian, where the communist rally was being held. Helpfully I pointed across the square, indicating the thousands of communists who were amassed there, and told her respectfully, "*Too – da Madam* [Over there Madam]."

The old lady thanked me and then informed me that she had been a tank driver in the Red Army during the Second World War. She also told me that she had fought at the battle of Kursk, which was the biggest ever tank battle in history.

I did not have the heart to tell her that I too had been a tank driver, but in the British army and that I had spent my time in Germany, during the late '60s, facing the Soviet Red Army in case of hostilities. I had much too much respect for her to have done that. She really was "A Hero of the Soviet Union".

Before she went off to join her fellow communists, she explained to me how she considered that everything that she and her *tovarichi* (comrades) had fought for was being stolen by the criminals and democrats, to the detriment of the ordinary, decent working people.

I watched her walk away, making her way to the demonstration and could understand her anger and disappointment at how the bulk of the people were being treated under the fictional democratic and capitalist society that had been foisted upon them.

After my latest brush with the luvvie brigade, it was back to making a couple more trips to the U.K. before Elena and Margarita flew in to Heathrow. Arriving back in England to start my holiday, I ended up in Sheppey, where John Marshall and my friend Bob Greensmith both lived.

John took over my truck and disappeared off to Kepstowe's. Bob took me round to his transport yard and showed me what he had bought for me.

He had promised to buy a car for me, that I could use for my holiday. And he had: a lime green, Lada Zhiguli, for which I gave him the £50 that it had cost him. How we laughed!

On the day that their flight arrived from Moscow, I drove to Heathrow and collected Elena and Margarita. When Elena saw our car, she burst out laughing. I can't think why.

Besides getting the car for me, Rob had also arranged for us to spend a week in a chalet at his family's chalet park at Eastchurch, on Sheppey. This was ideal for Margi' who used to run around on the huge grass area having a wonderful time. She also discovered an old couple who were living in one of the chalets and would disappear, visiting them. That was because, as I discovered, they were spoiling her with chocolate and cakes.

Meanwhile, living temporarily in the chalet, we were cooking for ourselves and I took Elena and Margi' to the local supermarket to buy the things that we needed. This gave Elena experience of food shopping in England and of what was available in our shops. When she had been in England before, she had not needed to cook, so this was an eye-opener for her.

After our week at Rob's, we drove to Great Yarmouth so that my mother could meet Margi'. Driving the old Lada was just like driving a tank; big, solid and slow to respond. But, it was a good car. We spent the following ten days in Yarmouth. While we were there, we used to take Margi' to a local park.

One day, as Elena and Margi' went into the park, a man approached me. "That your car?" he asked. I was not too sure that I wanted to admit to the fact, but he had obviously seen me get out of it. "I'll give you £250, for it," he offered. It turned out that he and some colleagues were buying up any Lada vehicles that they could lay their hands on. They were then stripping them down and putting them into 40ft containers. These were shipped to Leningrad and the parts were finding themselves back where they had started in Russia. This was because of the dire shortage of vehicle parts over there. I was slightly tempted to turn a profit, but Rob and I had decided that when I returned to Sheppey we were going to put the car through its paces across country, over the roughest terrain that you could imagine. So, I declined to sell it. Later, passing Ipswich, the complete, bloody exhaust system fell off it. Heap of bloody Russian crap!

I knew from having spoken to Kepstowe that John was in Moscow. So, you can imagine the way that I felt, when on October 4th 1993, I turned on my mother's T.V. to watch the news only to be confronted with live pictures from The White House on the bank of the Moskva River. The White House, which was now the home of the Russian Parliament.

Not only were there live pictures of the White House, but also of Russian tanks sitting on the Kutovsky bridge that spanned the river from the White House to the area of the Ukraina hotel. Not only that, but the tanks were firing live rounds of ammunition directly at the White House building. I called Elena and we watched, horrified, as the tanks kept firing, round after round. Smoke and flames poured from the building's shattered façade.

I immediately came to the conclusion that the town of Great Yarmouth really did not like Russia.

This was the second time that I had switched on the T.V. in Yarmouth and been confronted with bad news happening in Moscow. There was no way if Elena and I did come to live in Great Britain that we would end up inhabiting Great Yarmouth. If we did, then I could visualise Moscow being totally destroyed, within a couple of months. And I did not want to be held responsible for that.

I phoned Kepstowe to find out if they knew whether John was safe. It turned out that he had run to Moscow with Steve Clarke. They were both safely parked up in Octopus, well out of harm's way. It was then pointed out to me that my truck had been present, in Moscow, on both of the occasions when there had been insurrection in the city – '91 and now '93. If I was not careful, my truck would be banned from ever entering Moscow again. And I do not doubt that, at that very moment, the Mayor of Moscow, Yuri Lushkov, was in city hall tearing up the application for Moscow to twin with Great Yarmouth.

Of course, I had automatically worried about John's safety. I was not worried about my truck. If that had been damaged, it could be replaced. John could not.

But, what I did not know was at that very moment in time, Mark Hughes, the office manager at Octopus had his mother staying with him in his flat in Moscow. That flat was in Kutovsky Prospekt, very close to the Ukraina. Mark's mother was standing on the balcony of the flat, looking down at the tanks, when one of them fired the first round into the face of the White House. The tremendous concussion from the firing of that round sent a shockwave backwards, from the tank. The shockwave lifted Mrs. Hughes completely off her feet and threw her backwards, through the open doorway, into the living room. She was extremely lucky, not to sustain serious injury.

After Great Yarmouth, we travelled to Brighton, where we stayed with my brother, Chris, and his wife, Jane. From there, we returned to Sheppey for the last few days of the holiday. I took Elena and Margarita to Heathrow so they could catch their flight back to Moscow. I then returned to Sheppey to wait for John to return with my truck. When he turned up, he was full of the events in Moscow, but I don't think that he wanted to go back there ever again.

I paid him for the work that he had done and he, Bob and I had a good evening in a local pub. The next day I drove to London, so that I could get back on to the Kepstowe treadmill.

34

Keep on Trucking

BACK at work after my holiday, I sailed eastwards upon the good ship M.V. *Garden*. This involved another industrial strength drinking bout on the high seas. These marathon drinking sessions were beginning to become the kind of things of which legends are made. They were also the things that alcoholics were made of. Or rather for!

In Moscow, the winter had started in earnest and it was snowing heavily. I was waiting to go to Donetsk, in eastern Ukraine. The load that I had brought out on the *Garden* was safety equipment for a Russian coalmine in the Don Basin, just outside Donetsk.

While I was waiting to go on this trip, Pete Newlyn passed through Moscow on his way to Perm, 860 miles north-east of Moscow. I met him in Octopus as he passed through. Two weeks later I met him on his way back.

En route to Perm, he had come across a river, some 100 miles short of the city. There was no bridge, but there was a little steam ferryboat plying its way back and forwards across the river. He paid his money and loaded on to the ferry. The bridge of the boat was above the car deck and he would have to drive under it in order to offload from the ferry. However, unfortunately, it was too low for his vehicle and he hit the top of the truck against the underside of the bridge. Unable to drive off, the ferry crew helpfully suggested that he go back across the river with them, reverse off and then drive around, on a detour, to get to Perm. The problem with this plan of action, as he saw it, was that the detour was around 250 miles.

Using all his initiative and common sense, he bunged the crew a bribe, for them to reverse off the pier, turn the boat around and reverse back on to it. Then he could reverse back off the ferry on the right side of the river.

It must have been a rather large and substantial bung because when he returned after unloading in Perm they were ready to turn the boat around immediately for him. He reversed back on to it. No questions asked.

The delay in travelling to Donetsk was that the importer had not paid for the transportation of the goods. As soon as they did, I was under way, down to the extreme east of Ukraine. The snow was beginning to cover the landscape and as I drove south it picked up in intensity. The whole trip was again one of struggling through heavy snowfall.

Having tipped the safety gear at the coalmine just outside Donetsk, I was driving back through the city when, purely by chance, I came across Alan Johnson. He had been to Rostov and was on his way back to Moscow. He followed me and we crossed the city. The snow ploughs and gritters had been out and the roads were wet. In the gutters there were large puddles where the snow had melted. Passing a bus stop where crowds of people were waiting for their transport, the drive wheel of my truck lurched into a large dip at the side of the road. Johnno came on the C.B. straight away and said, "If I was you, I would get my foot down and keep going, non-stop to Moscow."

"Why's that?" I asked.

"Because you have just chucked up about a thousand litres of dirty water, which came back down over everybody in that bus queue."

I did no more, but took him at his word and floored the accelerator.

Arriving back at Octopus, I was allocated a trailer that was destined for Donetsk, again. This time it was for the Rank Xerox dealership in central Donetsk. I was not too pleased to be returning there so quickly. The people from that bus stop might recognise the truck if they saw it. However, off I went to deliver equipment for this brand new dealership's office. The load comprised of stands and promotional materials, etc. At that time the Donetsk dealership was the only one in the ex-Soviet Union that was exclusively privately owned. They were waiting for this equipment so they could open for business.

Once more, I struggled south through heavy snow. Reaching Donetsk, I tipped at the dealership and then left the city, heading north for the town of Orel (pronounced *Or–ee–yol*). At Orel, I had to load from the *pribelee* (thermostat) factory. Here I met Tatyana and her son, Alexie. Tatyana was the export clerk and translator at the factory. Alexie did not work there, but he had studied English, gaining a degree for it at Kharkov University. Therefore, Tatyana had called him when I arrived, so that he could meet me and practise his English. This became a regular occurrence when I went to Orel to load.

As I had arrived in the early afternoon, I could not load until the following morning. Alexie suggested that I accompany him into the city and stop the night at his father's flat where he lived, his mother and father being divorced. Arriving at the flat, we collected two large glass 5 litre bottles and then went out into the street and took a bus across town. We decamped from the bus and went into a beer shop, where the bottles were filled. We then went back to the flat, where we drained the bottles with the help of Alexie's dad. The next day, I loaded and set out for Moscow. Alexie saw me off and as I pulled out, he shouted "Keep on trucking" and gave me the thumbs up.

The load of thermostats was destined for Berlin. There, they were to be used in the construction of underground trains for the Berlin *U Bahn* (underground system). It was decided that I would take them to Berlin, tip them and then load for England. This meant that I would be on my way back to Russia just before Christmas.

In fact, I ended up sitting in a long queue of trucks on the Belarus–Russian border, near to Vitebsk, on Christmas Day. I eventually got home to Moscow on Boxing Day afternoon. For Christmas dinner, I had eaten tinned Irish stew. I really do know how to live.

Luckily I was back in Moscow in time for New Year, which meant that I could spend the Russian holiday with Elena and Margarita.

35

Not Too Happy a New Year

HAVING arrived in Moscow on Boxing Day '93, the following day I tipped the trailer into the Octopus warehouse. I was then taking the next two weeks off as holiday.

Moscow was cold and getting colder. It was already down to -20C and was expected to get even colder before too long. That did not stop us going out, though. We would go to the shops and the park. Margarita would march through the deep snow like a little tank, her cheeks puffed out and her little arms swinging back and forward across her body.

Thoroughly enjoying our time together, we rolled towards the New Year holiday without a care in the world. Other than that the outside temperature was now down to -30C.

On the Friday afternoon, New Year's Eve, Elena answered the phone to discover that the police at Vyazma were on the line. They informed her that Mike Mudie was there and wanted to speak to me. I answered the phone and Mike informed me that he had broken down. His engine would not run and he therefore had no heating in the vehicle. Mike told me that Alan Johnson was flying out to Moscow on the

Sunday and was going to phone me when he arrived in Moscow. When Alan rang, could I tell him about the situation at Vyazma?

I said that I would go down and get my truck running the following morning and drive out to Vyazma to see what we could do to get him going. He told me not to bother, that he was OK and could wait until Monday.

I did not like that idea, but he was insistent. So, I told him to use the 24/7 café kiosks there as a place to sit and keep warm. Have the occasional cup of coffee but above all keep himself warm.

Obviously, Mike had my phone number from when Kepstowe had been handing it out to everybody as an emergency number before they had the office at Octopus. So did Alan Johnson. That was fair enough. But why had Mike been adamant that he did not want me to drive to Vyazma on New Year's Day? If I had been broken down in those temperatures, I would have appreciated assistance as soon as possible. And why was Alan Johnson going to phone me when he got to Moscow? That was not a normal activity either. All very strange.

But, it was New Year's Eve. And we were going to celebrate.

Vyazma was situated between Moscow and Smolensk, about 150 miles West of Moscow and 100 miles from Smolensk. The town was set back from the road and in passing you saw nothing of the place. All you did see was the large crossroads with its police post and the kiosks scattered around the junction. Two of these kiosks were cafes where you could sit in the warm to eat or drink.

In the grand scheme of things, all Vyazma was for me was a marker as to how far I was from either Moscow or Smolensk.

We saw in the New Year watching the fireworks displays that were taking place across the north of Moscow. Then, we had dinner; roast beef. Elena began her round of telephone calls to all her friends and I watched the television. Margarita was sleeping.

The television programme was good, with Russian bands and singers providing the entertainment. But at the back of my mind there was the niggling thought, "What was Mike Mudie up to?"

The rise in the temperature, over the weekend, had been quite astounding. On the Friday, New Year's Eve, it had been -30C. By the Sunday afternoon it was a mere -20C. But this was perfectly normal in Moscow. A week of extremely severe cold weather, which ended abruptly.

At 8am, on Monday morning, the telephone rang and it was Alan on the line. He told me that his truck would not start and could I drive up to the Hungaro depot in northern Moscow and help him to get it started. I told him about Mike being broken down at Vyazma. I left the flat and went down to my truck. Luckily, the temperature was now only -15C and the truck started without too much bother. Although it ran unevenly to begin with, it soon settled down. Once it was running smoothly, I set out for the Hungarian depot about 5 miles away.

Arriving at the depot, I was admitted into the compound immediately, the gateman having recognised my truck. The yard was full of trucks and trailers.

They were all coated in a complete covering of ice and frost. The ground was one large slab of packed ice. Johnson's truck was frozen solid. I got out my jump leads and we connected them from my batteries, to his. I poured some petrol into his oil filler so as to thin out the oil in the sump.

We gave it ten minutes for the oil to thin. During this time we discussed Mike's situation. I said that we should drive to Vyazma together. Then if the broken down truck needed towing back to Moscow, he could pull the truck and I would pull the trailer. He dismissed my offer and said that he could sort the problem out alone. We fired up his truck, which at first belched clouds of white and grey smoke into the atmosphere. As soon as it was running smoothly, he set out for Vyazma and I drove home.

I spent the week with Elena and Margi'. We went out a few times for short walks to the park or down to the kiosks, all of us wrapped up nice and warmly. Margarita had a fur coat and fur hat on top of all of her normal clothes. The fur was a golden beige colour and she looked like a tiny little teddy bear.

The holiday over, I loaded and set off for Poland. I was due to swap trailers in Siedlce. During my time off in Moscow, I had not heard a word from Alan or Mike. I had no idea what had happened to them after Johnson had left the Hungaro depot.

I was approaching Brest on the motorway when I felt a lack of traction and realised that I was driving on black ice. I let my foot off and allowed the truck to slow down at its own pace. I passed what had been an old Mercedes saloon car until the driver had stuffed it against a length of Armco and taken the top off it. It was now a cabriolet, but without any windows. He was standing beside it, scratching his head.

I carried on, allowing the truck to decelerate, and passed under a flyover that carried traffic over the motorway at a junction. The truck was just moving as I went down through the gears, aiming to pull off the road once clear of the junction. Then I could wait for the gritters to appear and weave their magic.

The truck came to a rest where the slip road joined the motorway bringing traffic on to the dual carriageway. I had pulled on to the diagonal lines, separating the motorway from the slip road. I applied the handbrake and felt the truck begin to slide sideways. I stamped on the footbrake and this stopped the sideways momentum. So, for the next 30 minutes, I sat with my foot on the footbrake. Traffic was joining the motorway from the slip road and I did not want to slide into it, causing an accident.

Looking in my nearside mirror, I eventually picked out the flashing yellow lights of a gritter coming along the carriageway behind me. The gritter passed me and I was just about to pull away when I saw that the smashed up Mercedes was also coming. It was being towed by a breakdown truck. And, when I say being towed, I do not mean hitched up on to the back of it. They had tied a 10 metre length of strap from the wrecker to the car and the car was swinging from side to side on the carriageway behind the recovery vehicle, which was not hanging about. It was like a pendulum.

One moment the car would be grazing the central barrier and the next it had swung over to the hard shoulder. Then back again and so on. I watched this in the mirror and realised that if they timed it wrong he was going to crash into the side of my truck and create more havoc.

Luckily, as they passed me the car was out near the central Armco and then swung back over and went on to the slip road, some 20 metres in front of me. I sighed with relief, but then decided to give them a few minutes to piss off before I set out.

Darkness was falling as I moved on again and they had disappeared from sight, followed by a group of vehicles who were all following the gritter. Some 2 kilometres down the road I saw the Mercedes again. They had stuffed it into the concrete wall of a bridge. Once again the driver was standing there scratching his head. I reckoned that he could scratch it as much as he liked, but he would not get any feeling.

Arriving at Kukariki, I discovered that the border was completely empty. There were no other trucks at all, crossing in or out of Belarus. Despite becoming involved in protracted conversations with my Russian friends who were working there, I was through the border in just over an hour and, as snow began to fall, I made my way to Siedlce.

Arriving at the Hetmann, I discovered that Alan Johnson's and Mike's trucks were parked in the truck parking area. I parked alongside them and made my way into the motel. There was no sign of them in the restaurant, so I took it that they were having a shower. I sat down at a table, ordered a beer and thought about what I was going to have to eat.

I was sitting near to the huge, front picture window and looking out I saw Alan and Mike climbing into their trucks. I expected them to stow their washing gear and then return to the restaurant. It was obvious from the fact that my truck was parked there that I was in the vicinity.

Then, Johnson started his truck and I saw the smoke bellow from the exhaust. This was followed by Mike's truck starting up. I got up, told Anouska that I would be back shortly and made my way out of the building. I got to the two trucks just as they were beginning to pull out of the car park.

For a start, that far from home I did not consider this to be a particularly friendly way of carrying on. As I approached them they saw me and stopped.

I walked up to Mike's cab and he opened the driver's window. His face was partially lit by the floodlights around the truck park. Even in the semi-darkness, there was something strange about his appearance. He reached up and turned on his interior light and I could then see that his face was covered in large scabs. Not a nice sight.

Johnson walked around the front of the cab and stood beside me.

"Was it something I said?" I asked, shaking my head.

They told me that they were pulling out and heading for Poznan.

As the temperature was –10C I said that they were taking a risk with black ice, because the Poles did not grit their roads. In my opinion, they would be better off leaving in the morning, particularly as it was still snowing steadily. However, they were adamant that they were going. They said that they had both lost so much time over Mike's breakdown that they needed to get going. The truck was still sick and so was Mike. He needed to get proper medical attention.

I asked what had happened at Vyazma and it turned

out that Mike's truck had blown a brake valve. He had switched the engine off while he attempted to fix it and due to the intense cold the truck would not start again. What he had then done was either a sign of complete stupidity, or an indicator of a death wish.

Instead of doing as I suggested and holing up in the kiosk cafes, he had climbed into his sleeping bag. He had then spent from the Friday evening until the Monday afternoon laying there in the sleeping bag in a cab with no working heating system. The temperatures had been around -30C to -35C, both outside as well as inside the cab.

That was where the scabs on his face had come from. The intense cold.

I stood and watched as they pulled out of the motel grounds and drove their trucks down to the Siedlce bypass. Soon, their lights had disappeared into the darkness of the night and the swirling snow. I realised that snow was laying on my shoulders and was matted in my hair.

36

Technicalities?

WHEN you consider that I was living in Moscow illegally it is a wonder that I managed to survive as I did for so long, particularly with their obtrusive system of policing. Officially, I needed permission to live there from the Russian authorities, but I had never applied for it. I lived there on a casual basis. About as casual as you could possibly become. But that's my style.

However, in February 1994, I was caught carrying out my illegal working practice within Russia. An eagle eyed state transport officer at a newly opened control office at Tula inspected my paperwork. He realised from the date on my road permit that I had been in Russia for more than three weeks. Not only that, but I was not pulling the trailer with which I had entered the country. He therefore accused me of cabotage. This was carrying out a multitude of jobs within a country when your permit only authorised a single journey. You were not entitled to carry out internal haulage operations.

As I always say, "When in doubt lie". I told him that I had been ill in Moscow for a long while and that, regarding the trailer that I was pulling, the original truck it had entered Russia with had broken down. He did not believe me but could not prove any differently. However, he wrote all over my permit, invalidating it for any more cabotage.

Therefore, for the next two months, whenever I had to go to Tula or further south, instead of driving directly from Moscow on the M2, I used to drive to Kaluga, to the west of Tula, and then cut east, reaching the M2 to the south of the transport ministry control point. However, this was not a great alternative, as it was a long detour and the roads were not kept particularly clear of snow. Many nights, I struggled through snowstorms and drifting snow, just to avoid capture at Tula.

My work in the first half of 1994 was again a mixture of Moscow shunting, trips to Poland and journeys back to the U.K. Each trip to Britain found me returning to Moscow, via Finland, on the M. V. *Garden*. This was a real eye-opener when I saw the number of unaccompanied trailers that Kepstowe were sending to Russia, via the boat. At least thirty a week. Plus, the accompanied Kepstowe and subbies' trucks. The increase in their traffic over the four years that I had been running to Moscow was amazing. And it was obviously due to this vast increase in work, that, finding myself in London in April, I was called in to their office for "a chat".

The upshot of this chat was that Kepstowe wanted me to return to Moscow and stay there as the full-time resident shunter. Not run down to Poland. Not return to England, but to be based permanently in Moscow. They were going to send out six trailers, which would be my fleet. I would then run these trailers, tipping and loading them. A new pay structure was outlined that was very generous. I was on a £150 per day retainer, added mileage money, early and late start money and night out money.

So basically it was my choice. Take it, or leave it. I did not even have to think about it.

I took it!

Back in Moscow, I tipped my trailer at Octopus and then drove to Tula to reload it. I had a brand new permit and was legal. Arriving at Tula, I discovered that the transport ministry control post had closed. Life had now become so much easier.

The arrangement in Moscow was that I came completely under the control of the Moscow office. They decided my work. The six trailers arrived via Turku, pulled by Sovtransavto trucks. The Sovs had offloaded them in Moscow then dropped those trailers in Octopus. So, my first job was to reload the six trailers. They then stood in the yard until a truck came in with a loaded trailer. They dropped the loaded trailer and picked up one I had loaded for the U.K. They then headed back to England as soon as they wanted. This saved them the time it would have taken tipping and loading in Moscow.

As Moscow shunter I was allowed to use Kepstowe's computer equipment to complete my weekly invoices for the work that I had carried out. However, when other drivers were on site, I, like them, had to sit in my cab while waiting. This was because drivers were now banned from waiting around in the office due to the noise that they created.

We had a simple system for my payment. I wrote the invoice, Mark checked it and then forwarded it to London for payment into my bank account in England. I was drawing $500 per week for running and living costs, which was deducted before payment. I was very happy with the arrangement. So were Kepstowe and their customers.

As I knew all of the offloading and reloading sites and their procedures, as well as being able to speak Russian, things generally ran very smoothly.

I knew Moscow like the back of my hand and the location of all the sites outside the city. My knowledge of the Russian road system was very good and I was often asked to give directions to the other drivers. Another advantage that the drivers discovered was that if they were with me in a restaurant they could order what food they wanted. They did not have to have the courses dictated to them by the waitress, as normally occurred when they were on their own.

However, the main advantage that became apparent, of course, was for the subcontractors. Instead of losing days waiting to tip their trailers in Moscow, they merely turned up, dropped off the trailer that they had brought out from England and hooked straight up to one that I had preloaded. Their turnaround time was greatly reduced, which increased their profitability.

37

Dead Ends

FOR the last eight months of 1994, I led a varied existence. Although described as the Moscow shunter, some of my journeys took me well outside the Moscow area. Many would be relatively local, to destinations such as Tula and Razan, and I was still trotting off to Voronezh regularly with Yuri. However, I drove to further flung locations, as well: Orel, Donetsk, Dnepropetrovsk, Volgograd and Turku, numerous times. And all of this travelling led to me seeing many accidents and dead bodies.

The worst that I saw occurred on the streets of Moscow. I was driving through the city in relatively heavy traffic when in the distance ahead I saw a massive fireball rise above the roofs of the buildings that stood between me and the accident. The fireball was followed by an enormous cloud of black, oily smoke, which began to rise into the sky. The smoke began to billow up into the heavens continually. Soon, traffic was gridlocked and eventually everybody, including me, turned off the main road and followed their own diversion. I wanted to avoid the scene of destruction, which obviously lay ahead.

Having reached my destination, the trailer was

loaded and I returned along the normal route back through the city. This brought me directly to the scene of the earlier disaster. I came to a massive crossroads, which was controlled by traffic lights. I halted at the lights and witnessed the carnage that had occurred. The centre of the enormous crossroad junction was blocked by the debris of the earlier accident. A petrol tanker had crashed directly into the side of a trolley bus in the centre of the junction. I learned later that the tanker had been speeding and jumped the lights. Upon impact with the trolley bus, the tanker had exploded, which had created the massive fireball that I had seen. This fireball engulfed the trolley bus. All its passengers and driver had been burned to death instantly. So had the driver of the tanker. I looked at the remains of the trolley bus and could see the charred remains of the passengers, still seated, in the spot where they had perished. Around the two large vehicles, burned out cars and vans were littered. They too had been engulfed in the massive ball of flame.

When the lights changed, I picked my way around this scene of utter carnage and headed for Octopus.

Margarita was now two years old and Elena and I decided that when I went on long distance trips, where I would be away from home for some days, that they would accompany me. The first such trip was to Krasnodar. I was taking a load of cosmetics to a company there. They were the same sort of goods that Mark in Kiev imported: pound shop trash.

Now that I was based in Moscow, I had taken to travelling to Octopus on the Metro most days of the week. So, I used to buy monthly Metro season tickets. I kept these in my jacket, which I hung on the passenger side of the cab, over the bunk, when driving. On the way from Rostov to Krasnodar, I was pulled over by the G.A.I. on some spurious context. Of course, it was the standard procedure, whereby a short chat in Russian was followed by me handing my passport and a few Rouble notes out of the driver's window to the policeman. While the procedure took place, Margi' had gone to my jacket, got out the season ticket, which was in a plastic holder and some small sheets of scrap paper. This was her passport and money. She then came across the cab, leaned past me and handed them to the officer. He laughed, but still fined me. And he kept the slips of paper, the miserable, greedy bastard.

One thing that this demonstrated was that Margi' was well prepared for life on the road in Russia.

Another trip, in early September, saw us heading for Turku to swap trailers and return to Moscow. We travelled up from Moscow and soon came to the little town of Klin. The town had a small bypass, so that you avoided transiting through the town. I was driving around the bypass and we reached the northern end of it. Suddenly I came across the tail end of a queue. The queue moved forwards slowly and I kept moving up with it. Topping a slight hill, I could see the scene of an accident ahead.

There was a junction where a road ran off into Klin. In the centre of the junction, there was the remains of a Russian rural bus. The rural buses were basically a truck chassis, upon which they mounted a fibreglass box with seats and windows, a particularly crude contraption. The bus had been obliterated. The wrecked cab and twisted chassis lay in the centre of the junction. However, the bodywork in which the passengers would have been travelling no longer existed. It was strewn along the road in a million tiny pieces, totally shattered and destroyed by the force of the impact. The Russian police had recovered the bodies of the bus passengers and its driver. They were laid out at the side of the road, completely uncovered.

As I slowly edged past them in the queue, I was looking down upon them. I noticed that they were all women, except for one man, who I took to be the driver. They were dressed for the fields. Obviously, the bus was bringing agricultural workers back from work when the accident occurred. I noticed Margi' leaning over my shoulder and looking down on to the bodies. I moved her back, on to the bunk and drove away from the junction.

Further ahead, beyond the junction, I could see a Lithuanian truck standing on the dirt strip beside the road. As I passed it, I saw that the front of the tractor unit had been obliterated. I considered that to have continued that far down the road following the impact of the accident he must have been travelling at some speed when the crash occurred. It was reasonably obvious that the bus had been coming from the north and was turning left at the junction to drive into Klin. The truck had topped the brow of the slight hill, travelling too fast to avoid the bus. Passing the truck, I noticed the driver, still behind the steering wheel. He too was stone dead.

The total number of casualties from the collision therefore amounted to 16 dead. Strangely, all the dead farm workers' skin had turned to a sallow shade of yellow. I realised later that this was because, having been working all summer in the fields, they would have been extremely suntanned. The yellow pallor was from the blood ceasing to circulate and their colour fading away.

We had left Moscow on the Saturday morning to head for Turku. I needed to be in Turku by the Monday afternoon to register the trailer for the boat, which would arrive on Tuesday morning. I actually arrived there on the Sunday evening. I booked us into a hotel on the waterfront for two nights. After I had registered the trailer, on the Monday morning we went into town, where we bought Margi' clothing for the winter. Finland produces brilliant clothes for protection during the extreme cold that they experience every winter. With Margi' kitted out and having collected the trailer that I was waiting for, we headed back to Moscow. A journey of 1,300 kilometres.

On the way down from Leningrad, I was stopped by the G.A.I., for speeding. I had to accompany the policeman to look at his radar gun. As I walked away from the cab, Margi' jumped into the driving seat, turned to Elena and said, "*Nee boysa mamma. Papa noor pa pisset* [Don't worry mamma, dad's just gone for a piss]."

Having returned to Moscow, we then took a holiday, which I had booked. We flew to Cyprus, where we were booked into The Four Lanterns Hotel, on the seafront in Larnaca. We enjoyed the sun, the food and swimming in the Aegean. The water was crystal clear. The temperature all week was 27C. Quite a change from when we had left Moscow, where it had been -10C. On the flight south from Sheremetyevo the pilot had been gradually turning up the temperature in the plane. On the way back, he was busy turning it down. We returned to Moscow to discover that it was still -10C.

Back in Moscow, I was still carrying out my variety of tasks, tipping and loading all over the place. In November I went on a trip to Volgograd, but even though I was going to be away for some days, I went on my own. The load that I had to collect was extremely hazardous and I did not want to put Elena or Margarita in danger.

Volgograd was 1,000 kilometres from Moscow. Previously it had been known as Stalingrad. During the Second World War it was where the German advance was finally halted by the Soviet Red Army.

As I was leaving Moscow to drive to Volgograd I stopped at a kiosk to buy some cigarettes. While I was buying them, Steve Clarke pulled up at the kerb and joined me. He was on his way back in from Volgograd. Strangely, he began to relate a list of facts about Volgograd.

For instance, he told me that the city was situated on the west bank of the Volga River, that it was 54 kilometres long and was home to three car factories, 11 steel mills and four electrical power plants. On and on he went churning out facts and figures. As I drove away from Moscow after we had parted company, I wondered where in bloody hell he had accumulated all of that useless information.

The drive to Volgograd and back was carried out in a constant outside temperature of -18C. Not once did it vary either on the road, or during the three days that I spent in Volgograd. However, what was strange was the snow. All the way there, all the time that I was in the city and all the way back, it snowed. But the snow was what the Russians call *sookoy shnee-yek* (dry snow). It is like small, white coffee granules, which dropped out of the sky and bounced back up from the road surface. At Volgograd, one whole day was spent waiting as the workers from the factory constructed three wooden cradles in the trailer. I was collecting three metal tanks full of gas. The cradles were to support the tanks. When the gas had been finally loaded, a member of the factory staff, who could speak English, rode in the cab with me to the customs office.

As soon as we left the factory, he began to spout facts and statistics about Volgograd. So, that was where Steve had picked them up. However, having already heard them from Clarky, this regurgitation of the same information became extremely and utterly boring. I mean, in all honesty, who actually gave a shit? Not me for a start.

With Christmas '94 on the horizon, I made plans for a Christmas trip to England for Elena, Margarita and myself. So as to suit Kepstowe, it was decided that I would ship over to Harwich on the *Garden*, arriving in the U.K. on 23rd December.

The plan was that I would ship back out on the *Garden* the following Friday night, 30th December. That would mean spending New Year's Eve on the North Sea. As we were only going to be in England for a short while, I decided that we would spend the week at my mother's home and not bother trying to fit in everybody else. It was therefore arranged that I would leave my truck in Harwich and that my stepfather would collect us from there. Kepstowe, meanwhile, would have my trailer collected from Harwich and a replacement delivered there for me to take back to Moscow.

38

Snow Problem

AS I prepared to set out for Turku, western Russia was going through another of its spells of extremely low temperatures. The thermometers were holding at around -20C, day in and day out. There was also a considerable amount of snowfall. So, the trip to Turku was going to prove challenging, to say the least. Not least because on this little expedition I was to be joined by a brand new Kepstowe driver on his first trip to Russia. He was going to accompany me to Turku, but was then going to turn around and take a trailer back to Moscow. It was a job that I would have done, if I was not going to England. When I tell you that this driver now goes on social media with the handle Harry Monk, those of you that know what Harry Monk is rhyming slang for will sympathise with me.

Harry was driving Kepstowe's oldest Volvo truck and right from the off it was trouble. Despite the bad weather conditions, I had intended to make it as far as Leningrad on the first night. Novgorod, at worst. And it was even worse. We only made it to Tver. Harry's truck kept breaking down, but Harry was not inclined to repair it. He left that to me. So I repeatedly found myself laying in the snow, underneath his tractor unit, tightening air-line joints that were continually leaking. The loss of air was severe and meant that around every 50 miles or so he would have lost so much that the automatic brake system kicked in. This locked his brakes on so he could not move. Once again, I would be out in the cold, spanner in hand, tightening the worn joints. He had no spares and nothing with which to make a more permanent repair.

While I was laying under his truck, Harry would be sitting in the warmth in my cab drinking coffee.

Then, due to the intense cold, his diesel froze. Looking into the tank, I could see large chunks of ice floating on the surface. However, I sorted that out because we had stopped close to a Russian house, which had an enormous wood shed attached to it. The owner let me have some wood and I lit a large fire under Harry's tank. This de-iced the diesel and he was mobile again. It also stripped some paint. By the time that we reached Novgorod, things were becoming absolutely desperate. We pulled on to a fuel station forecourt and his air system gave up the ghost. I could not tighten it enough to build up sufficient air to get the truck mobile again. I told Harry that he would have to stop there overnight. I would go into Novgorod and in the morning speak to Sovtransavto. I would get them to come out to him and carry out repairs. I then drove to a hotel in Novgorod and booked Elena, Margi' and myself, in for the night. In the morning I went to Sovtransavto and asked them to go out to Harry and fix his truck. With that, I left Novgorod and headed for the Finnish border at Vaalimaa.

We had left Moscow on the Friday, hoping to be in Turku, by the Sunday night. Therefore we would have been in plenty of time to book in with the shipping company. However, we had ended up at Tver on the Friday night and Novgorod on the Saturday night. On the Sunday I drove to the Shell Truck stop at Kotka in Finland and stopped the night in the motel. Our motel room had a king size water bed. On the Monday I drove to Turku and booked in.

On Tuesday we loaded on to the ship and I discovered they had given us the use of the owner's cabin for the voyage. This was quite luxurious and much superior to the ordinary driver's cabins.

However, Elena and Margi' could not really enjoy the cabin, the food or the refreshments as they both became seasick as soon as the boat put out to sea. They slept for most of the three-day journey.

With no other drivers on the ship, I spent most of the voyage in the drivers' room or the bar. However, my bar bill for the crossing was considerably less than when I was sailing with other drivers in tow. It was just £10, instead of the usual £35.

We landed in Harwich late on Friday and spent the night sleeping in the cab. On Saturday morning, Christmas Eve, my stepfather arrived and drove us to Great Yarmouth. We spent Christmas there and on the Wednesday I received a phone call from Kepstowe, informing me that the *Garden* would not be sailing on the Friday night as the sailing had been cancelled. Therefore, we could have another week in England and ship out the following Friday, which we did. Sailing back to Finland, I was joined on board by four more of the Kepstowe crowd: Pete Newlyn, John Mantle, Nicky Reynolds and Gordon Jones.

However, the trip back to Turku was even rougher than the previous trip and all of these were affected by seasickness, as were Margi' and Elena. So, once again, I found myself drinking alone. Good job, because I was now drinking expensive Finnish black vodka. It was liquorice flavoured. Still, the bar bill was cheap again.

Arriving in Turku, I discovered that I had a blowout on one of the trailer tyres. So, I lost four hours having that sorted, while the others went ahead and drove towards Moscow. Unfortunately, a weather front came in. As they were ahead of it, their journey to Moscow was not too bad. But for me, it meant that I was driving into heavy snowfall all the way. They arrived in Moscow on the Wednesday night or early Thursday morning, but I did not get there until the Friday afternoon. Kepstowe thought that I had been taking the piss. This soured our relationship, both in Moscow and with London.

Also, the fact that I had left Harry Monk at Novgorod had not gone down very well. But, at the end of the day, what was I have supposed to have done? My priority was to get to Turku and catch the boat to England. As well as that, I had done everything to get him as far as Novgorod, while he had done absolutely nothing for himself. But, most importantly, I had Margi' and Elena with me. I was not prepared to subject them to sleeping in the cab of the truck when there was no need, especially in those weather conditions. To be honest, as far as I was concerned it was Kepstowe's fault. They had employed the wrong bloke for the job in the first place.

39

3 Wheels on My Wagon

MORE problems occurred with Kepstowe when one morning my truck, which was parked near the flat in Moscow, would not start. I knew that Mick Packham and Gordon Jones were at Octopus and called the office to ask whether they could come over to the flat and help to get the truck started. I was not working that day, but had merely checked the truck to see whether it was O.K. The batteries were flat.

I was told by Paul, quite clearly, that I did not work for Kepstowe. I was merely a subbie and that my truck was not their responsibility, so they would not send Mick or Gordon over to help me. I went out and got it started myself. I then drove to the Sovtransavto depot, where I had two brand new batteries fitted.

A couple of weeks later, I was in the flat and received a call from Paul telling me that a Kepstowe truck was broken down at Octopus and could I drive over there and help to get it started. I pissed myself laughing on the phone and then hung up. There is such a thing as Karma.

However, there is also such a thing as Rob Keir and later I received a call from him, from London, criticising my attitude and lack of co-operation. Obviously,

Paul had grassed me up. I explained the root cause of the situation and he appeared to be satisfied, but I think that "appeared" is all that it was. My relationship with him seemed to suffer from then on.

I was back to the daily grind, shuffling trailers around Russia and Ukraine. By now, the job had become tedious. Also, the fun of living in Moscow had evaporated. It was depressing to look out the windows of the flat and see the stark monochrome winter scene that existed nine floors below.

Elena and I had already decided that we were going to move to the U.K. that year. The truck was already paid for because I had paid off the last six instalments in one go. I had done this while we were in England for the Christmas and New Year. So, I had no financial need to stay in Russia. Then with no pressure financially, we were free to move to the U.K. and get Margi' into a playgroup. As she could only speak Russian, she could learn English there in preparation for beginning infants school.

The scenes that we had witnessed in Yarmouth of the tanks shelling the front of the Moscow White House had finally decided Elena that she did not want her daughter being brought up there, in such an uncivilised society as Russia. Therefore, England it was. However, before we moved there, Russia still had a few nasty surprises in store for me.

The first of which, courtesy of the trailer rental company, was that I jackknifed in Moscow. The trailer, a fridge, had a braking problem. When I braked, the trailer brakes did not come on at first. Then they snatched on hard. I was driving through Moscow on my way back to Octopus. Coming down a hill, in heavy snow, I noticed that at the bottom of the hill, a group of cars had crashed into one another. Obviously, they were sliding around in the snowy conditions.

I braked to slow my descent, but the trailer brakes did not work at first. Then, they snatched on, violently, out braking the unit. Due to this, I had the unit trying to push forwards and the trailer holding it back. Taking the line of least resistance, the front of the unit swung to the right and I crashed headlong into a lamp post. The lamp posts in Moscow are solid and the truck bounced backwards, causing the rear offside of the cab to meet the side of the trailer. Both the trailer and the truck cab were damaged by the collision.

My insurance company had to pay for the damage to the trailer, which came to £3,500. This increased my premiums significantly. As I had not taken the trailer back to the U.K. myself, I could not get the rental firm to admit to the fault with the trailer brakes.

Some months later, Kepstowe recalled me to the U.K. to discuss their new plans for the Russian operations. I listened to how they had decided that, instead of shunting, I would be making weekly trips to Turku, swapping trailers and returning to Moscow. I did not inform them at that time that I would shortly be leaving Russia for good. I merely said that I would think about it and let them know.

Driving back to Moscow from London, I was pulling a rental tilt trailer. I was sent back via Dover and not Harwich. Crossing Belgium, I noticed that there was smoke coming from one of the trailer axles. Then it burst into flames. Pulling up, I took the super single wheel off the axle and strapped it to the top of my diesel tank. The hub had obviously burned out, due to lack of grease, so there was no point replacing the wheel. Luckily, on the Van Hool trailers, they had a steel bond, which stopped the axle from dropping to the ground. I drove to the rental depot at Antwerp. Even though it was a Saturday, they were shut. Unable to have the problem rectified, I carried on.

When I reached Belarus, another of the wheels actually fell off the trailer. I managed to recover it and now headed for Moscow with a three-axled trailer that only had four wheels instead of six in contact with the ground. In Moscow, Sovtransavto, who were the trailer rental company's agents, packed the axles with grease and replaced the wheels. However, what they should have done but didn't was to check all the axle hubs because as two of the hubs had obviously not had any grease in them then it was odds on that the others were in the same condition.

At this time the Russian customs were creating problems over the procedure that Kepstowe were using. Trailers that were coming into Russia from Finland were then returning to England via Poland. The customs at Vaalimaa therefore had no proof that custom clearance had taken place in Moscow. This meant that the goods may not have been presented to customs at all. Due to this they were making things exceedingly difficult on the Finnish border for all Kepstowe's trailers. This attitude was also beginning to take effect on the Polish border. Due to this, I had to take this trailer back to Berlin, where I would swap with one coming out.

I left Moscow, running with Steve Clarke. Obviously, I had told him about losing the wheels from the trailer on the way to Moscow. He was running behind me and it came as no surprise to me when he came on the C.B. to tell me that I had lost another trailer wheel. No surprise, because I knew that it was a piss take, trying to wind me up. At the time, we were driving through the night and were between Smolensk and Orsha. When we eventually stopped at the border, I saw that he had actually been telling the truth. However, as I pointed out to him, it was too late to go back and look for it. Either it would have rolled off deep into the surrounding countryside, or if it had dropped at the roadside, somebody would have seen it and made off with it. All in all, I was not going back. So we continued on our merry way.

We reached Poznan and then separated. He went into Poznan, to load from an exhibition, while I carried on to Schwedt, heading for Berlin. Just as I reached the Polish side of the border, another wheel fell off. Luckily, I was going very slowly, approaching the bridge. I limped on to the border itself and the German Police went mad. They told me that under no circumstances was the trailer to be moved, that it must be repaired at the border. They called the rental firm's local depot, which was actually in Schwedt. When their fitter arrived, he pronounced that the fix could not be made at the border. I was therefore instructed that I was to drive to the depot and nowhere else. So I did.

Luckily I had decided not to make a break for it and head for Berlin. That is because I had a police escort from the border to the depot. Backing into the workshop, another wheel slowly and gently came away from an axle and ended up lying beside the trailer. The fitters inspected the trailer and pronounced that all the axles would have to be replaced. That was because, with the hubs not having grease, all of them were burned out beyond repair. The drawback to this was that the axles would have to come from Stuttgart and, as it was a Friday, they would not be able to be fitted until Tuesday. I immediately informed Kepstowe, who were less than delighted with the situation. However, the upshot of it all was that the rental firm's Slough depot had to bear all of the cost. They also had to shell out £900 in demurrage costs for the waste of my time. Shame, I thought!

In the last few months before quitting Russia I was sent to Dnepropetrovsk to load. The women who made up the loading crew were talking to me during a tea break. They asked me how many children I had.

I told them that I had five, four in England and a daughter in Moscow. As people were relatively poorer in Russia, they could not afford big families. The women came to the conclusion that I must be well off. "You must be very rich," one said. At the time, Russian T.V. was showing a soap opera entitled *Boogata toja platchet* (The rich also cry).

Joking, I said, "*boogata toja platchet.*"

The women, instead of laughing, thought that this was a very deep and sincere statement. They considered me to be a philosopher. Really, I was just a piss taker.

Another time, in Orel, a few of the middle-aged women from the loading crew were having a look into my cab. They saw the fur hat draped over the coffee machine and asked what it was there for as it was May. Joking, I said that it was to keep my head warm when I was in bed.

One of the women said, "You do not need a hat, Micky. What you need is a woman." I immediately replied, "Come on then. Get up in to the cab."

The gang of women immediately scuttled off, laughing and giggling like schoolgirls.

40

Dasvidaniya, Tanya

AND so I came to the end of my time in Moscow. I had made plans for our return to England. We had been offered a chalet at Rob Greensmith's family's chalet park to use as a base until we could find permanent accommodation. I had a buyer for the truck lined up, courtesy of Channel Commercials. There was also a business opportunity with my brother, which appeared positive.

I had informed Kepstowe that I was leaving and would not take up the option of running from Moscow to Turku weekly. I don't think that it was a popular decision. With Kepstowe that is.

It was popular with me.

Mid-May was my choice for leaving Moscow, but Kepstowe asked me to stay on until a Petro-Gas exhibition in Baku had taken place. That was because Mark and Paul from the Moscow office were going to it and I was asked to keep an eye on the office, shunt goods and help the subbies, while they were away.

I actually met up with the ten-truck convoy to Baku near Rostov, where I had tipped a trailer. Among the drivers there were my friends, Pete Newlyn, Nicky Reynolds and John Mantle. They had driven out through Moscow, where one driver had not enjoyed the trip that far and threw his hand in.

Had I been in Moscow I would have probably taken the trailer to Baku. However, another driver had been flown out from London to take over the truck. To be fair, I was not disappointed. I just wanted to get back to the U.K. and start our new life.

Arriving back in Moscow, I saw Mark and Paul just before they flew to Baku. I then shunted out of the new office, which Kepstowe had just opened in north Moscow. We had withdrawn from Octopus and moved into the new premises. My part was now shunting between the two, carrying goods from one warehouse to the other. I was kicking my heels until I could leave Moscow for the last time. A big shame was that the new office was only about a fifteen-minute drive from our flat.

While I was waiting in Moscow, killing time until we finally moved to England, Gordon Jones passed through on his way to Irkutsk, 3,225 miles away, in deepest Siberia. Twice the distance from Moscow to London.

He was pulling a trailer for an American Tobacco Company. They were putting on road shows in all the major cities east of Moscow. Gordon was going to be spending four months in Siberia. He would get back to Moscow just before the winter started. I wished him luck, he was going to need it. To the best of my knowledge, Gordon was the English driver who travelled the furthest into Russia.

Mark and Paul returned from Baku and I was taken out to lunch by them as thanks for all of my hard work in Moscow. They presented me with a huge book that contained pictures of Moscow's sights and landscapes. My last series of work involved shunting for an exhibition in Krasnaya Presnaya. The last load out of the exhibition was the one that I was to take back to the U.K. at the beginning of June.

With the goods loaded and the trailer ready to go, I took the truck home to Voikovskaya so that we could load our possessions into the cab. We did not take much as we could buy most things that we needed when we arrived in England. Vera came down to the truck, to say goodbye.

As she stood beside the truck and I turned on the engine, she began to cry. This started Elena crying. As I pulled away from the kerb, Margi' turned to Elena and said, "Don't cry mamma. Dad's not angry."

The final sting in the tail and the ex-Soviet Union's attempted parting shot was that when I arrived at Grodno, Mr Stand By Gents discovered that the customs at K.P. had not sealed the trailer properly again.

Once again, he told me to return to Moscow, or take my chances at Brest. However, I was not taking Margi' and Elena to Brest, to swelter in a 48-hour queue. The temperature at the time was in the mid-30s. He knew full well about the queues at Kukariki. He knew from the cab control that I had Elena and Margi' with me. So, I kicked off. Not usual for me, but I had taken enough from him.

The noise brought the border chief out of his office and he wanted to know what was wrong. When the situation was explained to him he ordered Mr Stand By Gents to open the trailer, check the freight and then reseal it with a new seal.

This was what the lazy twat should have done when Mick and I were sent back to Brest. It was obvious that he was too bone idle and arrogant, so had not bothered. Now, he was being made to do his job properly.

As the customs chief walked away, I heard him say, "*Hoy doorak*". He must have known that female news-reader, in Moscow, as well. With the trailer resealed, I took my leave of Mr Stand By Gents. His sullen face surrounded hate-filled eyes, as he wished me a very insincere, "Good Bye".

How Micky Packham would have been proud of me, as in reply I wished Stand By a very calm, cold and clinical "F@ck off".

41

Backword

AS I drove out of the border at Grodno, heading into Poland, I climbed a slight incline on to a low ridge. On the top of the ridge, I looked into my driving mirror and caught the last ever view of the ex-Soviet Union that I would get from the cab of my truck. I stuck my arm out of the window, raised it and gave the two-fingered salute. This was not for Russia. This was for Mr Stand By Gents.

And so, what was supposed to have been a one-year contract driving between Venray and Klyazma, finally came to an end, after just over five years. From those five years I had obtained the three things that I had set out to achieve: money, adventure and learning the Russian language. But I had achieved so much else as well, the greatest of my achievements being my little daughter, Margarita, who was sat in the cab on the way to a brand new adventure for her in England.

As I drove away from the border, heading into Poland, I thought of all the people that I had met, places that I had seen and adventures that I had experienced. So much more than I have been able to describe in this narrative.

It had been a good five years, one that I would have repeated without hesitation, if asked to do so. There had been more good times than bad times. Despite the hardships, those good times had out-weighed the danger and the low periods.

I had enjoyed subcontracting to Kepstowe and been brilliantly looked after by Channel Commercials. All in all, the whole five years had been the adventure of my life.

But now, as I looked at my little family, riding with me in the truck, heading for the U.K., I knew that a whole new experience was just beginning for all three of us.

But, that is another story.